And Yet . . .

And Yet . . .

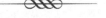

ESSAYS

Christopher Hitchens

Atlantic Books
London

First published in the United States in 2015 by Simon and Schuster, a division of CBS Corporation, New York.

This edition published in Great Britain in e-book in 2015 and in hardback in 2016 by Atlantic Books, an imprint of Atlantic Books Ltd.

The essays in this book originally appeared, sometimes in slightly different form, in the following publications: *The Atlantic*, *Foreign Policy*, *The New York Review of Books*, *Slate*, *Vanity Fair*, *The Wall Street Journal*, *The Wilson Quarterley*.

10 9 8 7 6 5 4 3 2 1

A CIP catalogue record for this book is available from the British Library.

Hardback ISBN: 978 1 78239 455 6
Trade paperback ISBN: 978 1 78239 456 3
E-book ISBN: 978 1 78239 457 0

Printed and bound by CPI Group (UK) Ltd, Croydon, CR0 4YY

Atlantic Books
An Imprint of Atlantic Books Ltd
Ormond House
26–27 Boswell Street
London
WC1N 3JZ

www.atlantic-books.co.uk

Contents

Che Guevara: Goodbye to All That — 1

Orwell's List — 19

Orhan Pamuk: Mind the Gap — 29

Bring on the Mud — 39

Ohio's Odd Numbers — 45

On Becoming American — 53

Mikhail Lermontov: A Doomed Young Man — 57

Salman Rushdie: Hobbes in the Himalayas — 63

My Red-State Odyssey — 71

The Turkey Has Landed — 83

Bah, Humbug — 87

A. N. Wilson: Downhill All the Way — 91

Ian Fleming: Bottoms Up — 97

Power Suits — 105

Blood for No Oil! — 115

How Uninviting — 123

Look Who's Cutting and Running Now — 127

Oriana Fallaci and the Art of the Interview — 131

Imperial Follies — 141

Clive James: The Omnivore — 147

Gertrude Bell: The Woman Who Made Iraq — 153

Physician, Heal Thyself — 159

Edmund Wilson: Literary Companion   *163*

On the Limits of Self-improvement, Part I:
    Of Vice and Men   *169*

On the Limits of Self-improvement, Part II:
    Vice and Versa   *177*

On the Limits of Self-improvement, Part III:
    Mission Accomplished   *185*

Ayaan Hirsi Ali: The Price of Freedom   *193*

Arthur Schlesinger: The Courtier   *197*

Paul Scott: Victoria's Secret   *203*

The Case against Hillary Clinton   *211*

The Tall Tale of Tuzla   *215*

V. S. Naipaul: Cruel and Unusual   *217*

No Regrets   *225*

Barack Obama: Cool Cat   *229*

The Lovely Stones   *235*

Edward M. Kennedy: Redemption Song   *243*

Engaging with Iran Is Like Having Sex with
    Someone Who Hates You   *247*

Colin Powell: Powell Valediction   *251*

Shut Up about Armenians or We'll Hurt
    Them Again   *261*

Hezbollah's Progress   *265*

The Politicians We Deserve   *269*

Rosa Luxemburg: Red Rosa   *273*

Joan Didion: Blue Nights   *281*

The True Spirit of Christmas   *283*

Charles Dickens's Inner Child   *291*

G. K. Chesterton: The Reactionary   *299*

The Importance of Being Orwell   *311*

What Is Patriotism?   *321*

Index   *323*

One should strive to combine the maximum of impatience with the maximum of skepticism, the maximum of hatred of injustice and irrationality with the maximum of ironic self-criticism. This would mean really deciding to learn from history rather than invoking or sloganizing it.

—from *Letters to a Young Contrarian*

And Yet . . .

Che Guevara:
Goodbye to All That

———— ⌀⌀⌀ ————

W HEN, SHORTLY AFTER the triumph of the Castro revolution, Ernesto Guevara took over the direction of the Cuban
National Bank, it became his duty to sign the newly minted ten- and
twenty-peso notes. This he did with a contemptuous flourish, scrawl-
ing the bold nom de guerre "Che" on both denominations. By that
gesture, which made those bills a collectors' item in some quarters of
the left, he expressed an ambition to move beyond the money economy
and what used to be termed "the cash nexus." It was a stroke, at once
Utopian and puritanical, that seemed to sum up his gift both for the
improvised and the determined.

Revisiting Havana recently, for the purpose of making a BBC
documentary on the thirtieth anniversary of Guevara's murder, I discovered that there are now four legal currencies in circulation. The
most proud and salient, of course, is the United States dollar. Nowhere
outside the Panama Canal Zone has any Latin American economy
capitulated so utterly to the usefulness of this green symbol. Once
the preserve of the Cuban *nomenklatura* and of those with access to

Review of *Che Guevara: A Revolutionary Life*, by Jon Lee Anderson, and *The
Motorcycle Diaries: A Journey around South America*, by Ernesto Che Guevara,
translated by Ann Wright

special diplomatic "dollar stores," the money of *Tío Sam* is now the preferred streetwise mode of exchange, and also the essential legal tender in hotels and newly privatized restaurants. Next in importance is the special "INTUR" money, printed by the Cuban Ministry of Tourism for the exclusive use of foreign holidaymakers. Large tracts of Cuba, especially the Varadero beach section outside Havana, have been turned into reservations for this special breed of "internationalist." Third comes the *peso convertible*, a piece of scrip with a value pegged to that of the dollar. And last we find the Cuban peso, a mode of exchange so humble that windshield washers at intersections, when handed a fistful, will wordlessly hand it back.

On this last currency appears the visage of Che Guevara. It certainly, if somewhat ironically, demonstrates the regime's fealty to his carelessness about money. Meanwhile, under stylized poster portraits of the heroic comandante, and within sight of banners reading—rather gruesomely, perhaps—"*Socialismo o Muerte*," the youth of Havana sell their lissome bodies as they did in the days of the Sam Giancana and George Raft dispensation. Junk tourist artifacts are sold from stalls outside Hemingway's old Bodeguita. The talk among the liberal members of the writers' union, as also among the American expatriate veterans, is all of the surge in street crime and delinquency. With unintentional comic effect, these conversations mimic their "deprived or depraved?" counterparts in Los Angeles and New York. Is it the lack of jobs and opportunities? Or could it be the decline in the moral basis of society? After all, it's not that long since Martha Gellhorn instructed her readers that mugging in Havana was unknown. The old "moral versus material" debate continues in a ghostly form, as if there were a pentimento of Che concealed behind the partly gaudy and partly peeling façade.

Leaving Cuba and landing in Cancún, Mexico, I buy the *Miami Herald* and the *New York Times*. On the front page of the *Herald* is the news that Hector Silva, candidate of the Farabundo Martí Liberation Front, has been elected mayor of San Salvador. The paper mentions that many of Silva's enthusiasts "still sport" lapel buttons bearing the likeness of Guevara. When I interviewed him in 1987, the brave and eloquent Señor Silva was a much likelier candidate for assassination than election.

The front page of the *New York Times* reports from Zaire, and carries the claim of Laurent-Désiré Kabila that his rebel forces will be in the capital city by June. The paper's correspondent, citing the inevitable "Western diplomatic sources," quotes them as saying that they will be surprised if it takes as long as that. One of Guevara's first acts, after the overthrow of Batista, was to extend hospitality and training to the embryonic forces of the Sandinista and Farabundo Martí fronts. And one of his last acts, before embarking for Bolivia, was to spend some time on the shores of Lake Tanganyika, attempting to put a little fiber and fervor into the demoralized anti-Mobutu guerrillas. (At this time, he formed a rather low opinion of M. Kabila, whose base and whose tactics were too tribal, who demonstrated a tendency toward megalomania, and who maltreated deserters and prisoners.) Still, Mobutu had been the jewel in the CIA's African crown. So perhaps not all the historical ironies turn out to be at Guevara's expense.

The superficial account of Che's significance is narrated chiefly in symbols and icons. Some of these constitute a boutique version: Antonio Banderas plays a sort of generic Che in the movie rendition of Sir Andrew Lloyd Webber's *Evita*. As photographed by Alberto Korda with an expression of untamable defiance, Che became the poster boy of the vaguely "revolutionary" generation of the 1960s. (And of that generation's nemesis: the Olivetti conglomerate once used a Che poster in a recruiting advertisement with the caption "We would have hired him.") The Cuban government recently took legal steps to stop a popular European beer being named after its most popular martyr.

Much of the attraction of the cult has to do with the grace of an early and romantic death. George Orwell once observed that if Napoléon Bonaparte had been cut down by a musket ball as he entered Moscow, he would have been remembered as the greatest general since Alexander. And not only did Guevara die before his ideals did, he died in such a manner as to inspire something akin to superstition.

He rode among the poor of the altiplano on a donkey. He repeatedly foresaw and predicted the circumstances of his own death. He was spurned and betrayed by those he claimed to set free. He was by calling a healer of the sick. The photographs of his corpse, bearded and half-naked and lacerated, make an irresistible comparison with paintings of the deposition from Calvary. There is a mystery about his last resting place. Alleged relics are in circulation. There have even been sightings. . . .

The CIA and its Bolivian military allies chopped off Guevara's hands in order to make a positive fingerprint comparison with records in Argentina: the preserved hands were later returned to Cuba by a defector from La Paz. We may be grateful that the Castro regime did not choose to set up an exhibit of mummification on the model of Lenin's tomb. Though I did discover, during my researches in Havana, that the pictures of Guevara's dead body have never been shown in Cuba. "The Cuban people," I was solemnly told at the national film archive, "are used to seeing Che Guevara alive." And so they do, night after night on their screens—cutting cane as a "volunteer," greeting parties of schoolchildren, orating at the United Nations or the Alliance for Progress, posing in a clearing in the Sierra Maestra or the Bolivian uplands.

One of the special dramas of the Latin American region is that of the desaparecido, or "disappeared person." From Buenos Aires to Guatemala City, there are still committees of black-draped *madres* who demand to know the whereabouts of their sons and daughters. And there are also "truth commissions" which have come up with the most harrowing evidence of what did happen. Che Guevara is the most famous "disappeared person" in the hemisphere. When Jon Lee Anderson, the author of this intelligent and intriguing biography, published his findings last year on the probable burial site of Guevara's remains (still undetermined, but very probably underneath the runway of a military airport at Vallegrande in Bolivia), he had the incidental effect of igniting a movement of relatives of the desaparecidos in Bolivia itself.

Another way of describing, and incidentally of de-trivializing, the legacy of Guevara is to place him as a founding figure of "magical realism." In his *Motorcycle Diaries*, an account of a continental road trip he took as a young medical student in the early 1950s, we read in Guevara's own youthful prose about his fact-finding tour of the leper colonies of Latin America. He celebrated his twenty-fourth birthday at one such colony in the Peruvian Amazon. The patients threw him a party at the conclusion of which, flown with locally distilled pisco, he made a speech and said:

> The division of America into unstable and illusory nations is a complete fiction. We are one single mestizo race with re-markable ethnographic similarities, from Mexico down to the Magellan Straits. And so, in an attempt to break free from all narrow-minded provincialism, I propose a toast to Peru and to a United America.

As he later described the same occasion in a letter home to his mother:

> Alberto, who sees himself as Peron's natural heir, delivered such an impressive demagogic speech that our well-wishers were consumed with laughter. . . . An accordion player with no fingers on his right hand used little sticks tied to his wrist, the singer was blind and almost all the others were hideously deformed, due to the nervous form of the disease which is very common in this area. With the light from lamps and lanterns reflected in the river, it was like a scene from a horror film. The place is very lovely. . . .

The boy "Che" drunkenly spouting pan-Americanism to an audi-ence of isolated lepers in a remote jungle—here is a scene that Werner Herzog might hesitate to script, or Gabriel García Márquez to devise. (Márquez once said in the hearing of a friend of mine that in order to write about Guevara he would need a thousand years or a million pages. His nonfiction "Operation Carlotta," a straightforwardly not to say panegyrically Fidelist account of the Cuban expedition to Angola, does deal briefly with Guevara's earlier foray into the Congo.) But writers as diverse as Julio Cortázar and Nicolás Guillén* have taken Guevara as an inspiration, and indeed one of his more lasting memorials may be in the regional literary imagination.

If we take this as Anderson does—as a chronicle of a death foretold— then it may be related as an intelligible series of chapters and parables. First we have the rebel: the James Dean and Jack Kerouac type. The young "Che"—the nickname is distinctively Argentine and translates roughly as *"copain,"* or pal—came from an Irish-Spanish family of impoverished aristocrats with the patronymic of Lynch. He was always a charmer and a wit, and always a troublemaker and heartbreaker. His period of youthful sexual repression seems to have been short: an appealing candor about the physical and libidinous runs through all his writings as it does with very few professional revolutionaries. His family was anti-Nazi and anti-Peronist during a time when this could be perilous in Argentina.

Ernesto took an active if rather theatrical part in local youth and student activism, helping out refugees from Republican Spain and cheeking pro-Nazi teachers and professors. The boy is not yet the father to the man except in two respects: he does not dislike Peron as much as his family does, because Peron is at least a nationalist and a foe of the Yanqui. And he is gravely debilitated by asthma, an affliction which he refuses to allow to incapacitate him. The story of his body-building, sporting enthusiasm, and outdoor effort, all aimed at

---

*The imagery of these texts tends to be nationalist-heroic rather than socialist or revolutionary. Though a highly orthodox Communist himself, and a contemporary of Neruda, Nicolás Guillén composed an ode in 1959 comparing Guevara to Martí and San Martín. Julio Cortázar wrote a death-paean for Che, offering his own hands and pen as a replacement for the hands chopped off by the killers.

putting strength into a feeble frame, reminds one of nothing so much as (of all people) Theodore Roosevelt. From this derives an emphasis on "the will" which is essential to the story.

Parable two concerns his resolve to become a physician. Not only did this expose him to encounters with veteran socialist doctors, but it also gave him a firsthand experience of the misery of the region. The *Motorcycle Diaries*, which reinforce the Dean-Kerouac scapegrace image at one level, also contain some very moving and detailed accounts of this part of his education. A monograph could easily be written on the "radicalizing" effect of medical training on young idealists of the middle class. Guevara was much influenced, on his rattling around the southern cone, by an encounter with the Peruvian leprologist and Marxist Dr. Hugo Pesce. This man, the author of a book on Andean underdevelopment entitled *Latitudes del Silencio*, was the recipient ten years later of an inscribed copy of Guevara's first book, *Guerrilla Warfare*. Clearly its author was interested in more than socialized medicine. (Another attentive reader of that first edition was President John F. Kennedy, who had it rapidly translated for him by the CIA and who then ordered the setting up of the "Special Forces"—materializing Régis Debray's thesis that "the Revolution revolutionizes the Counter-Revolution.")

Parable three brings us to the consummate internationalist. Of mixed nationality to begin with, Guevara married a Peruvian woman and took out Mexican citizenship for his children. He was awarded, and later renounced, Cuban nationality. He died in a country named for Simón Bolívar, and near a town named for one of Bolívar's lieutenants. His favorite self-image was that of Don Quixote, the rootless wanderer and freelance righter of wrongs. "Once again," as he wrote on quitting Cuba, "I feel Rosinante's ribs creaking between my heels." (It was Alasdair MacIntyre who first compared this observation to one made by Karl Marx, who drily noted that "knight errantry is not compatible with all forms of society.") Indeed, Guevara came late to

Marxism. For him, the great personal and political crux occurred as a result of his stay in Guatemala in 1954, where he was a direct witness to the ruthless and cynical destabilization of the Arbenz government by the CIA.

This story has been well told before, notably by Stephen Schlesinger and Stephen Kinzer in their book *Bitter Fruit*. Our knowledge of the coup, of the complicity of the United States, and of the hellish consequences for all Guatemalans but especially for the descendants of the Mayan *indigenes*, has recently been sharply enhanced by disclosures from the archive of the Central Intelligence Agency, and by the excavation of an archipelago of unofficial mass graves across the Guatemalan countryside.* In the Kinzer-Schlesinger narrative, Guevara rated only a glancing mention. Jon Lee Anderson has reconstructed his part in the events with punctilious detail.

Guevara arrived in Guatemala in December 1953, at the end of his long period of bumming around the continent. He decided to stay, and resolved to become more serious about himself, because he could scent both revolution and counterrevolution in the air. Nor were his instincts at fault. The election of the reformist Jacobo Arbenz had set in motion the two things that the reformists most feared—namely the rising expectations of the revolutionaries and the poor, and the direst forebodings on the part of the United States. (The febrile atmosphere of the place and the moment is well caught in Gore Vidal's novel *Dark Green, Bright Red.*) Guevara decided to offer his credentials as a physician to the new regime, and hoped to be employed as a "barefoot doctor" among the peasants. Discouraged by the bureaucratic response to this proposal, he mingled at first rather ineffectually with the milieu of stateless rebels and revolutionaries who had converged on Guatemala City: the losers in the battles with Somoza and Trujillo and Batista. As he was arriving, Guevara had written home to say that:

---

*See, especially, Peter Kornbluh, *The New York Times*, "The CIA's Foreign Policy," Op-Ed page, May 31, 1997, on the CIA's published plans to assassinate the Guatemalan then-leadership, and Larry Rohter, "Guatemala Digs Up Army's Secret Cemeteries," *The New York Times*, June 7, 1997.

Along the way, I had the opportunity to pass through the dominions of the United Fruit, convincing me once again of just how terrible these capitalist octopuses are. I have sworn before a picture of the old and mourned comrade Stalin that I won't rest until I see these capitalist octopuses annihilated. In Guatemala I will perfect myself. . . .

Fidel Castro's failed but already legendary attack on the Moncada barracks in Cuba had taken place the preceding July, and Guevara fell in (initially as a doctor for one of their number) with some of his exiled comrades. The talk was all of a coming confrontation with the colossus to the north, and its local octopus clientele. And indeed, the script for the events reads like a primer in elementary Leninism. The Dulles brothers and their corporate friends did embark on an armed destabilization of the elected Arbenz government. They did engage the support of neighboring oligarchs such as General Anastasio Somoza. They did find and pay a military puppet named Castillo Armas. And they did invade Guatemala with a mercenary force. Guevara and his "internationalist" friends watched all this with a mixture of shame and incredulity, convinced that their predictions about the uselessness of gradualism were being confirmed, so to speak, before their very eyes. But they were impotent.

Chased into the sanctuary of the Argentine embassy by the coup he had long foreseen and tried vainly to resist, Guevara spent some very concentrated time with desperate militants who would, in the succeeding decades, become guerrilla commanders in El Salvador, Nicaragua, and Guatemala itself. Together, they reviewed the lessons of the defeat. Chief among these, they felt, was Arbenz's failure to distribute arms to the people. Next came his refusal to take action against the CIA's clever manipulation of the local press. It was a crucible moment: a young man receiving an indelible impression at a formative age. Up until then, Guevara had even by his own account been playing at revolution. Henceforth, he would not joke about Stalin. Rather, he would school himself in the intransigence of the "socialist camp," and begin to study the canonical work of its lately deceased but not-yet-disowned General Secretary.

In the succeeding parable, Guevara decides that he has found a mission in life. Guatemala must be avenged. Imperialism must pay for its arrogance and cruelty. To a friend he writes an agonized letter, saying that the Arbenz government was defeated and betrayed, just like the Spanish Republic, but without the same courage and honor in its extremity. Indignantly, he repudiates the stories about atrocities committed by pro-Arbenz forces, adding ominously: "There *should* have been a few firing squads early on, which is different; if those shootings had taken place the government would have retained the possibility of fighting back."

Chased from Guatemala to Mexico, when he encounters the young Fidel Castro he needs no persuading that this meeting was meant to happen. Before long, he is pursuing a more intensive study of Communist literature and a rigorous training as a guerrilla fighter.* (Iconographic note: when the rebel-bearing vessel *Granma* beaches on Cuban shores and runs straight into an ambush, all later accounts stress that this left the nucleus of revolutionary disciples at the numinous number twelve.)

Trotsky once remarked that what distinguished the revolutionary was not his willingness to kill but his readiness to die. The anti-Batista war conducted by Castro, Guevara, Camilo Cienfuegos, and Frank País was, by most standards, a near-exemplary case of winning "hearts and minds" and recruiting popular enthusiasm. Some informers and deserters and backsliders were executed out of hand, but Guevara seems at first to have shown no relish for such work. Indeed, he cashiered one of his deputies in Camagüey province, a bizarre American freebooter named Herman Marks, because of his undue eagerness to take part in reprisal killings or on-the-spot battlefield punishments. Yet Ander-

---

*According to Aleksandr Fursenko and Timothy Naftali in *"One Hell of a Gamble"*: *Khrushchev, Castro, and Kennedy, 1958–1964* (New York: Norton, 1997), which is based on recently released Soviet archives, Guevara went to the length of becoming a formal member of the Cuban Communist Party as early as 1957.

son has unearthed a suggestive detail. Once in power in Havana, and immediately charged by Castro with purging and punishing Batista's police apparatus, Guevara set up an improvised drumhead tribunal at the harbor fortress of La Cabaña, where he sent for Marks again and reemployed him as an executioner.

Some justified this kind of "people's court" as utilitarian. Herbert Matthews of the *New York Times* had a go at defending them "from the Cuban's perspective." (The paper wouldn't print his efforts.) But other foreign correspondents were appalled by the lynch trials, ordered by Fidel Castro himself, that were held in the Havana sports stadium. Raúl Castro went even further in the city of Santiago, machine-gunning seventy captured Batistianos into a ditch dug by a bulldozer. When challenged by friends and family, Guevara resorted to three defenses. First, he claimed that everybody at La Cabaña had had a hearing. The speed at which the firing squads operated made his argument seem exiguous. Second, as reported by Anderson, "he never tired of telling his Cuban comrades that in Guatemala Arbenz had fallen because he had not purged his armed forces of disloyal elements, a mistake that permitted the CIA to penetrate and overthrow his regime." Third, and dropping all pretense, he told a protesting former medical colleague: "Look, in this thing either you kill first, or else you get killed."

Methods and rationalizations of this kind have a way of establishing themselves, not as "emergency measures" but as administrative means of dealing with all opposition. That was the point made by Rosa Luxemburg in her original criticism of Leninism. The Luxemburg example was brought up in a fascinating interview given by Guevara to the American socialist academic Maurice Zeitlin on September 14, 1961. In this discussion, the new minister came out firmly for "democratic centralism," praised the Soviet example, and flatly opposed the right of factions or dissidents to make their views known even within the Communist Party itself. Asked by Zeitlin about Luxemburg's warnings on this score, Guevara replied coolly that Luxemburg had died "as a consequence of her political mistakes" and that "democratic centralism is a method of government, not only a method of conquering power."

It was clear, in other words, that his authoritarian stance was taken on principle and not in response to "tactical" considerations. Huber Matos and other allegedly "bourgeois" supporters of the original revolution who were imprisoned had already found this out, as had the Trotsky-ists who dared to criticize Fidelism from the "left."*

The final parable is the one in which Guevara recognizes that, in a sense, his kingdom can never be of this world. Those who sympathized with the Cuban revolution at the time very often did so because they explicitly hoped for a non-Soviet model. In the figure of "Che," some of them, at least, thought they had found their exemplar. And they were, in one unintended sense, not mistaken. Guevara *was* privately critical of the Soviet bloc, already well into its post-Stalinist phase, on the grounds that it was too soft. It wanted "peaceful coexistence" with the American imperium abroad, and a system of capitalist emulation at home. There is a good deal of evidence that he privately sympathized with the emerging position of the Maoists—especially for the "coun-tryside versus city" theses of Lin Piao, where the immiserated peasants of the world were supposed to surround the debauched metropoles and overwhelm them by sheer force of numbers—and might have done so more openly if not for the close yet surreptitious friendship between the Castro brothers and Moscow.

It is certain that he was enraged by Khrushchev's compromise with Kennedy over the missiles, and by the generally lukewarm attitude of the Warsaw Pact toward revolution in the third world. In February 1965, while addressing an "Afro-Asian Solidarity" meeting in Algiers, he went so far as to describe the Kremlin as "an accomplice of impe-rialism" for its cold-cash dealings with impoverished and insurgent states. This, and the general chaos arising from his stewardship of

---

*The entire interview, which is replete with the most lugubrious orthodoxy, can be found as an appendix to Robert Scheer and Maurice Zeitlin, *Cuba: An American Tragedy* (New York: Penguin, 1964). Until relatively recently, it was the custom among certain apologists for Castro to say that United States policy was "driving him into the arms of the Soviet Union." Now that the Cuban one-party state has outlived the Soviet one, this excuse is at least no longer vulnerable to the charge that the embrace of the Soviet Union had been the preferred destination in any case.

the Ministry for Industry, made him an easy target for inner-party attacks by the unsmiling elements among the Cuban Communist Party: people for whom the very words "romanticism" and "adventurism" were symptoms of deviation. His dismissal from the ministry followed immediately on his return from Algiers, and he soon afterward set off for Africa with no very clear mandate or position.

The word "romantic" does not make a very good fit with his actual policies as industry minister. The French economist René Dumont, one of the many well-meaning Marxists who advised Cuba during this period, recalls making a long study of the "agricultural cooperatives." He told Guevara that the workers in these schemes did not feel themselves to be the proprietors of anything. He pressed him to consider a system of rewards for those who performed extra tasks in the off-season. As Dumont records, Guevara's reaction was tersely dismissive. He demanded instead:

> A sort of ideal vision of Socialist Man, who would become a stranger to the mercantile side of things, working for society and not for profit. He was very critical of the industrial success of the Soviet Union [!] where, he said, everybody works and strives and tries to go beyond his quota, but only to earn more money. He did not think the Soviet Man was really a new sort of man. He did not find him any different, really, than a Yankee. He refused to consciously participate in the creation in Cuba "of a second American society."

It's worth noting at this point that Guevara made almost no study of American society, scarcely visited the country except as a speaker at the United Nations, and evinced little curiosity about it in general. When asked once, again by Maurice Zeitlin, what he would like the United States to do, he replied, "Disappear."

In view of the resemblance of Guevara's Spartan program to other celebrated fiascos and tragedies like the Great Leap Forward, it deserves to be said that he was unsparing of himself. He worked unceasingly, was completely indifferent to possessions, and performed heavy lifting and manual labor even when the cameras were not turning. In the same way, he wanted to share in the suffering and struggle of those, in Africa and elsewhere, who were receiving the blunt end of the Cold War. The murder of Patrice Lumumba in the Congo, for example, seems to have affected him in very much the same personal way as did the overthrow of Jacobo Arbenz. He was, perhaps, one of those rare people for whom there is no real gap between conviction and practice.

And he did have a saving element of humor. I possess a tape of his appearance on an early episode of *Meet the Press* in December 1964, where he confronts a solemn panel of network pundits. When they address him about the "conditions" that Cuba must meet in order to be permitted the sunshine of American approval, he smiles as he proposes that there need be no preconditions: "After all, we do not demand that you abolish racial discrimination. . . ." A person as professionally skeptical as I. F. Stone so far forgot himself as to write: "He was the first man I ever met who I thought not just handsome but beautiful. With his curly, reddish beard, he looked like a cross between a faun and a Sunday School print of Jesus. . . . He spoke with that utter sobriety which sometimes masks immense apocalyptic visions."

Those whom the gods wish to destroy, they probably begin by calling "charismatic." The last few years of Guevara's life were a study in diminishing returns. He drove himself harder and harder, relying more and more on exhortation and example, in order to accomplish less and less. In the case of the Cuban economy, the argument over "moral" versus "material" incentives became muddied, with the system eventually resolving itself into one of material non-incentive, periodically prodded by slogans, along Eastern European lines.

On the front of the "world revolution," which is more fully treated by Anderson, Guevara's tricontinental activity (Asia, Africa, Latin America) was sometimes ahead of its time and sometimes behind, but never quite on target. For example, he lent his support to a catastrophic guerrilla operation in the wilds of his native Argentina—catastrophic in the sense that it was an abysmal failure and led to the deaths of most of its members as well as of a few civilians, but catastrophic, too, in that it began the quasi-bandit phase of radical politics in Argentina. Like Trotsky in exile, his guesswork sometimes allowed him to make important predictions, or even to compose moving postmortems. But he could do no more than dream of a new "international."

He was among the first to appreciate the central importance of the war in Vietnam: a place where the hated American empire had made itself morally and militarily vulnerable. But his most celebrated speech on the subject, which called for replicating the Vietnamese experience across the globe, sounded bombastic at the time and reads even more so today. His voyage to Africa, to combat Mobutu and his white mercenaries in the Congo and to open a second front against apartheid and colonialism, was conducted on a moral and material shoestring. He was humbled on the battlefield as well as sabotaged by the anti–Ben Bella coup in Algeria and an outbreak of second thoughts by the Tanzanians. As Guevara scuttled his last positions on Lake Tanganyika in 1965, he did not try to delude himself:

> A desolate, sobering and inglorious spectacle took place. I had to reject men who pleaded to be taken along. There was not a trace of grandeur in this retreat, nor a gesture of rebellion . . . just some sobbing, as [I], the leader of the escapees, told the man with the mooring rope to let go.

Guevara's health—another subject on which he did not delude himself—had deteriorated further in Africa, and his fortieth birthday was looming up. It was evident to him that he had only one more chance to deal a decisive stroke at the detested imperial power. He had had Bolivia in mind for a long time, because its altiplano abutted several other countries and a guerrilla *foco*, properly inserted there, might act as a lever on an entire region. The extreme altitude, desolation, and underdevelopment of the area do not seem to have struck him as a disadvantage until far too late, although it was at this time that he began to recur to the subject of his own death, which he always prefigured as a defiant one in the face of hopeless odds.

Anderson's reconstruction of the Bolivian campaign is exhaustive and convincing. It is clear that the Bolivian Communists regarded Guevara's adventures as an unpardonable intrusion into their "internal affairs," and that they had the sympathy of Moscow in so doing. The persistent rumor that Castro, too, was glad to be rid of a turbulent comrade is rated by Anderson as less well founded. A successful revolution or even upheaval in Latin America would have strengthened his hand and perhaps helped end his isolation and dependence: Havana kept in touch with the doomed expedition for as long as it could.

But of course it also had, in the case of a defeat, the option of declaring an imperishable martyrdom. Since 1968, the "Year of the Heroic Guerrilla," Cuban children have been instructed in almost Baden-Powell tones that if they seek a "role model," they should comport themselves *como el Che*. This strenuous injunction only emphasizes the realization that Guevara's Cromwellian, ascetic demands on people bordered on the impossible: even the inhuman. The grandson who is said most to resemble him—a young man named Canek—has quit the island in order to pursue the vocation of a heavy-metal guitarist in Mexico, and it is a moral and material certainty that many of his generation wish they could do the same.

Having been captured in the first days of October 1967, Guevara was killed in cold blood. The self-serving account of his last hours given by Felix Rodriguez, the Cuban-American CIA agent on the scene, at least makes this clear.* Rodriguez wastes a lot of time explaining that he was full of doubt and remorse, and that he had no authority to overrule the Bolivian military, but succeeds only in drawing a distinction without a difference. The Bolivian Special Forces would have done what they were told and it seems that, Rodriguez notwithstanding, they knew what was wanted of them. As always in

---

Shadow Warrior: The CIA's Hero of a Hundred Unknown Battles, by Felix I. Rodriguez with John Weisman (New York: Simon and Schuster, 1989).

these cases, a "volunteer" executioner was eager and on hand. Che's surviving disciples managed to escape in a wretched state across the Chilean border, where they were met by a then-obscure physician named Salvador Allende and given by him a safe-conduct to Easter Island and home.

Guevara's exemplary final days, which Rodriguez describes as suffused with "grace and courage," demonstrated yet again and conclusively that he was no hypocrite. The news of his murder somehow helped to inaugurate the "hot" period of the 1960s, in which, however much the image of "Che" was to the fore, it was the hedonist Utopians rather than the rigorous revolutionary puritans who made the running. Thus, in a slightly bizarre manner, the same Che was able to achieve the impossible, or at least the incompatible, by simultaneously summoning an age of chivalry and an age of revolution. That posthumous accomplishment was necessarily brief.

Our own age of sophists and calculators has thrown up some of the surviving actors in secondary roles. Felix Rodriguez, for example, having gone on to serve the CIA in Vietnam and El Salvador, surfaced again as George Bush's embarrassing underling in the Iran-contra scandal. He was stunned, while being questioned on other matters by Senator John Kerry's committee of investigation into illegal drugs and guns, to be asked from the chair why he had not tried to save Che Guevara's life.

As Jon Lee Anderson's work serves to remind us, when Che Guevara first spurred Rosinante into the field the world was a radically different place. Most of South and Central America was in the safekeeping of military caudillos. The Portuguese empire was secure in Africa. Vietnam was still (just) a French colony. The Shah of Iran had been crammed back on his throne. Nelson Mandela was a semi-clandestine human-rights lawyer. Algeria was French and the Congo was Belgian. The Suez Canal Zone was British. In the processes that overturned this situation, Guevara was a nebulous and elusive but nonetheless real presence. The very element that gave him his certainty and courage—his revolutionary Communism—was also the element that condemned him to historical eclipse. In setting down the whole story in such a respectful but objective manner, Jon Lee Anderson has succeeded in writing, for himself and I suspect for many others, a nuanced goodbye to all that.

(*The New York Review of Books*, July 17, 1997)

Orwell's List

———⚬⚬⚬———

IT IS EASY enough for me to say that George Orwell was essentially right about the three great twentieth-century issues of fascism, Stalinism, and empire, and that he was enabled to be right by a certain insistence on intellectual integrity and independence. The question arises, Was it possible for him to uphold all these positions, and in that way, simultaneously?

I choose a representative quotation from Paul Lashmar and James Oliver's book *Britain's Secret Propaganda War*,* a history of the Information Research Department (IRD) of the British Foreign Office:

> George Orwell's reputation as a left-wing icon took a body-blow from which it may never recover when it was revealed in 1996 that he had cooperated closely with IRD's Cold Warriors, even offering his own black-list of eighty-six Communist "fellow-travelers." As the *Daily Telegraph* noted, "To some, it was as if Winston Smith had willingly cooperated with the Thought Police in *1984*."

---

*Stroud, Gloucestershire: Sutton, 1998.

This, or something like it, is a recounting of events that now enjoys quite extensive currency. It is easy to demonstrate, if only by the supporting evidence presented by Lashmar and Oliver, that it is wholly mistaken. And I have selected their synopsis because it is free of the Orwell-hatred that disfigures many other versions of the story.

Just as a matter of record, then:

1. The existence of Orwell's list of Stalinized intellectuals was not "revealed" in 1996. It appears in Professor Bernard Crick's biography, which was first published in 1980.

2. A blacklist is a collection of names maintained by those with the power to affect hiring and firing. To be blacklisted is to be denied employment for political reasons unconnected to job performance. The word does not now have, and never has had, any other meaning.

3. Even if the *Daily Telegraph* says so, and although it has not chosen to specify the "some" who chose to think it, the Information Research Department was unconnected to any "thought police," to say nothing of the thought police as they actually feature in the pages of *Nineteen Eighty-Four.*

This is by no means to exhaust the utter distortion of Orwell's motives and methods that is involved in the rapid but shallow dissemination of this "disclosure." The simple facts of the case are these. Together with his friend Richard Rees, Orwell had for some time enjoyed playing what Rees himself called a "parlor game." This game consisted of guessing which public figures would, or would not, sell out in the event of an invasion or a dictatorship. Orwell had been playing this game, in a serious as well as a frivolous way, for some little time. On New Year's Day 1942 he wrote, in a lengthy dispatch for *Partisan Review*, about the varieties of defeatist opinion to be found among British journalists and intellectuals. His tone was detached; he noted the odd alliances between widely discrepant factions. He also analyzed the temptation among intellectuals to adapt themselves to power, as instanced by developments across the Channel:

> Both Vichy and the Germans have found it quite easy to keep a façade of "French culture" in existence. Plenty of intellectuals were ready to go over, and the Germans were quite ready to make use of them, even when they were "decadent." At this moment Drieu de la Rochelle is editing the *Nouvelle Revue Française*, Pound is bellowing against the Jews on the Rome radio, and Céline is a valued exhibit in Paris, or at least his books are. All of these would come under the heading of *kulturbolschewismus*, but they are also useful cards to play against the intelligentsia in Britain and the U.S.A. If the Germans got to England, similar things would happen, *and I think I could make out at least a preliminary list of the people who would go over* [my italics].

Notice the date of this. It should be borne in mind here that until recently the Soviet Union had been in a military alliance with Hitler—an alliance loudly defended by Britain's Communists—and that Moscow Radio had denounced the British naval blockade of Nazi Germany as a barbaric war on civilians. The German Communist Party had published a statement in 1940 in which it was discovered that for dialectical reasons the British Empire was somewhat worse than the National Socialist one. Orwell never tired of pointing these things out; they were the sort of illusions or delusions that could have real consequences. Nor did he omit to mention and specify the sorts of intellectual—E. H. Carr being a celebrated instance—who could transfer his allegiance with sinister smoothness from one despotic regime to another.

No less to the point, he had discovered in Spain that the Communist strategy relied very heavily upon the horror and terror of anonymous denunciation, secret informing, and police espionage. At that date, the official hero of all young Communists was Pavlik Morozov, a fourteen-year-old "Pioneer" who had turned in his family to the Soviet police for the offense of hoarding grain. The villagers had slain him as a result; statues of the martyr-child were commonplace in the USSR and it was the obligation of a good Party member to emulate his example.

Orwell's disgust at this culture of betrayal was not confined to the visceral style by which he portrayed and condemned it in *Nineteen Eighty-Four*. He showed a lifelong hatred for all forms of censorship, proscription, and blacklisting. Even when Sir Oswald Mosley was released from prison at the height of the Second World War—a piece of lenience which inspired many complaints from supposed antifascists—Orwell commented that it was unpleasant to see the left protesting at the application of habeas corpus. He took the same line with those who objected to lifting the government ban on the publication of the *Daily Worker*, only taking time to notice that this habit of intolerance had been acquired by many people from the *Daily Worker*'s own editors. In May 1946 he wrote that the main danger from any Communist-led split in the Labour movement was that it "could hardly result in a Communist-controlled government, but it might bring back the Conservatives—which, I suppose, would be less dangerous from the Russian point of view than the spectacle of a Labour government making a success of things."

This last sentence approaches the crux of the matter. The extreme left and the democratic left had concluded in different ways that Stalinism was a negation of socialism and not a version of it. Orwell had seen the extreme left massacred by Stalin's agents in Spain, and he was one of the few to call attention to the execution of the Polish socialist Bund leaders Henryk Erlich and Victor Alter on Stalin's orders in 1943.* For him, the quarrel with the "Stalintern" was not an academic question, or a difference of degree. He felt it as an inti-

---

*Later information tells us that Henryk Erlich hanged himself in prison in May 1942 while Victor Alter was shot in February 1943. In announcing the deaths, which took place in Moscow, Molotov had not troubled to make this distinction. See Gennadi Kostyrchenko, *Out of the Red Shadows* (Amherst, NY: Prometheus, 1995).

mate and very present threat. And the campaign to ban or restrict his books—to "blacklist" him and his writing—had been led by surreptitious Communist sympathizers who worked both in publishing and in the offices of the British state. It was a bureaucrat in the Ministry of Information named Peter Smolka who had quietly helped orchestrate the near suppression of *Animal Farm*. One might therefore put it like this: in the late 1940s Orwell was fighting for survival as a writer, and also considered the survival of democratic and socialist values to be at stake in the struggle against Stalin.

Was it possible to conduct this struggle without lending oneself to "the forces of reaction"? In everything he wrote and did at the time, Orwell strove to make exactly that distinction. He helped to organize and circulate a statement from the Freedom Defence Committee which objected to the purge of supposed political extremists from the Civil Service, insisting that secret vetting procedures be abolished and that the following safeguards be implemented:

(a) The individual whose record is being investigated should be permitted to call a trade union or other representative to speak on his behalf.

(b) All allegations should be required to be substantiated by corroborative evidence, this being particularly essential in the case of allegations made by representatives of MI5 or the Special Branch of Scotland Yard, when the sources of information are not revealed.

(c) The Civil Servant concerned, or his representative, should be allowed to cross-examine those giving evidence against him.

Signed by, among others, Orwell, E. M. Forster, Osbert Sitwell, and Henry Moore, this statement was first published in the *Socialist Leader* on August 21, 1948. (I cannot resist noting that this was twenty years to the day before the Soviet occupation of Czechoslovakia, and saw print at the time when Czechoslovakia was being efficiently Stalinized, as well as ethnically cleansed of its German-speaking inhabitants, with the collaboration of many apparently "non-Party" front organizations. Orwell was one of the few to inveigh against either development, anticipating both Ernest Gellner and Václav Havel in seeing the anti-German racism as a demagogic cover for an authoritarian and nationalist state.) These details do not appear in any published book on the subject of Orwell's supposed role as a police spy, most accounts preferring to draw back in shock at the very idea that he had any contact with the British Foreign Office.

What, then, was the extent of this contact? On March 29, 1949, Orwell received a visit at his hospital bedside from Celia Kirwan, who was among other things an official of the IRD. She was also the sister-in-law of Arthur Koestler, and Orwell had already, in that capacity, met her and proposed marriage to her. They discussed the necessity of recruiting socialist and radical individuals to the fight against the Communists. This subject was already close to Orwell's heart, as can be seen from the story of his effort to get *Animal Farm* circulated clandestinely in Eastern Europe. Ms. Kirwan was close to his heart also, and some defenders of Orwell have kindly suggested that this, together with his much-etiolated physical condition, may have led to a moment of weakness. I find this defense both sentimental and im-probable. He told her what he would have told anyone, and what he said in print whenever the opportunity afforded itself, which was that many presentable leftists of good reputation were not to be trusted when it came to the seductions of Moscow. On April 6 he wrote to Richard Rees asking him to find and forward his "quarto notebook with a pale-bluish cardboard cover," in which could be found "a list of crypto-Communists & fellow-travellers which I want to bring up to date." This in itself shows that Orwell had not originally drawn up the list at the behest of the state. No doubt there was another notebook with the names of the old Nazi sympathizers and potential collaborators, but no matter. Orwell is not today being impeached for keeping lists, merely for keeping them on the wrong people.

The incurable inanity of British officialdom and "official secrecy" means that the list of thirty-five names given to Celia Kirwan is still not open to our scrutiny. The Public Record Office states demurely and fatuously that "a document has been withheld by the Foreign Office." It was at one point conceivable that this measure was taken to protect living people from Orwell's posthumous opinion; even that absurd pretext must now have decayed with time. However, we have the notebook if not the "update" and we do not require official permission to make up our own minds.*

The list certainly illustrates Orwell's private resentments and eccentricities. Very little of it, in point of fact, materializes Rees's confirmation that "this was a sort of game we played—discussing who was a paid agent of what and estimating to what lengths of treachery our favourite *bêtes noires* would be prepared to go." To be exact, only one person is ever accused of being an agent, and even there the qualifying words "almost certainly" are applied. This was Peter Smolka, alias Smollett, a former Beaverbrook newspaper executive and holder of the OBE, who was the very official in the Ministry of Information who had put pressure on Jonathan Cape to drop *Animal Farm*. It has since been conclusively established that Smolka was indeed an agent of Soviet security; this represents a match of 100 percent between Orwell's allegation of direct foreign recruitment and the known facts. As he phrased it rather mildly in his letter to Celia Kirwan, in which he enclosed his list, it wasn't "very sensational and I don't suppose it will tell your friends anything they don't know . . . If it had been done earlier it would have stopped people like Peter Smollett worming their way into important propaganda jobs where they were probably able to do us a lot of harm." The "us" here is the democratic left.

On the very same day, Orwell wrote to Richard Rees, saying that

---

*Professor Peter Davison, the only scholar with comprehensive access to the archives, points out that the original Rees-Orwell notebook (which included names such as that of Orwell's tax inspector) is not the same as "the list." For example, the names of Charlie Chaplin and Stephen Spender are not on the list as it was received by the IRD, and Orwell himself crossed out the names of J. B. Priestley and Tom Driberg. Paul Robeson—correctly listed as a Stalinist in the notebook—was also spared the ordeal of being identified to the IRD. Hardly surprising, since this body was asking only for sincere socialists who opposed the Soviet design.

just because a certain Labour MP was a friend of the flagrant and notorious Konni Zilliacus, this did not prove he was "a crypto." He added: "It seems to me very important to attempt to gauge people's *subjective* feelings, because otherwise one can't predict their behaviour in situations where the results of certain actions are clear even to a self-deceiver. . . . The whole difficulty is to decide where each person stands, & one has to treat each case individually." The staffers of Senator Joseph McCarthy did not possess even the inklings of this discrimination.

Few of the thumbnail sketches run to more than a dozen or so freehand and laconic words. And many of them stand the test of time remarkably well. Who could object to the summary of Kingsley Martin as "Decayed liberal. Very dishonest"? Or, to take another and later editor of the *New Statesman*, to the shrewd characterization of Richard Crossman as "??Political Climber. Zionist (appears sincere about this). Too dishonest to be outright F.T. [fellow traveler]"? The latter has a nice paradox to it; Orwell had a respect for honest Leninists. Almost one-third of the entries end in the verdict "Probably not" or "Sympathizer only," in the space reserved for Party allegiance. J. B. Priestley is recorded as making huge sums from advantageously published Soviet editions of his works; well, so he did, as it now turns out.

Some critics, notably Frances Stonor Saunders in her book *Who Paid the Piper?*, have allowed a delicate wrinkling of the nostril at Orwell's inclusion of details about race, and what is now termed "sexual preference." It is true that Isaac Deutscher is listed as a "Polish Jew," and it is also true that he was a Polish Jew. But then Louis Adamic is identified—and why not?—as "Born in Slovenia not Croatia." The protean Konni Zilliacus, then a very influential figure, is queried rather than identified as "Finnish? 'Jewish'?" (He was both.)

I have to admit that I laughed out loud at seeing Stephen Spender described as having a "Tendency towards homosexuality," which would not exactly define him, and at seeing Tom Driberg written down as merely "Homosexual," which was not to say the half of it. Ms. Saunders comments haughtily that accusations of that kind could get a chap into trouble in those days. Well, not in the British Secret Service or Foreign Office, they couldn't.

Hugh MacDiarmid, the Stalin-worshiping Scots poet, was described by Orwell as "Very anti-English." My friend Perry Anderson, editor of the *New Left Review*, made something of this, too, until I pointed out that MacDiarmid had listed "Anglophobia" as one of his recreations in *Who's Who*. And it was Perry Anderson who published, in his "Components of the National Culture" in the *New Left Review* in 1968, a chart giving the ethnic and national origins of the Cold War émigré intellectuals in Britain, from Lewis Namier, Isaiah Berlin, E. H. Gombrich, and Bronisław Malinowski to Karl Popper, Melanie Klein, and indeed Isaac Deutscher. He reprinted the diagram in his book *English Questions* in 1992. I defended him both times. These things are worth knowing.

There are some crankish bits in the list, as when Paul Robeson is written off as "Very anti-white." But even some of the more tentative judgments about Americans are otherwise quite perceptive. Henry Wallace, as editor of the *New Republic*, had already caused Orwell to cease sending contributions to a magazine in which he could sense a general softness on Stalin. In 1948, Wallace's campaign for the American presidency probably ruined and compromised the American left for a generation, because of his reliance on Communist Party endorsement and organization. Veteran leftist critics of the Truman administration, notably I. F. Stone, were mentally and morally tough enough to point this out at the time.

All too much has been made of this relatively trivial episode, the last chance for Orwell's enemies to vilify him for being correct. The points to keep one's eye on are these: the IRD was not interested or involved in domestic surveillance, and wanted only to recruit staunch socialists and Social Democrats; nobody suffered or could have suffered from Orwell's private opinion; he said nothing in "private" that he did not consistently say in public. And, while a few on "the list" were known personally to Orwell, most were not. This has its importance, since a "snitch" or stool pigeon is rightly defined as someone who betrays friends or colleagues in the hope of plea-bargaining, or otherwise of gaining advantage, for himself. By no imaginable stretch could Orwell's views of Congressman Claude Pepper, or of Vice President Wallace, fall into this category. Nor could it (or did it) damage their careers. And there is no entry on "the list" that comes anywhere near, for sheer sulfuric contempt, Orwell's published challenge to Professor J. D. Bernal, and the other editors of the *Modern Quarterly*, to come clean about whether they were conscious agents of Stalin or not.

This was the period during which Orwell's samizdat editions of *Animal Farm* were being confiscated in Germany by American officers and either burned on the spot or turned over to the Red Army. It was indeed difficult for him to oppose Stalinism and Western imperialism at the same time, while attempting to hold on to his independence. But the stupidity of the state only helped to make certain that, at any rate while he lived, he was always its victim and never its servant. The British Foreign Office, which had been erring on Stalin's side for almost a decade, suddenly needed anti-Stalinist energy in the mid-1940s. It had nowhere to turn, in its search for credible and honest writers, but to the *Tribune* left. This is not, to take the medium or the long view of history, the most disgraceful moment in the record of British socialism. It is also part of the reason why there was no McCarthyite panic or purge in Britain. The *trahison des clercs* was steadily opposed, in both its Stalinoid and its conservative forms, by groups like the Freedom Defense Committee. Orwell cannot posthumously be denied his credit for keeping that libertarian and honest tradition alive.

(*The New York Review of Books*, September 26, 2002)

Orhan Pamuk: Mind the Gap

WELL BEFORE THE fall of 2001 a search was in progress, on the part of Western readers and critics, for a novelist in the Muslim world who could act the part of dragoman, an interpretive guide to the East. In part this was and remains a quest for reassurance. The hope was (and is) that an apparently "answering" voice, attuned to irony and rationality and to the quotidian rather than the supernatural, would pick up the signals sent by self-critical Americans and Europeans and remit them in an intelligible form. Hence the popularity of the Egyptian Naguib Mahfouz, who seemed in his Cairo café-society mode to be potentially "one of us"—even more so when he had the misfortune to be stabbed in the neck by a demented fundamentalist. There was a much lesser vogue for spikier secular writers, such as the late Abdelrahman Munif, author of the Cities of Salt quintet, and the late Israeli Arab Emile Habibi, whose novel *Saeed the Pessoptimist* is the favorite narrative of many Palestinians (and who also had the grace to win Israel's national prize for the best writing in Hebrew). In some ways those two were not quite "Muslim" enough for the purposes of authenticity.

Orhan Pamuk, a thoughtful native of Istanbul who lived for three

Review of *Snow* by Orhan Pamuk

years in New York, has for some time been in contention for the post of mutual or reciprocal fictional interpreter. Turkey is, physically and historically, the "bridge" between East and West, and I have yet to read a Western newspaper report from the country that fails to employ that cheering metaphor. (I cannot be certain how many "Eastern" articles and broadcasts are similarly affirmative.) With his previous novel, *My Name Is Red*, Pamuk himself became a kind of register of this position, dwelling on the interpenetration of Islamic and Western styles and doing so in a "postmodern" fashion that laid due emphasis on texts, figures, and representations. After 9/11 he was the natural choice for the *New York Review of Books*, to which he contributed a decent if unoriginal essay that expressed horror at the atrocities while admonishing Westerners not to overlook the wretched of the earth. In Turkey he spoke up for Kurdish rights and once refused a state literary award. Some of his fellow secularists, however, felt that he was too ready to "balance" his views with criticism of the Kemalist and military forces that act as guarantors of Turkey's secularism.

In a Bush speech to the new membership of NATO, delivered in Istanbul last June, one of the president's handlers was astute enough to insert a quotation from Pamuk, to the effect that the finest view of the city was not from its European or its Asian shores but from—yes—the "bridge that unites them." The important thing, as the president went on to intone from Pamuk, "is not the clash of parties, civilizations, cultures, East and West." No; what is important is to recognize "that other peoples in other continents and civilizations" are "exactly like you." *De te fabula narratur.*

Human beings are of course essentially the same, if not exactly identical. But somehow this evolutionary fact does not prevent clashes of varying intensity from being the norm rather than the exception. "Remember your humanity, and forget the rest," Albert Einstein is supposed to have said. This already questionable call to amnesia translates badly in cultures that regard Einstein himself as a Satanic imp spawned from the hideous loins of Jewish degeneration.

In his new novel Pamuk gives us every reason to suppose that he is far more ambivalent about this facile "bridge-building" stuff than he has so far let on. The plot is complex yet susceptible of summary. Narrated by Pamuk, with the advantages of both foresight and hindsight, it shows an anomic young Turk named Kerim Alakusoglu, a poet with a bad case of literary sterility and sexual drought, as he negotiates a moment of personal and political crisis in the city of Kars, on the Turkish-Armenian frontier. Disliking his given name, the man prefers to go under the acronym formed by his initials: "Ka." Having taken part in the violent and futile Marxist-Leninist student movement that was eventually obliterated by the military coup of 1980, and having followed so many of his ex-comrades into exile in Germany, Ka is a burned-out case. Pretending to seek a journalistic assignment in this remote town, which has recently witnessed an epidemic of suicide by young girls thwarted in their desire to take the Muslim veil, he is in fact magnetized by the possibility of seeing Ipek, the lost flame of his youth. As he arrives, a blizzard isolates the city and almost buries it in snow—for which the Turkish word is *kar*. One might therefore deploy a cliché and say that the action is frozen in time.

When frozen in the present, the mise-en-scène discloses a community of miserably underemployed people, caught among a ramshackle state machine, a nascent Islamism, and the claims of competing nationalist minorities. A troupe of quasi-Brechtian traveling players is in town, and it enacts a "play within a play," in which the bitter violence of the region is translated with shocking effect directly onto the stage. Drawn into the social and religious conflict, Ka seems to alternate between visions of "snow" in its macrocosmic form—the chilly and hostile masses—and its microcosmic: the individual beauty and uniqueness of each flake. Along the scrutinized axes that every flake manifests he rediscovers his vocation and inspiration as a poet and arranges a cycle of verses. This collection is lost when, on his return to Frankfurt, he is shot down in a street of the red-light district.

In terms of characterization the novel is disappointing, precisely because its figures lack the crystalline integrity of individuals. Ipek, for example, appears on almost every page yet is barely allowed any quality other than her allegedly wondrous beauty. The protagonists speak their lines as Islamists, secularists, conformists, and opportunists. And the author leaves no room for doubt that he finds the Islamists the most persuasive and courageous. This is true in spite of the utter nonsense that he makes them spout. A couple of Muslim boys corner Ka and demand that he answer this question, about a dead girl he never met:

> Now we'd like to know if you could do us both a favor. The thing is, we can both accept that Teslime might have been driven to the sin of suicide by the pressures from her parents and the state. It's very painful; Fazil can't stop thinking that the girl he loved committed the sin of suicide. But if Teslime was a secret atheist like the one in the story, if she was one of those unlucky souls who don't even know that they are atheists, or if she committed suicide because she was an atheist, for Fazil this is a catastrophe: It means he was in love with an atheist.

I should caution the potential reader that a great deal of the dialogue is as lengthy and stilted as that, even if in this instance the self-imposed predicaments of the pious, along with their awful self-pitying solipsism, are captured fairly well. So is the superiority/inferiority complex of many provincial Turks—almost masochistic when it comes to detailing their own woes, yet intensely resentful of any "outside" sympathy. Most faithfully rendered, however, is the pervading sense that secularism has been, or is being, rapidly nullified by diminishing returns. The acting troupe is run by a vain old Kemalist mountebank named Sunay Zaim, who once fancied himself an Atatürk look-alike, and his equally decrepit and posturing lady friend. The army and the police use torture as a matter of course to hang on to power. Their few civilian supporters are represented as diseased old ex-Stalinists whose leader—one Z. Demirkol, not further named—could have leapt from the pages of Soviet agitprop. These forces take advantage of the snowstorm to mount a coup in Kars and impose their own arbitrary will, though it is never explained why they do this or how they can hope to get away with it.

In contrast, the Muslim fanatics are generally presented in a favorable or lenient light. A shadowy "insurgent" leader, incongruously named Blue, is a man of bravery and charm, who may or may not have played a heroic role in the fighting in Chechnya and Bosnia. (Among these and many other contemporary references, the Taliban and al-Qaeda are never mentioned.) The girls who immolate themselves for the right to wear head-covering are shown as if they had been pushed by the pitiless state, or by their gruesome menfolk, to the limits of endurance. They are, in other words, veiled quasi-feminists. The militant boys of their age are tormented souls seeking the good life in the spiritual sense. The Islamist ranks have their share of fools and knaves, but these tend to be ex-leftists who have switched sides in an ingratiating manner. Ka himself is boiling with guilt, about the "European" character that he has acquired in exile in Frankfurt, and about the realization that the Istanbul bourgeoisie, from which he originates, generally welcomes military coups without asking too many questions. The posturing Sunay at least phrases this well:

No one who's even slightly westernized can breathe free in this country unless they have a secular army protecting them, and no one needs this protection more than intellectuals who think they're better than everyone else and look down on other people. If it weren't for the army, the fanatics would be turning their rusty knives on the lot of them and their painted women and chopping them all into little pieces. But what do these upstarts do in return? They cling to their little European ways and turn up their affected little noses at the very soldiers who guarantee their freedom.

A continuous theme of the novel, indeed, is the rancor felt by the local inhabitants against anyone who has bettered himself—let alone herself—by emigrating to an undifferentiated "Europe" or by aping

European manners and attitudes. A secondary version of this bitterness, familiar to those who study small-town versus big-city attitudes the world over, is the suspicion of those left behind that they are somehow not good enough. But this mutates into the more consoling belief that they are despised by the urbane. Only one character—unnamed—has the nerve to point out that if free visas were distributed, every hypocrite in town would leave right away and Kars would be deserted.

As for the past tense in which Kars is also frozen, I have to rely on a certain amount of guesswork. Although Ka's acronym could ostensibly have been drawn from any pair of consonant/vowel first and last names, I presume from Pamuk's demonstrated interest in codes and texts that K and A were chosen deliberately. There seem to be two possibilities here: one is "Kemal Atatürk," the military founder of modern secular Turkey; the other is "Kurdistan and Armenia," standing in for the national subtexts of the tale.

Pamuk supplies no reason for his selection, but the setting of Kars means that he might intend elements of both of the above. The city was lost by Ottoman Turkey to Russia in 1878, regained in 1918, and then briefly lost again to an alliance of Bolsheviks and Armenians until, in late 1920, it became the scene of a Turkish nationalist victory that fixed the boundary between Turkey and then-Soviet Armenia that endures to the present day. (This event was among the many negations of Woodrow Wilson's postwar diplomacy, which had "awarded" the region to the Armenians.) From Kars, also in 1920, the legendary Turkish Communist leader Mustafa Suphi set out along the frontier region, dotted with magically evocative place-names like Erzurum and Trebizond, and was murdered with twelve of his comrades by right-wing "Young Turks." This killing was immortalized by Nâzim Hikmet in a poem that is still canonical in Turkey. (Hikmet himself, the nation's unofficial laureate, was to spend decades in jail and in exile because of his Communist loyalties.) The outright victor in all those discrepant struggles was Mustafa Kemal, who had helped defeat two "Christian" invasions of Turkish soil in his capacity as a soldier, and who went on to assume absolute political power and to supervise and direct the only lasting secular revolution that a Muslim society has ever undergone. His later change of name to Kemal Atatürk was only part of his driving will to "westernize" Turkey, Latinize its script, abolish male and female religious headgear, adopt surnames, and in general erase the Islamic caliphate that today's fundamentalists hope to restore.

Pamuk is at his best in depicting the layers of the past that are still on view in Kars—in particular the Armenian houses and churches and schools whose ghostly reminder of a scattered and desecrated civilization is enhanced in its eeriness by the veil of snow. Nor does he omit the sullen and disaffected Kurdish population. The price of Kemalism was the imposition of a uniform national identity on Turkey, where ethnic and religious variety was heavily repressed, and where the standard-issue unsmiling bust of Atatürk—pervasive in Pamuk's account of the scenery and most often described as the target of terrorism or vandalism—became the symbol of military rule. (Atatürk was a lifelong admirer of the French Revolution, but Turkey, as was once said of Prussia, is not so much a country that has an army as an army that has a country.) In these circumstances it takes a certain amount of courage for any Turkish citizen to challenge the authorized version of modern statehood.

However, courage is an element that this novel lacks. Some important Turkish scholarship has recently attempted an honest admission of the Armenian genocide and a critique of the official rationalizations for it. The principal author in this respect is Taner Akçam, who, as Pamuk is certainly aware, was initially forced to publish his findings as one of those despised leftist exiles in Germany—whereas from reading *Snow* one might easily conclude that all the Armenians of Anatolia had decided for some reason to pick up and depart en masse, leaving their ancestral properties for tourists to gawk at. As for the Kurds, Pamuk tends to represent them as rather primitive objects of sympathy.

Ka's poetic rebirth involves him, and us, in a comparable fatalism and passivity. Early in the story he is quite baldly described as feeling a predetermined poem coming on, and is prevented from completion of the closing lines only by a sudden knock at the door. I managed to assimilate the implied allusion to Coleridge's "Kubla Khan." But about fifty pages later, when another poem was successfully delivered from Ka's subconscious, I was confronted with a full-out deadpan account of the person from Porlock who had interrupted Coleridge at the critical moment. Pamuk's literalism and pedantry are probably his greatest enemies as a writer of fiction; he doesn't trust the reader until he has hit him over the head with dialogue and explanation of the most didactic kind. Throughout the remainder of the novel, though, we are invited to believe in the miraculous rather than the mundane: Ka quite simply sits himself down at odd moments and sets out near faultless poems (never quoted) on whatever paper is handy. The necessary cliché about "automatic writing" is eventually employed, somewhat heavily, to account for this. But I was inevitably put in mind of the Koran, or "recitation," by which the Prophet Muhammad came to be the supposed medium of the divine.

Ka is presented to us as a man who has assumed or affected his atheism as a kind of protective epidermis. His unbelief is of a piece with his attempt to deaden his emotions and decrease his vulnerability. His psyche is on a knife edge, and he is always ready to be overwhelmed by the last person he has spoken to. Yet he can watch an educator being shot in cold blood by a Muslim zealot and feel nothing. Only when in the company of beaming Dervishes and Sufis—those Islamic sects that survived Atatürk's dissolution of clerical power—does he become moist and trusting and openhearted. Yet "rising up inside him was that feeling he had always known as a child and as a young man at moments of extraordinary happiness: a prospect of future misery and hopelessness." Like the Danish prince who had a version of the same difficulty, Ka finds a form of cathartic relief in helping to produce the violent stage play that expresses his own fears and dreads. Pamuk drops in many loud references to Chekhov, and the gun that is on the mantelpiece from the beginning of the action is at last duly and lethally discharged. (It is described as a "Canakkale" rifle, Canakkale being the Turkish name for the Dardanelle Straits and the site of Gallipoli—the battle that was Atatürk's baptism as a leader.) The handgun that goes off later, and extinguishes Ka's life, is heard only offstage. But it is clear that Islamist revenge has followed him to the heart of Europe and punished him for his ambivalence.

Prolix and often clumsy as it is, Pamuk's new novel should be taken as a cultural warning. So weighty was the impression of Atatürk that ever since his death, in 1938, Western statecraft has been searching for an emulator or successor. Nasser was thought for a while to be the needful charismatic, secularizing strongman. So was Sadat. So, for a while, was the Shah of Iran. And so was Saddam Hussein . . . Eager above all to have a modern yet "Muslim" state within the tent, the United States and the European Union have lately been taking Turkey's claims to modernity more and more at face value. The attentive reader of *Snow* will not be so swift to embrace this consoling conclusion.

(*The Atlantic*, October 2004)

Bring on the Mud

———⟨∞∞⟩———

IN HIS CLASSIC post–World War I novel *The Good Soldier Schweik*, the Czech writer Jaroslav Hašek makes mention of "The Party for Moderate Progress within the Boundaries of Law," the very sort of political formation the powers-that-be have always dreamed of. With such respectful parties, there's no danger of any want of decorum, or challenge to the consensus, or spreading of misgiving about authority or institutions. Instead, or rather: "There's much to be said on both sides of the case." "The truth lies somewhere in between." "Lurid black and white must perforce give way to reputable gray."

Satire defeats itself, as usual. A political formation that could readily be considered absurd by intelligent readers in the stultified Austro-Hungarian Empire is now considered the beau ideal by the larger part of the American commentating class. What's the most reprehensible thing a politician can be these days? Why, "partisan," of course. What's the most disapproving thing that can be said of a "partisan" remark? That it's "divisive." What's to be deplored most at election time? "Going negative" or, worse, "mudslinging." That sort of behavior "generates more heat than light" (as if there were any source of light apart from heat).

The selection of these pejoratives tells us a good deal, as does the near-universal acceptance by the mass media of the associated vernacular. To illustrate what I mean, consider a celebrated recent instance. Senator John Kerry was not adopting any "issue" when he proposed himself for the presidency by laying heavy stress on his record as a warrior. (That is to say, he clearly could not have intended to assert that Democrats had been more gung-ho than Republicans during the Vietnam War.) The "issue" was his own record, and ostensibly no more. But when that record was challenged, with varying degrees of rancor and differing levels of accuracy, the response was immediate. I have in front of me as I write a full-page ad in the *New York Times* of August 27, 2004, attacking the "Swift Boat Veterans for Truth" who challenged Kerry. This costly proclamation states, and then demands: "It can be stopped. All it takes is leadership. Denounce the smear. Let's get back to the issues."

Never mind the truth or falsehood of the allegations for now. What's worth notice is that the ad does not deny their truth so much as say that nobody has the right to make the allegations in the first place. Thus, having himself raised a subject, the candidate is presumed to enjoy the right to have his own account of it taken at face value. Anything else would be indecorous. The slight plaintiveness of this is underscored by the call to "get back to the issues." But surely Kerry had made his military service an "issue." At the bottom of the ad appear the legend "Paid for by the Democratic National Committee" and the accompanying assurance that "this communication is not authorized by any candidate or candidate's committee." Even the law requires us to believe these days that, for purposes of fund-raising, the organs of a party are independent of its nominee (which is why the members of the "Swift Boat" group had to pretend to be above politics in the first place, thereby leaving themselves vulnerable to the charge of being sinister proxies).

But is there any place "above politics"? Is there a subject that can avoid becoming "a political football" or a resource out of which "political capital" cannot be made? The banality of the automatic rhetoric is again suggestive here. Since every other electoral metaphor is sports oriented, from the top of the ninth to the ten-yard line to the playing of "offense" and "defense," why should there not be a ball or two in play? (Surely, to move to a market image, it's short-term dividends rather than actual capital that one hopes to accrue.)

Opinion polling shows how far cognitive dissonance on this point has progressed. When asked, millions of people will say that the two parties are (a) so much alike as to be virtually indistinguishable, and (b) too much occupied in partisan warfare. The two "perceptions" are not necessarily opposed: party conflict could easily be more and more disagreement about less and less—what Sigmund Freud characterized in another context as "the narcissism of the small difference." For a while, about a decade ago, the combination of those two large, vague impressions gave rise to the existence of a quasi-plausible third party, led by Ross Perot, which argued, in effect, that politics should be above politics, and that government should give way to management. That illusion, like the touching belief that one party is always better than the other, is compounded of near-equal parts naïveté and cynicism.

The current discourse becomes odder and emptier the more you examine it. We live in a culture that's saturated with the cult of personality and with attention to the private life. So much is this the case that candidates compete to appear on talk shows hosted by near therapists. In so doing, they admit that their "personalities" are under discussion and, to that extent, in contention. Even I, who don't relish the Oprah world, say, "Why not?" There must be very few people who choose their friends or their lovers on the basis of their political outlook rather than their individual qualities. Yet just try to suggest that the psychopathic element in a politician, whether Richard Nixon or Bill Clinton, is itself a consideration, and see how fast you're accused of "personalizing" or "witch-hunting" or "mudslinging." This charge will most often come from someone who makes his or her living as the subsidiary of a party machine and has an idealized or personalized photo or portrait of a mere human being or "personality" in a position of honor somewhere near the mantelpiece.

By definition, politics is, or ought to be, division. It expresses, or at least reflects, or at the very least emulates, the inevitable difference of worldview that originates, for modern purposes, with Edmund Burke and Thomas Paine. This difference can be muddied, especially in a highly disparate society, but it cannot be absolutely obscured. So given the inevitable tendency of the quotidian, the corrupt, and the self-interested to muddy differences and make sinuous appeals to all sides, might we not place a higher value on those who seek to make the differences plainer and sharper?

Yet we seemingly dread controversy, almost as a danger in itself. The consequence is that there are large and important topics that the electoral "process" is almost designed to muffle or muzzle. Let me select three important topics that everybody knew in advance could not break the surface in an election year: the "war on drugs," the death penalty, and the Pledge of Allegiance. It's quite simply assumed, across the political class, that no candidate interested in forwarding his or her own cause would depart from the presumed consensus on all three—which is that we must persist in the "war on drugs," come what may; that the death penalty is a necessary part of law and order; and that the pledge should recognize the Almighty. Each of these "issues" is symbolic of a greater one—the role of the state in the private life of the citizen, the posture of the United States toward international legal norms, and the boundary of separation between religion and government—and there is good evidence that the extent of apparent agreement on all three is neither as wide nor as deep as is commonly supposed. In any event, could we not do with more honest and more informed disagreement on these subjects? Is not the focus on the trivial a product, at least in part, of the repression of the serious? In much the same way, the pseudo-fight over Senator Kerry's valor in the Mekong Delta is a distorted and packaged version of the "debate" over the conflict in Iraq, in which both parties pretend to agree with each other on the main point, while in fact not even agreeing genuinely with themselves. The general evasiveness and cowardice surely call for more polarization rather than less.

Just as hypocrisy is the compliment vice pays to virtue, so, I sometimes think, the smarmy stress on "bipartisanship" is a tribute

of a kind to American diversity. A society so large and plural must
depend, to a great degree, on the observance of an etiquette of "non-
offensiveness"—to give this affectation the off-putting name it deserves.
In fact, that very diversity demands *more* political variety rather than
less. The consensus that slavery in America was too toxic and divisive
an "issue" to become a political subject only postponed the evil time
when it became the cause of an actual civil war.

That reflection, on its own, puts paid to the vague, soft view that
politics used to be more civil in the good old days, and that mudslinging is a new invention. Leave aside the relative innocuousness of the
supposed mudslinging that now takes place; it is simply flat-out mytho-
logical to suppose that things were more polite in the golden past. Yes,
there was Adlai Stevenson in the mid-twentieth century saying that
he'd rather lose the election than tell a lie, but earlier in the century
there was also Ed "Boss" Crump of Memphis, Tennessee, charging
that his opponent would milk his neighbor's cow through a crack in
the fence. When I was a boy, the satirical pianist-and-songster duo
Michael Flanders and Donald Swann made several excellent albums.
One of their hits was a rousing ditty about the basking habits of the
hippopotamus. The refrain went as follows:

Mud, mud, glorious mud!
Nothing quite like it for cooling the blood!
So follow me, follow—down to the hollow
And there let us wallow
In glorious mud!

Michael Flanders's daughter Laura is now a punchy presenter on
Al Franken's Air America station, where people can say whatever they
like about Dick Cheney and Halliburton, George W. Bush and Osama
bin Laden, the Carlyle Group and other elements of the invisible
government. Bring it on, I say. Where would we be without the tradition of American populism, which adopted for itself the term hurled
as an insult by Teddy Roosevelt—"muckraker"? What goes for muck

should go for mud. Who would wish to be without that "used-car salesman" innuendo against Richard Nixon, or the broad hint that Barry Goldwater was itchy in the trigger finger? Just let's have no whining when the tables are turned.

In the election that pitted Thomas Jefferson against John Adams, the somewhat more restricted and refined electorate had its choice between the president of the American Philosophical Society and the president of the American Academy of Arts and Sciences. "What could possibly have been more civilized and agreeable?" breathes the incurable nostalgic. Yet it's worth looking up what was said, especially about Jefferson, in those days: he was called adulterer, whoremaster, atheist, even deserter in the face of the enemy. There's no doubt that the emergence of parties or "factions" after the retirement of George Washington gave voters a set of clear and often stark choices—and a good thing that was, too.

The United States makes large claims for itself, among them the claim that the nation is the model for a society based simultaneously on democracy and multiethnicity. It's certainly no exaggeration to say that on the success or failure of this principle much else depends. But there must be better ways of affirming it than by clinging to an insipid parody of a two-party system that counts as a virtue the ability to escape thorny questions and postpone larger ones.

(*The Wilson Quarterly*, Autumn 2004)

Ohio's Odd Numbers

—◅◅◅▻▻▻—

I F IT WERE not for Kenyon College, I might have missed, or
skipped, the whole controversy. The place is a visiting lecturer's
dream, or the ideal of a campus-movie director in search of a setting.
It is situated in wooded Ohio hills, in the small town of Gambier,
about an hour's drive from Columbus. Its literary magazine, *The Kenyon Review*, was founded by John Crowe Ransom in 1939. Its alumni
include Paul Newman, E. L. Doctorow, Jonathan Winters, Robert
Lowell, Chief Justice William Rehnquist, and President Rutherford B.
Hayes. The college's origins are Episcopalian, its students well man-
nered and well off and predominantly white, but it is by no means
Bush-Cheney territory. Arriving to speak there a few days after the
presidential election, I found that the place was still buzzing. Here's
what happened in Gambier, Ohio, on decision day 2004.

The polls opened at 6:30 a.m. There were only two voting machines
(push-button direct-recording electronic systems) for the entire town
of 2,200 (with students). The mayor, Kirk Emmert, had called the
board of elections ten days earlier, saying that the number of registered
voters would require more than that. (He knew, as did many others,
that hundreds of students had asked to register in Ohio because it
was a critical "swing" state.) The mayor's request was denied. Indeed,

instead of there being extra capacity on Election Day, one of the only two machines chose to break down before lunchtime.

By the time the polls officially closed, at 7:30 that evening, the line of those waiting to vote was still way outside the community center and well into the parking lot. A federal judge thereupon ordered Knox County, in which Gambier is located, to comply with Ohio law, which grants the right to vote to those who have shown up in time. "Authority to Vote" cards were kindly distributed to those on line (voting is a right, not a privilege), but those on line needed more than that. By the time the 1,175 voters in the precinct had all cast their ballots, it was almost four in the morning, and many had had to wait for up to eleven hours. In the spirit of democratic carnival, pizzas and canned drinks and guitarists were on hand to improve the shining moment. TV crews showed up, and the young Americans all acted as if they had been cast by Frank Capra: cheerful and good-humored, letting older voters get to the front, catching up on laptop essays, many voting for the first time and all convinced that a long and cold wait was a small price to pay. Typical was Pippa White, who said that "even after eight hours and fifteen minutes I still had energy. It lets you know how worth it this is." Heartwarming, until you think about it.

The students of Kenyon had one advantage, and they made one mistake. Their advantage was that their president, S. Georgia Nugent, told them that they could be excused from class for voting. Their mistake was to reject the paper ballots that were offered to them late in the evening, after attorneys from the Ohio Democratic Party had filed suit to speed up the voting process in this way. The ballots were being handed out (later to be counted by machine under the supervision of Knox County's Democratic and Republican chairs) when someone yelled through the window of the community center, "Don't use the paper ballots! The Republicans are going to appeal it and it won't count!" After that, the majority chose to stick with the machines.

Across the rest of Ohio, the Capra theme was not so noticeable. Reporters and eyewitnesses told of voters who had given up after humiliating or frustrating waits, and who often cited the unwillingness of their employers to accept voting as an excuse for lateness or absence. In some way or another, these bottlenecks had a tendency to occur in working-class and, shall we just say, nonwhite precincts. So did many disputes about "provisional" ballots, the sort that are handed out when a voter can prove his or her identity but not his or her registration at that polling place. These glitches might all be attributable to inefficiency or incompetence (though Gambier had higher turnouts and much shorter lines in 1992 and 1996). Inefficiency and incompetence could also explain the other oddities of the Ohio process—from machines that redirected votes from one column to the other to machines that recorded amazing tallies for unknown fringe candidates, to machines that apparently showed that voters who waited for a long time still somehow failed to register a vote at the top of the ticket for any candidate for the presidency of these United States.

However, for any of that last category of anomaly to be explained, one would need either a voter-verified paper trail of ballots that could be tested against the performance of the machines or a court order that would allow inspection of the machines themselves. The first of these does not exist, and the second has not yet been granted.

I don't know who it was who shouted idiotically to voters not to trust the paper ballots in Gambier, but I do know a lot of people who are convinced that there was dirty work at the crossroads in the Ohio vote. Some of these people are known to me as nutbags and paranoids of the first water, people whose grassy-knoll minds can simply cancel or deny any objective reasons for a high Republican turnout. (Here's how I know some of these people: in November 1999, I wrote a column calling for international observers to monitor the then upcoming presidential election. I was concerned about restrictive ballot-access laws, illegal slush funds, denial of access to media for independents, and abuse of the state laws that banned "felons" from voting. At the end, I managed to mention the official disenfranchisement of voters in my hometown of Washington, DC, and the questionable "reliability or integrity" of the new voting-machine technology. I've had all these wacko friends ever since.) But here are some of the non-wacko reasons to revisit the Ohio election.

First, the county-by-county and precinct-by-precinct discrepancies. In Butler County, for example, a Democrat running for the state supreme court chief justice received 61,559 votes. The Kerry-Edwards ticket drew about 5,000 fewer votes, at 56,243. This contrasts rather markedly with the behavior of the Republican electorate in that county, who cast about 40,000 fewer votes for their judicial nominee than they did for Bush and Cheney. (The latter pattern, with vote totals tapering down from the top of the ticket, is by far the more general—and probable—one nationwide and statewide.)

In eleven other counties, the same Democratic judicial nominee, C. Ellen Connally, managed to outpoll the Democratic presidential and vice-presidential nominees by hundreds and sometimes thousands of votes. So maybe we have a barn-burning, charismatic future candidate on our hands, and Ms. Connally is a force to be reckoned with on a national scale. Or is it perhaps a trick of the Ohio atmosphere? There do seem to be a lot of eccentrics in the state. In Cuyahoga County, which includes the city of Cleveland, two largely black precincts on the East Side voted like this. In Precinct 4F: Kerry, 290; Bush, 21; Peroutka, 215. In Precinct 4N: Kerry, 318; Bush, 11; Badnarik, 163. Mr. Peroutka and Mr. Badnarik are, respectively, the presidential candidates of the Constitution and Libertarian Parties. In addition to this eminence, they also possess distinctive (but not particularly African-American-sounding) names. In 2000, Ralph Nader's best year, the total vote received in Precinct 4F by all third-party candidates combined was eight.

In Montgomery County, two precincts recorded a combined undervote of almost 6,000. This is to say that that many people waited to vote but, when their turn came, had no opinion on who should be the president, voting only for lesser offices. In these two precincts alone, that number represents an undervote of 25 percent, in a county where undervoting averages out at just 2 percent. Democratic precincts had 75 percent more undervotes than Republican ones.

In Precinct 1B of Gahanna, in Franklin County, a computerized voting machine recorded a total of 4,258 votes for Bush and 260 votes for Kerry. In that precinct, however, there are only 800 registered voters, of whom 638 showed up. Once the "glitch" had been identified, the president had to be content with 3,893 fewer votes than the computer had awarded him.

In Miami County, a Saddam Hussein–type turnout was recorded in the Concord Southwest and Concord South precincts, which boasted 98.5 percent and 94.27 percent turnouts, respectively, both of them registering overwhelming majorities for Bush. Miami County also managed to report 19,000 additional votes for Bush after 100 percent of the precincts had reported on Election Day.

In Mahoning County, *Washington Post* reporters found that many people had been victims of "vote hopping," which is to say that voting machines highlighted a choice of one candidate after the voter had recorded a preference for another. Some specialists in election software diagnose this as a "calibration issue."

Machines are fallible and so are humans, and shit happens, to be sure, and no doubt many Ohio voters were able to record their choices promptly and without grotesque anomalies. But what strikes my eye is this: *in practically every case* where lines were too long or machines too few the foul-up was in a Democratic county or precinct, and *in practically every case* where machines produced impossible or improbable outcomes it was the challenger who suffered and the actual or potential Democratic voters who were shortchanged, discouraged, or held up to ridicule as chronic undervoters or as sudden converts to fringe-party losers.

This might argue in itself *against* any conspiracy or organized rigging, since surely anyone clever enough to pre-fix a vote would make sure, just for the look of the thing, that the discrepancies and obstructions were more evenly distributed. I called all my smartest conservative friends to ask them about this. Back came their answer: Look at what happened in Warren County.

On Election Night, citing unspecified concerns about terrorism and homeland security, officials "locked down" the Warren County administration building and prevented any reporters from monitoring the vote count. It was announced, using who knows what "scale," that on a scale of one to ten the terrorist threat was a ten. It was also claimed that the information came from an FBI agent, even though the FBI denies that.

Warren County is certainly a part of Republican territory in Ohio: it went only 28 percent for Gore last time and 28 percent for Kerry this time. On the face of it, therefore, not a county where the GOP would have felt the need to engage in any voter "suppression." A point for the anti-conspiracy side, then. Yet even those exact same voting totals have their odd aspect. In 2000, Gore stopped running television commercials in Ohio some weeks before the election. He also faced a Nader challenge. Kerry put huge resources into Ohio, did not face any Nader competition, and yet got exactly the same proportion of the Warren County votes.

Whichever way you shake it, or hold it to the light, there is something about the Ohio election that refuses to add up. The sheer number of irregularities compelled a formal recount, which was completed in late December and which came out much the same as the original one, with 176 fewer votes for George Bush. But this was a meaningless exercise in reassurance, since there is simply no means of checking, for example, how many "vote hops" the computerized machines might have performed unnoticed.

There are some other, more random factors to be noted. The Ohio secretary of state, Kenneth Blackwell, was a state cochair of the Bush-Cheney campaign at the same time as he was discharging his responsibilities for an aboveboard election in his home state. Diebold, which manufactures paper-free, touch-screen voting machines, likewise has its corporate headquarters in Ohio. Its chairman, president, and CEO, Walden O'Dell, is a prominent Bush supporter and fund-raiser who proclaimed in 2003 that he was "committed to helping Ohio deliver its electoral votes to the president next year." (See "Hack the Vote," by Michael Shnayerson, *Vanity Fair*, April 2004.) Diebold, together with its competitor, ES&S, counts more than half the votes cast in the United States. This not very acute competition is perhaps made still less acute by the fact that a vice president of ES&S and a Diebold director of strategic services are brothers.

I would myself tend to discount most of the above, since an oligarchy bent on stealing an election would probably not announce itself so brashly as to fit into a Michael Moore script. Then, all state secretaries of state are partisan, after all, while in Ohio each of the eighty-eight county election boards contains two Democrats and two Republicans. The chairman of Diebold is entitled to his political opinion just as much as any other citizen.

However, there is one soothing explanation that I don't trust anymore. It was often said, in reply to charges of vote tampering, that it would have had to be "a conspiracy so immense" as to involve a dangerously large number of people. Indeed, some Ohio Democrats themselves laughed off some of the charges, saying that they too would have had to have been part of the plan. The stakes here are very high: one defector or turncoat with hard evidence could send the principals to jail forever and permanently discredit the party that had engaged in fraud.

I had the chance to spend quality time with someone who came to me well recommended, who did not believe that fraud had yet actually been demonstrated, whose background was in the manufacture of the machines, and who wanted to be anonymous. It certainly could be done, she said, and only a very, very few people would have to be "in on it." This is because of the small number of firms engaged in the manufacturing and the even smaller number of people, subject as they are to the hiring practices of these firms, who understand the technology. "Machines were put in place with no sampling to make sure they were 'in control' and no comparison studies," she explained. "The code of the machines is not public knowledge, and none of these machines has since been impounded." In these circumstances, she continued, it's possible to manipulate both the count and the proportions of votes.

In the bad old days of Tammany Hall, she pointed out, you had to break the counter pins on the lever machines, and if there was any vigilance in an investigation, the broken pins would automatically incriminate the machine. With touch-screen technology, the crudeness and predictability of the old ward-heeler racketeers isn't the question anymore. But had there been a biased "setting" on the new machines it could be uncovered—if a few of them could be impounded. The Ohio courts are currently refusing all motions to put the state's voting machines, punch-card or touch-screen, in the public domain. It's not clear to me, or to anyone else, who is tending the machines in the meanwhile. . . .

I asked her, finally, what would be the logical grounds for deducing that any tampering had in fact occurred. "Well, I understand from what I have read," she said, "that the early exit polls on the day were believed by both parties." That, I was able to tell her from direct experience, was indeed true. But it wasn't quite enough, either. So I asked, "What if all the anomalies and malfunctions, to give them a neutral name, were distributed along one axis of consistency: in other words, that they kept on disadvantaging only one candidate?" My question was hypothetical, as she had made no particular study of Ohio, but she replied at once: "Then that would be quite serious."

I am not any sort of statistician or technologist, and (like many Democrats in private) I did not think that John Kerry should have been president of any country at any time. But I have been reviewing books on history and politics all my life, making notes in the margin when I come across a wrong date, or any other factual blunder, or a missing point in the evidence. No book is ever free from this. But if all the mistakes and omissions occur in such a way as to be consistent, to support or attack only one position, then you give the author a lousy review. The Federal Election Commission, which has been a risible body for far too long, ought to make Ohio its business. The Diebold company, which also manufactures ATMs, should not receive another dime until it can produce a voting system that is similarly reliable. And Americans should cease to be treated like serfs or extras when they present themselves to exercise their franchise.

(*Vanity Fair*, March 2005)

On Becoming American

A S WE WERE waiting for the cameras to roll in a Washington studio just before Christmas, my *faux bonhomme* host, Pat Buchanan, inquired offhandedly as to my citizenship and residency status. I innocently told him that my paperwork for naturalization was in the system, but that Homeland Security had racked up an immense backlog of applications. Then up came the music for the next segment—which was to be about the display of religious symbols on public land—and before I knew it, Buchanan was demanding to know by what right I, a foreign atheist, could presume to come over here and lecture Americans about their Christian heritage.

Synthetic outrage is de rigueur in the world of American cable-TV news, and I was almost as surprised by the authenticity of my own fury as I had been by the extreme inexpensiveness of Buchanan's ambush. More than two decades in Washington—and all that time beseeched by Buchanan to be a guest! Three children born in the country, and all three as American as the day is long! An unblemished record of compliance with boring correspondence from the IRS! As the blush of anger left my cheek, however, I dimly realized that I was not resentful of Buchanan's abuse of his own hypocritical hospitality. Rather, I felt that my very own hearth was being profaned. Don't be telling me to go home, big boy. I *am* home.

Seething a little more in the limo that bore me away, I understood why I had not even thought of one possible riposte: "Don't you take that tone with me, you German-Irish fascist windbag. I don't have to justify my presence to riffraff like you. Tell it to Father Coughlin and Charles Lindbergh—and meanwhile, don't stab our boys in Iraq in the back." Had I said that, or anything like it, I would truly have been sorry, at the time as well as later. (On the other hand, I shall always covertly wish I *had* said it—though had I done so, the prefix to "bag" would not have been "wind." One hopes to keep one's well of meticulous English pure and undefiled; but then again, there's no demotic abuse like American demotic abuse.)

In writing a biography of President Clinton, who was our contemporary at Oxford, my English friend and colleague Martin Walker had some success with a book titled *The President We Deserve*. The volume was also published in London, with the no less eloquent title *The President They Deserve*. I had just completed work on a short biography of another president, Thomas Jefferson, and had found myself referring in the closing passages to "our" republic and "our" Constitution. I didn't even notice that I had done this until I came to review the pages in final proof. What does it take for an immigrant to shift from "you" to "we"?

No loyalty oath, no coerced allegiance, was involved. In the course of writing thousands of columns and making hundreds of media and podium appearances, many of them highly critical of the government of the day, I had almost never been asked by what right I did so. My offspring were Americans just by virtue of being born here (no other country in the world is or has ever been this generous). As soon as I got my green card, immigration officers started saying "welcome home" when I passed through. Moreover, as one who is incompetent to do anything save writing and speaking, I stood under the great roof of the First Amendment and did not have to think (as I once had to think) of the libel laws and the other grand and petty restraints that oppress my craft in the country of my birth.

But this wasn't my thinking. Anyone who has read this far may already be muttering, "Easy for *you* to say. English-speaking. White.

Oxford-educated." Semiconsciously, I had been thinking the same way. *You're lucky enough as it is, and anyway who will ever mistake you for anything but a Brit?* Yet osmosis was at work somehow, or so I must now suppose, and when it came to a critical point, it did so in the form I would most have wanted to resist: namely, that of a cliché. For me, September 11, 2001, really did "change everything." In exploring the non-clichéd but most literal forms of that observation, and its ramifications, I began to read the press—the American press—as if it were held up to some kind of mirror. Each time I was instructed that such-and-such a fatuity was the view of "the Europeans," I decided not that my Anglo-Celtic-Polish-German-Jewish heritage was being parodied (though it was) but that someone whose claim to be "European" was at least as good as M. Chirac's should assure his American friends that they need not feel unsophisticated or embarrassed. *Au contraire . . .*

One cannot hope or expect to keep such a feeling—which I claim is of the mind as well as of the heart—within bounds. I had lived in the nation's capital for many years, and never particularly liked it. But when it was exposed to attack, and looked and felt so goddamn vulnerable, I fused myself with it. I know now that no solvent can ever unglue that bond. And yes, before you ask, I could easily name Arabs, Iranians, Greeks, Mexicans, and others who felt precisely as I did, and who communicated it almost wordlessly. I tried my hardest in 2001 to express it in words all the same. The best I could do was to say that in America your internationalism can and should be your patriotism. I still rather like the clumsiness of what I said. In finishing my Jefferson book I concluded more sententiously that the American Revolution is the only revolution that still resonates. I suppose I could narrow this a bit and add that the strenuously nativist and isolationist Pat Buchanan still strikes me, as he always did, as chronically un-American.

(*The Atlantic*, May 2005)

Mikhail Lermontov:
A Doomed Young Man

———❦———

THE POINT TO be marked in a study of *A Hero of Our Time*," observed Vladimir Nabokov, "is that, though of tremendous and at times somewhat morbid interest to the sociologist, the 'time' is of less interest to the student of literature than the 'hero.'" With this characteristically lofty ruling—which helped introduce his own co-translation of the novel in 1958—Nabokov proposed a false antithesis, or a distinction without a difference. The "student of literature" must needs be to some extent a student of history, if not exactly of "sociology." Much of the fascination that the book continues to exert is owing to its context, and none of the editions I possess, including Paul Foote's 1966 translation and now this very deft version by Hugh Aplin, has failed to include quite a deal of background material without which Mikhail Lermontov's brief, intricate masterpiece is difficult to appreciate. These five nicely chiseled stories, giving *Rashomon*-like perspectives on the short life of a doomed young man, are in a most intriguing way "of their time."

The equally pleasurable elements of time and heroism are in fact united in the most common description of the novel and its author:

———

Review of *A Hero of Our Time* by Mikhail Lermontov, translated by Hugh Aplin both are referred to as "Byronic." And the similitude is fair in either case. Early Russian literature was intimately connected to the Europeanizing and liberal tendency of the "Decembrist" revolution of 1825, which was enthusiastically supported by Pushkin and his inheritor Lermontov. And the debt of those rebels to Byron's inspiration was almost cultish in its depth and degree. Lermontov even published a short poem in 1832 titled "No, I'm Not Byron." In it he wrote,

> No, I'm not Byron: set apart
> Like him, by Fate (though I'm
>   unknown yet) . . .
> I started sooner, I'll end sooner:
> But little work will I complete . . .

Those last two lines surely betray a foreknowledge of—almost an ambition for—an early and Romantic death. A few months before his actual death, in 1841, Lermontov set down this even more premonitory verse:

> In noon's heat, in a dale of Dagestan,
> With lead inside my breast, stirless
>   I lay;
> The deep wound still smoked on;
>   my blood
> Kept trickling drop by drop away.

Dagestan, like Chechnya and Ossetia, is part of the southern Caucasus, which czarism was at that time engaged in conquering and disciplining. (This was the Russian end of the "Great Game" that Kipling later described as extending all the way to the North-West Frontier Province of India and Afghanistan.) Lermontov served twice in the Caucasus as a cavalryman, both times as punishment. On the first occasion he had offended the authorities by writing a poem implying that Pushkin's death, in a duel in 1837, had been orchestrated by the czar's regime. On the second occasion he was in trouble for fighting a duel himself, with the son of the French ambassador to St. Petersburg. In 1841 he fought another duel, with a brother officer in the Caucasus, not far from the spot where Pechorin fights his duel in *A Hero of Our Time*, and was killed instantly. This obsession with single combat and possible self-immolation is admitted by Nabokov to be poignant because, as he bluntly put it, "the poet's dream came true." Well, then: we should by all means be as much aware of the surrounding conditions as he was.

Lermontov, like Byron, was of partly Scottish origin, being descended from a seventeenth-century mercenary named George Learmont. (Pushkin himself was of part-Ethiopian descent, so multiculturalism and multiethnicity had their role to play in the evolution of Russian letters; but Sir Walter Scott was also a kind of gold standard in those days, and his *Old Mortality*, of all novels, is respectfully mentioned as the book that Pechorin reads on the night before the duel.) Lermontov recurs to Byron with attention throughout *A Hero of Our Time*. Pechorin's close friend, Werner the physician, is described as having "one leg shorter than the other, like Byron." His chief female target, Princess Mary, is described admiringly as one "who's read Byron in English and knows algebra." (Most Russians of the period would have read Byron in French.) In a moody moment Pechorin reflects, "How many people, beginning their lives, think they'll end them like Alexander the Great or Lord Byron, but then remain titular councillors an entire lifetime?" He speaks appreciatively of a poem titled "The Vampyre," which was then believed to be Byron's work.

It is when we move from the Byronic to the ironic that difficulties arise. The publication of the novel, in 1840, aroused a pitch of criticism that was based on the very title itself. How could such a louche, amoral young man as Pechorin be presented as a hero? In a languid preface to the second edition Lermontov commented, "Our public is still so young and ingenuous that it does not understand a fable if it does not find a moral at the end of it. It does not get a joke, does not sense an irony; it is simply badly brought up." But where is the irony of the title to be discovered? Once again it is necessary to be daring enough to disagree with Nabokov. Quite plainly, Pechorin is not presented as a "hero" of any kind. Even when described by others who admire him, such as the staunch old soldier Maxim Maximych (one of a series of diminishingly reliable narrators), he appears affectless and irresponsible even if charismatic. To himself, he is bored and detached on the outside and moved by nameless discontents within. To the objective reader, if such there be, he seems callous and occasionally sadistic. At the very end of the last story he demonstrates a bit of initiative and élan in subduing a homicidal Cossack; but in the wider war to repress the natives of the Caucasus he does mainly as he is told. If this is Byronic at all, it is of the Byron of "The Corsair": a consummate egotist. Not a hint of idealism or principle is permitted to occur—or not ostensibly, at any rate.

No, the irony must be about the "time." Pechorin, and Lermontov, treat society and the military exactly as they find them. Russia's slavishness and torpor are taken for granted: there is a matter-of-fact mention of the knout, and later of a dowry of fifty serfs. Drunkenness is endemic in the army; snobbery and favoritism are the rule at the aristocratic health resorts in which the Caucasus abounds. The glorious Russian war to civilize the Muslim tribes is a squalid and brutal business on both sides. In these circumstances why should Pechorin rouse himself to care about anything? Meeting old Maxim Maximych by chance, in what is for me the most tragic scene in the novel, he snubs him like any young Prince Hal turning away a superfluous Falstaff. Women are creatures whose influence on men is to be resented; if the opportunity arises, revenge can and should be taken for this. Thus the scandal of the novel was occasioned by a young officer of good family who said, in effect, Here is a mirror. Look into it if you care to, but don't be hypocritical about what you see.

It might be more rewarding to trace the hidden influence of Pushkin than the relatively blatant traces of Byron. Before his own pointless death Pushkin had begun, to Lermontov's infinite disgust, to compromise with the czar and the establishment. Even in the poem

Lermontov wrote on his own hero Pushkin's suspicious end ("The Death of the Poet"), he inquired angrily about the way the idol had gone soft: "Why did he shake hands with worthless slanderers? / Why did he trust false words and flattery?"

The hero of Pushkin's *Eugene Onegin* took his name from the river Onega, in northern Russia. The "hero" of Lermontov's *A Hero of Our Time*, Grigory Pechorin, was named for the river Pechora, somewhat farther to the north. One Russian critic has pointed out that whereas the Onega flows smoothly to the sea, the Pechora is turbulent and wild. It was obviously part of Lermontov's fictional plan to be more remote and more extreme than his predecessor. This becomes plain when, by a fantastic process of eavesdropping and coincidence, Pechorin learns that the duel into which he is to be provoked will also be a setup for his murder. In riposte he adopts a strategy that allows him to kill his adversary, Grushnitsky, with no more compunction than he would have felt in killing a cockroach. His casual remark to Dr. Werner, and to the landscape, as Grushnitsky's corpse topples into a ravine is a masterpiece of the laconic: *"Finita la commedia!"*

One is more than tempted to speculate that Lermontov made Pechorin do what Pushkin could not: discover the plot against his life and then act with ruthlessness and cold decision to ensure that it was the assassin who was assassinated. This makes it the more eerie that he was incapable of such resolution in his own life and death. Czar Nicholas I had denounced *A Hero of Our Time* in a clumsy letter to his wife. (As Anthony Powell, a superior contriver of literary and social coincidence, once phrased it, "In spite of Russia's great size, the number of people who actually operated things politically, socially, culturally, was very small. Thus a poetry-writing subaltern could be a real thorn in the side of the Tsar himself.") When Lermontov was brought to the field of honor, he apparently declined to fire on the fool who had provoked the duel. Slain on the spot, he never heard the czar's reported comment: "A dog's death for a dog." His unflinching indifference on the occasion, however, drew on two well-rehearsed nineteenth-century scenarios: the contemptuous aristocrat on the scaffold, and the stoic revolutionary in front of the firing squad. The Decembrists, in their way, admired and emulated both models.

One remaining question will probably never be cleared up. Doris Lessing alludes to it slyly in her foreword to Aplin's translation. "I often wonder," Pechorin says, "why I'm so persistent about winning the love of a young girl I don't want to seduce and will never marry. What's the point of this feminine coquetry?" The "feminine coquetry" here is not in the female. Nabokov makes the same point in a different way, by remarking,

> Lermontov was singularly inept in his descriptions of women. Mary is the generalized young thing of novelettes, with no attempt at individualization except perhaps her "velvety" eyes, which however are forgotten in the course of the story. Vera is a mere phantom, with a phantom birthmark on her cheek; Bela, an Oriental beauty on the lid of a box of Turkish delight.

The Casanova complex—a hectic and indiscriminate pursuit of women who are not truly desired—is sometimes suspected of being a masking symptom of the repressed homosexual. Byron's frantic activity in this sphere (or do I mean in these spheres?) has long been a subject in its own right. Powell mentions that although the duel that extinguished Pushkin was apparently about his wife's supposed adultery, "there were also homosexual undercurrents in the circles involved."

Pechorin is described from several perspectives in the novel: by his old friend, by himself, and by a third party, who speaks of his skin as having "a sort of feminine delicacy." Lermontov himself, according to Turgenev, was considerably stooped and bowed by childhood maladies, giving him an appearance that—at least in youth—was fascinating rather than repulsive. The feminine fictional character seems to have had some will to live, whereas the masculine actual one had a strong need to throw his life away.

(*The Atlantic*, June 2005)

Salman Rushdie:
Hobbes in the Himalayas

———— ⬿⬿⬿ ————

TAKE THE ROOM-TEMPERATURE op-ed article that you have read lately, or may be reading now, or will scan in the future. Cast your eye down as far as the sentence that tells you there will be no terminus to Muslim discontent until there has been a solution to the problem of Palestine. Take any writing implement that comes to hand, strike out the word "Palestine," and insert "Kashmir." Then spend as much time as you can afford in elucidating the subject. And then . . . I was about to say "read this novel," but realized that I should instead recommend it as a means of motivating yourself to embark on the elucidation in the first place.

This may seem a banal and literal way in which to introduce a complex and intriguing work of fiction, but I make no excuse for it. Like Palestine, Kashmir used to be a part of the British Empire (and it is the setting for many of the better-wrought scenes in Paul Scott's *The Raj Quartet*). Like Palestine, it was subject to simultaneous independence and partition in the course of a British scuttle in 1947–1948. It is the only Muslim-majority state in India, and it has long been claimed by the Islamic Republic of Pakistan. Several "conventional"

Review of *Shalimar the Clown* by Salman Rushdie

wars have been fought over it, and "unconventional" guerrilla and counterguerrilla warfare has been in progress for decades, and it has more than once been the occasion for a short-fuse nuclear confrontation. If anything calamitous in the thermonuclear line does occur in the next few years, it is most probable that Kashmir will be the trigger. Moreover, it was the lakes and valleys and mountains of Kashmir that made the crucible in which the Pakistan–Taliban–al-Qaeda "faith-based" alliance was originally formed. The bitterest and longest battle between Islamic jihad and its foes is a struggle not between jihad and the West, or jihad and the Jews, but between jihad and Hindu/secular India. It is a matter not of East versus West but of East versus East.

I know this from a little study and also from a visit to the Pakistani-held side of Kashmir, where I was reminded that although human beings will always fight over even the most arid and desolate prizes, there are some places so humblingly beautiful that it is possible to imagine dying for them oneself. Salman Rushdie knows it in his core: he is Kashmiri by family, Muslim by birth, Indian by partition, and now (shall we say perforce?) something of a Western cosmopolitan. After various grueling excursions he here wheels back to the sacred and profane territory that made him celebrated before he became notorious: the still contested territory of *Midnight's Children* and *Shame*.

He would object to the simplicity of my paragraphs above, preferring to state that the Kashmiri identity is in itself polymorphous and polycentric, and deserving of rescue from both its clumsy and patronizing big brothers. Indeed, this is why he opens the story in Los Angeles, where the landscape and the ecology also shift from neighborhood to neighborhood, and where all forms and aspects of "diversity" receive their chance, and where one of the first people we meet—the brawny lady "super" of an apartment building—is matter-of-factly described as "the last surviving descendant of the legendary potato witches of Astrakhan." (That this mighty maternal figure speaks a Yiddish patois is an unlooked-for bonus.) Her task is to comfort the lovely India, a heavenly girl who resents her given name and secretly practices the martial arts of self-defense.

Next onto the stage is Max Ophuls, India's father and an American diplomat of surpassing polish and dash. He, too, like his directional namesake, originates from contested and burned-over territory—on the Alsatian frontier between France and Germany. He has the seismic instincts of the imperiled Jew, and a way with women that is principally his own way. The story opens with his murder in California at the hands of a manservant named Shalimar, and the novel is the backstory that eventuates in this crime. Only then do we move to Kashmir, setting of Shalimar itself—Shalimar being the ancient name for "the great Mughal garden . . . descending in verdant liquid terraces to a shining lake."

Rushdie does not by any means neglect what is magical and mythical about Kashmir, or the effect that it produces on visitors and interlopers. The Indian army's Colonel Hammirdev Suryavans Kachhwaha, a Rajput martinet posted to keep the ungrateful locals in line, finds himself subject to a version in reverse of what happens to the people of Márquez's Macondo: not an attack of insomnia that results in amnesia but an over-access of mnemonic that results in insomnia. And he, with his craving for the order and respect that never come to him, is cousin to the hapless, trapped colonels and majors in Joseph Heller and Paul Scott. The young acrobat and clown Shalimar is born as Noman Sher Noman, and this nominal echo of Odysseus in the cave of Polyphemus is underlined by an allusion to the old Indian epic *Ram Leela*, in which "Sita the pure was kidnapped and Ram fought a war to bring her back." When Noman swears a fierce oath to his first love, vowing to kill her and all her children if she ever leaves him, we know we are in the presence of a great hubris.

The solemnity of this is not unrelieved by Rushdie's characteristic humor. (I never understand why his reputation is so grave when he can be, and is, so consistently funny.) Here is the *wazwaan*, the far-famed "Banquet of Thirty-Six Courses Minimum," surpassed only by the rarely attempted "Banquet of Sixty Courses Maximum." Village leaders vie with one another in the matter of cuisine and cooking pots and in the related matter of pre- and postprandial (not to speak of midprandial) dramatic entertainments. Indian interpreters do their stuff in faultless Anglo-Indian or IndoAnglian ("Actually her given name is Bhoomi, the earth, but her friends are calling her by this Boonyi cognomen which, sir, is the beloved tree of Kashmir").

But tragedy, both in the Attic sense of the fatal flaw and in the Hegelian sense of a conflict of rights, is to be the master theme. At one point Rushdie gives what is in effect a short modern history of the Kashmiri conflict. He does so by telling the story "straight," as it were, but interleaving Max Ophuls, as the American ambassador to New Delhi, into the factual record. It is breathtakingly well done, like a pentimento beneath the figures of John Kenneth Galbraith and Daniel Patrick Moynihan, and it helps to illustrate the degeneration of Kashmiri life and Kashmiri ethics. Generally pacific and staunchly nonsectarian for many generations, the Kashmiris found themselves under assault by a divide-and-rule policy that made the most of confessional differences. The Pakistanis stressed Islam for obvious reasons, while the Indian authorities sometimes exploited Muslim strains in order to isolate the secular nationalists. We see this cynicism through the increasingly bleary eye of the newly promoted General Kachhwaha, whose mandate expands to fit the nickname of his "base" at "Elasticnagar," and who becomes less and less choosy about his methods. And we feel it through the lives of the villagers, who find poisonous distrust and sectarianism undoing the friendships of generations. Soon enough the mirthless robots of al-Qaeda are at work, symbolized by a mullah made out of scrap iron. (Ophuls's Jewish parents in Strasbourg have already died in the vain belief that their ancestral library will "outlast whatever iron men come clanking across our lives.")

Who suffers most when the forces of holiness and certainty decide to create a burned-over district? The ancient and modern answer is that women suffer most. Rushdie understands this intimately.

Firdaus Noman shook her head. "How can a woman's face be the enemy of Islam?" she asked angrily. Anees took her hands in his. "For these idiots it's all about sex, *maej*, excuse me. They think it is a scientific fact that a woman's hair emits rays that arouse men to deeds of sexual depravity. They think that if a woman's bare legs rub together, even under a floor-length robe, the friction of her thighs will generate sexual heat which will be transmitted through her eyes into the eyes of men and will inflame them in an unholy way." Firdaus spread her hands in a gesture of resignation. "So, because men are animals, according to them, women must pay. This is an old story. Tell me something else."

But the "old story" is the grand narrative after all. Every woman in the novel is made miserable, or fat, or afraid, or afraid for her children, or afraid of her children, by her husband or her lover or some gangster. In the voices and faces of the Gegroo brothers, and of the Karim brothers, one can feel the moment when vicious testosterone and plebeian resentment combine, and when the tendrils of fascism and sadism are both uncoiled and conjoined.

In Kashmir the traditional exorcism of such demons took place by way of the playactor's art. But this catharsis is ruthlessly denied the victims of modernity. The village troupe may hope to produce a performance in honor of the good old king Zain-ul-abidin, who tried to synthesize all the discrepant and multifarious faiths of the country, but the streets outside the theater are soon filled with a yelling crowd and then with the sounds of tanks and gunfire. In these latitudes it may take a village to nurture the feelings of kinship and solidarity that transcend tribal or religious allegiances, but it takes only a few fanatics to destroy in a short while the comity that took generations to evolve. This awful lesson is not for Kashmir alone.

In a series of reports from Kashmir in the *New York Review of Books* in 2000, the Indian writer Pankaj Mishra came to the arresting conclusion that it was now impossible to know, or to discover, what was really happening there. If, say, a village was burned out, the number of possible competing perpetrators, and the number of "false-flag" tactics employed by them, made a mockery out of any analysis. Rushdie captures this Hobbesian nightmare very well, by means of a reverie of General Kachhwaha.

> Already the army had made contact with renegade militants around the country and when extrajudicial activity was required these renegades could be used to kill other militants. After the executions the renegade militants would be given the use of uniforms and would bring the corpses to this or that house belonging to this or that individual and place the corpses in the same location with guns in their hands. The renegades would then depart and be relieved of their uniforms while the armed forces attacked the house, blew it to bits and murdered the dead militants all over again for public consumption.

Through this tournament of shadows the figure of Shalimar/ Noman moves inexorably, kept alive by his unslakable thirst for private revenge on the American Jew who so deftly seduced his beautiful wife. From the frozen mountains of the north he beams a telepathic message to Los Angeles: *Everything I do prepares me for you and for him. Every blow I strike, strikes you or him. The people leading us up here are fighting for God or for Pakistan but I am killing because it is what I have become. I have become death.*

That last line is easily recognizable from another Indian epic, the Bhagavad Gita—"I am become death: the shatterer of worlds." These, as I recall, were the very words mouthed by Robert Oppenheimer as he saw the flash and felt the fire at Alamogordo.

This fusion of the psychopathic with the apocalyptic—surely the essence of "terror" in our time—is transferred to America by another "factive" passage, this one interleaving Noman's presence in Los Angeles with the riots of 1992 and with the first attempt to bring down the World Trade Center, in 1993. Anonymous though he may prefer to be, Noman actually fits rather well into the crazed world of LA celebrity defendants, special wings for same in the LA county jail, and special attorneys for same in the LA courts. He also mingles fairly effortlessly with the city's proliferating gang-and-maximum-security scene. One of his targets, meanwhile (I seek to give away as little as possible), has become an adept in the parallel world of private security—the latter being an area of expertise in which Mr. Rushdie requires no lessons from anyone.

This is a highly serious novel, on an extremely serious subject, by a deeply serious man. It is not necessary to assimilate all the details of the conflict in Kashmir in order to read it. Nor is it necessary to favor one or another solution, though we get a hint from the epigraph page—Mercutio's "plague on both your houses," from *Romeo and Juliet*—of Rushdie's opinion of Indian and Pakistani policy. Rather than seek for anything as trite as a "message," I should guess that Rushdie is telling us, No more Macondos. No more Shangri-las, if it comes to that. Gone is the time when anywhere was exotic or magical or mythical, or even remote. Shalimar's clown mask has been dropped, and his acrobatics have become a form of escape artistry by which he transports himself into "our" world. As he himself says in closing his ominous message of Himalayan telepathy, *I'll be there soon enough.*

(*The Atlantic*, September 2005)

My Red-State Odyssey

T ISN'T RECENT, this psychic partition between the red and the
blue states of our Union. One hundred years after the Emancipation Proclamation, the late Daniel Patrick Moynihan—a quintessential
northeastern big-city boy, even if he was born in Tulsa, Oklahoma—
was an assistant secretary in the "New Frontier" administration when
he heard the news that his president had been shot dead in Dallas.
While everyone else in Washington was rushing around, shouting
importantly about going to the shelters or about "the loss of American
innocence," Moynihan called everyone he knew. The main thing, he
insisted, was to "get Oswald out of Dallas." If anything happened to
him while he was in the custody of the Dallas PD, the tragedy and
the mystery would last forever. Before everything, before anything,
secure the prisoner Oswald.

That's it, in a way, for a lot of people I know. The states of the former Confederacy are not quite American. The inhabitants—of course
one strives to avoid cliché, let alone the deadly word "stereotype"—are
perhaps slightly too much given to dark thoughts and bloody recreations; to snickering at out-of-state license plates in the intervals of
their offenses against chastity with either domestic animals or (the
fact must be faced) with members of their immediate families. An area
where all politics is yokel.

Moynihan's suggestive choice of phrase was to be echoed very quickly, when, in 1964, Lyndon Johnson had to defend his tragic and accidental incumbency against Barry Goldwater. Senator Goldwater had been visiting New York, where he tried to cash an Arizona check and to his fury was refused. It might be better for all concerned, he harrumphed, if the northeastern seaboard were sawed off the country and allowed to float away. He was later stomped and whomped by LBJ in the election (the last election in which both nominees were Southerners, unless you count George Bush Sr. as a Texan), but never since has a majority of white males, let alone in the South, voted for a Democrat. In 1956, when Adlai Stevenson was being trounced by Dwight Eisenhower and Richard Nixon, Democrats on Election Night could cheer as Alabama and Mississippi and the Carolinas came through for them, as they nearly always had ever since Reconstruction.

So in some ways we are looking at an inversion of an old picture. Not that it lacks contradictions: I interviewed Barry Goldwater for *Vanity Fair* on the occasion of his retirement from the Senate, and he was at his most vocal when denouncing the arrogant behavior of the Christian right. ("Kicking Jerry Falwell in the ass" was, I clearly recall, among his ambitions.) More recently, I was speaking with my friend Philip Bobbitt, the nephew of LBJ and a famous Texas liberal, who teaches law at the University of Texas at Austin, opposes capital punishment, and was a senior director on Clinton's National Security Council. "If I am traveling overseas and people ask me where I'm from," he said as we looked out onto Austin's capitol dome, which had been inaugurated by his great-grandfather (and built to be fourteen feet higher than the original, in Washington), "I always say I'm from Texas."

Like Moliere's M. Jourdain in *Le Bourgeois Gentilhomme*, who was astonished to find that he had been speaking prose all his life, I was startled to realize when I embarked on this voyage that I have lived in the South for twenty-three years, or for most of my adult life.

The Mason-Dixon Line is well to the north of us Washingtonians, dividing the country where Maryland becomes Pennsylvania and just below the stretch of high ground consecrated to Gettysburg. Aspects of the District of Columbia are Dixie-ish enough: it gets very hot and muggy in the summer, and its neighborhoods are very segregated. Its very existence is the result of a dinner-table carve-up between Thomas Jefferson and Alexander Hamilton, whereby Hamilton got his national debt–consolidation scheme and the Virginian slavers got a huge land deal for a plot of swamp. But our memorials tend to commemorate the Union more than the Confederacy, and we have the World Bank and the International Monetary Fund, and at election times in the District they weigh the votes rather than count them, and the Democrats always win either way.

Opinions differ about how far you have to drive into Virginia before you have entered the South proper. Some say Fredericksburg, hometown of the great Florence King, authoress of *Wasp, Where Is Thy Sting?* "Redneck" is only a rude word for Wasp. In any case, I have long believed that the acronym certainly doesn't need its *W* and barely needs its *p*. (William F. Buckley Jr. is Waspy despite being Irish and Catholic; George Wallace could never have achieved Waspdom in spite of being aggressively white, Anglo-Saxon, and Protestant. That's because "Wasp" is a term of class, not ethnicity—another trick you can learn in DC.)

Anyway, by the time you hit Richmond the argument is over, and the South has begun. Here was the capital of the Confederacy, and its sylvan streets and squares, enclosing Monument Avenue and the massive statues of Lee and Davis and Jackson, are as firmly genteel and traditional as the heart could wish. (The recent addition of a silly statue of Arthur Ashe, waving a tennis racket while the others flourish their swords and banners and cannons, is exactly the sort of gesture that has allowed Southern courtesy to survive.) I have come here to bypass the chivalry and head straight to the NASCAR event. All right—NASCAR has its chivalry, too. Its heroes are known as "gladiators with radiators."

You often notice, in the South, that people don't at all mind if they live up to their own clichés and stereotypes. In the environs of the Richmond International Raceway, stretching to the horizon, are great tracts of pickups and trailers, fuming with barbecue and hot dogs and surmounted by flags. Old Glory predominates, but quite often the Stars and Bars is flown as well (though always underneath) or separately. I got close-up to one freestanding Confederate flag, to find that it had the face of Hank Williams Jr. on it, and the refrain of his song "If the South Woulda Won (We'd a Had It Made)." I liked the tone of self-parody. The black flag of the POW/MIA movement is frequent. The tailgates groan with huge coolers, and groan even more when proud, gigantic rear ends are added. People wear shorts who shouldn't even wear jeans. Tattoos—often belligerent—are not uncommon. T-shirts featuring the late Dale Earnhardt, the Galahad of NASCAR chivalry, who went into a wall at 160 mph in 2001, are everywhere. Should you desire to remove the right to bear arms from these people, you might well have to pry away a number of cold, dead, chubby fingers. Bailey's cigarettes ("Smooth Start! Smokin' Finish!") are advertised and endorsed by NASCAR celebrities. The whole NASCAR tradition actually began with the drivers of souped-up cars who raced on dirt roads through the night, outrunning the authorities in the scramble to bring moonshine liquor to all who desired it. The showstopping sideshow at this event is provided by one Doug Bradley, who has converted a gas-powered lawn trimmer into a blender that can generate fifty frozen margaritas per tank at something close to warp speed. Agents of the Bureau of Alcohol, Tobacco and Firearms—the only Washington job I ever wanted—must find NASCAR weekends their busiest time.

Indulgence ceases for a moment as the drivers finish their lap of recognition and the loudspeakers call for prayer. Baseball caps come off. Then all hands smite the breastbone as "The Star-Spangled Banner" is sung, and at the wavering climactic high note there comes a heart-thudding *wham* as four F-16 jets, in diamond formation, streak low over the racetrack and, to thunderous applause, head back to

Sandston. The air force had a recruiting stand to justify this huge expense, and the army, navy, National Guard, Coast Guard, and Marine Corps each had a driver and a car in the weekend's races, competing with Twizzlers, M&M's, Advil, Home Depot, and Viagra. A beer stand just off the track advertised itself as being run by volunteers from the Marine Corps Weapons Training Battalion at Quantico ("Just raising funds for our annual ball," the smart young man in charge told me).

You could certainly get the impression, from hanging out here, that god was a Republican, with a good chance of being white. The GOP has been registering voters at NASCAR events since February 2004—there were 180,000 people at this event alone—and Senator George Allen, the former governor of the state who has been making both godly and presidential noises, took care to be present. But so did the current governor, Mark Warner, who is "mentionable" as a future Democratic nominee. And, on the second night I was there, the Pledge of Allegiance was led by the mother of Private First Class Leslie Jackson, a young black woman who lost her life in Iraq. (NASCAR is doing a big "outreach" to African Americans, though it boasts only one black driver on its three circuits, and has recruited Magic Johnson to a "diversity" committee while banning the Confederate colors from anything that it franchises.)

Embraced by a couple of guys near the beer stand, I soon came to appreciate that they were using me the way drunks use lampposts: in other words, more for support than illumination. Charlie's lard-like pallor was enhanced by the closing stages of a spectacular intake of fuel—he swayed gigantically as he leaned on my shoulder and sobbed out the story of his one-man rig: "Haul any fucking thing," he said brokenly. "Any fucking thing." He was just on that cusp between instant friendship and instant menace. His friend Mike was lean and wolfish and rather handsome, and able to talk quite fast as long as he employed the crutch of obscenity. In short order, I found that he got on well with the "sand people"—local Arab immigrants—who ran the gas stations; had a child with a Puerto Rican girl; owned three guns; couldn't get along with black males who were any younger than he;

and had a father and grandfather who had seen service. (He wouldn't join up himself, because the Iraq war was "just for a fuckin' barrel of oil.") For all that, I doubt he was a swing voter. He was a carpenter, and when one of his favorite drivers had switched sponsorship from Home Depot to Lowe's, he took his business right along to the new sponsor. "The thing to know about NASCAR fans," said Jerry Reid, a local enthusiast and sportswriter, "is that if their man was endorsed by Viagra they'd start taking it even if they didn't need it." When the race is over, the victor does a lap of honor in the opposite direction—a NASCAR tradition hallowed ever since Alan Kulwicki started it seventeen years ago. He was later to die in a plane crash, of all things, the plane belonging to his sponsor, namely Hooters. In his honor, this gesture is called "the Polish victory lap."

West Virginia went the other way in the Civil War, cleft from Virginia and staying with the Union. And as you push deeper into the hills, you start to pick up the kinds of songs that make you know you are in territory that was once fought over. Naturally, you get a lot of self-pitying wails from country-music types. ("If you play one of these backwards," I was told, "you eventually get sober and then you get your car, your dog, and your wife back.") But there's some fire-breathing defiance, too, as from Lee Greenwood's 1984 smash, "God Bless the USA," now played at Republican conventions.

This time, though, I am in search of the genteel. At the Greenbrier resort, in White Sulphur Springs, you need a coat and tie to dine, and many of the staff are descended from previous staff. Verdancy is the keynote, with thick woods and immaculate lawns and golf courses stretching toward the misty Allegheny Mountains. In a cottage on the grounds, five pre–Civil War presidents (Van Buren, Fillmore, Pierce, Buchanan, and Tyler) passed agreeable summer vacations while beaux and belles came to take the waters. It's easy to see—from the Southern perspective, and if things had gone the other way just a teeny, tiny bit—how natural it would have been to have the capital of the United States in, say, Richmond. As it is, if things had gone just a teeny, tiny bit the other way during the Cold War, the Capitol of the United States would have been at the Greenbrier. In complete secrecy, during the Eisenhower administration, a provisional Capitol was built in a deep shelter right beside this palatial hotel. The bunker was encased in several feet of reinforced concrete and buried 720 feet into the hillside. Its western entrance was protected by a 25-ton steel door. The "chambers" for the Senate and the House have the right number of seats but not quite the same amount of space. There's a power plant that could supply about 1,100 people for up to 40 days—this was as far ahead as planners could think when they contemplated the blast and radiation that would have been twilight's last gleaming. This is where our final laws would have been passed. The Greenbrier would have been the last resort.

It says something for the locals that, during nearly three years of massive excavation, drilling, blasting, and cement pouring, nobody uttered a single word. The local construction industry had a serious boom, and many people now tell you that they sure knew something was going on, but between the start of work, in 1958, and the revelation of the place's existence by the *Washington Post* in 1992, the rest of the country was quite unaware that Washington was only its provisional capital. Even today, one can't help noticing that White Sulphur Springs has a very large airport for so small a town, and a direct rail link with DC from a nearby station. The bunker has been decommissioned now, and Homeland Security has taken a different form. In one of the spacious lobbies of the Greenbrier, I met Mr. John P. Carter, a fine man with a shield and crest embossed on his business card. He had had quite enough of being jerked around at airport security, and decided to get a pilot's license and his own plane so that he could make business trips without being humiliated by the federal government. Old Cessna aircraft, he told me, were "quite good and quite cheap: cheaper in the long run." I don't exactly know how I could or would prove this, but there was something Southern in his attitude.

Take a short drive from the Greenbrier and pass through Lexington, Virginia, where the Virginia Military Institute stands like a fortress, and where the campus of Washington and Lee University has not only the sarcophagus of Robert E. Lee but also the grave of his favorite horse. Press on toward the small town of Natural Bridge, where US 11 passes over a rock crossing that is 215 feet high and 40 feet wide. Its arch, which appears uncannily man-made in its symmetry, spans 90 feet. This astonishing site was surveyed by George Washington in 1750 and then acquired as a property by Thomas Jefferson. But the people who run the place, and who charge you admission to see it, and who have made it tacky with waxwork and haunted monster museums, won't leave you to admire the wonders of nature. Instead, every evening in season they put on a program entitled "Drama of Creation," with readings from Genesis accompanied by devotional music. What could possibly be more ridiculous? The "design" of the world is conspicuous for its lack of natural bridges. The "designer" didn't bother to connect Marin with the San Francisco peninsula, or Manhattan with Brooklyn. That had to be left to mere evolved humans, operating with hard-won scientific rules. One of the pioneers of this work was Thomas Paine, unacknowledged Founding Father and among the first to design an iron bridge, who ridiculed the Bible as a long fairy tale of crime and fantasy. His friend and patron Thomas Jefferson took a razor to the New Testament and cut out everything that was evil, silly, or mythical. This left him with a very short edition. These were the men who actually founded the secular United States, but on Jefferson's home turf the pious believers now sell bubble gum and crappy souvenirs, and credit divine authority for an accidental rock formation.

But as fast as the South can get you down, it can pick you up again. The next Lexington I saw—Massachusetts has no monopoly on this place-name—was in Kentucky. Kentucky is also one of the states that were calved from Virginia, more peacefully this time, and its nicely named Transylvania University is even older than Mr. Jefferson's University of Virginia. A bit like Cuba's, Kentucky's economy depends

almost entirely on things that are good for you but are said to be bad
for you: Cuba has sugar, rum, and tobacco; and Kentucky has bourbon, tobacco, and horse racing. When you see the Derby run on TV,
the cameras linger on opulence in hats and horseflesh, and the farms
often look like rolling feudal estates in Normandy or Oxfordshire, but
if you go to the Keeneland racetrack at Lexington you see a crowd
not unlike the NASCAR one: real popular participation in the sport
of kings. My tour of a bourbon distillery was a slight disappoint-
ment, in that you no longer get offered a free sample, but later, in a
Lexington restaurant, I was heartened to see the bar area full of blue
smoke, only a year after the city had passed a no-smoking ordinance.
"I guess," said one of the patrons cheerfully, "that we just don't take
the law that seriously in these parts." All over town, though, you can
see the fading painted signs on what used to be tobacco warehouses
and auction houses. The end of the tobacco price supports is also the
end of "small tobacco" as a hereditary living, and with the vanishing
of "Tobacco Road" the whole texture of the Old South will change
in ways that we can't predict.

Was I supposed to be looking for patterns? If you look for them, you
find them. But it wouldn't be unfair to speculate, at this juncture,
that if you consider yourself a Southerner you are more likely to
come from a large family, more likely to have a family connection
to the military or to the military-industrial complex, more likely to
have some relationship—however twisted—with a personal savior,
and more likely to take a "screw you" attitude to the federal government. To this one might add that you are more likely to live where
your ancestors lived, and to feel the presence of American history. In
Huntington, West Virginia, where the souvenirs at the airport tend
to be made from coal, I was told quite simply, "You'll like it here.
Most people hereabouts are English." Indeed, H. L. Mencken, that
great Anglophobe, who originated the term "Bible Belt," also alluded
to "the hook-worm belt" of Anglo-Saxondom to put down Dixie.

"The same people, living in the same place," as T. S. Eliot rather more mildly put it in his famous lecture "After Strange Gods" at the University of Virginia. Many American cities and counties have some kind of "heritage" campaign, but one way of telling that you are in the South is the prevalence of roadside markers, battlefield memorials, equestrian statues, and plaques. This is by no means "the United States of Amnesia" that Gore Vidal scorns—it's an area where the past is taken seriously.

This goes double for Texas, as Texans invariably think no matter what the subject is. It was actually in Marshall, Texas, that the last headquarters of the Confederacy was located: there were just that many secessionist dead-enders who held on for the few days between the burning of Richmond and the ceremony at Appomattox. Doomed last stands are a special subject in this territory, but the Alamo also symbolizes the fact that Texas had its own declaration of independence, its own revolution, and its own statehood, as well as a disastrous adventure in confederation, before rejoining the Union. You can still see where the French embassy to Texas used to be, in Austin, just as you can still see where the Texas embassy used to be on St. James's Street in London. Schoolchildren in Texas have to recite the pledge to the Texas flag every morning, just after the Pledge of Allegiance.

One always strives to avoid "land of contrast" clichés, but in Texas the more people live up to their reputation, the more they don't. And the more it stays the same, the more it changes. You may be surprised to know that the famous bumper sticker "Don't Mess with Texas," now seen on the back of many a pickup that is also insured by Smith & Wesson, was originally a green slogan, for a statewide antilittering campaign. I went to call on Kinky Friedman, at his combination ranch and animal-rescue center in the fabulously beautiful Hill Country outside Austin. The Lone Star State's most famous Jew and bohemian, now running for governor on a platform to be determined, was full of praise for the cowboy spirit. "'Cowboy' is a great word. Gandhi was a cowboy, Jesus was a cowboy, Mandela was a cowboy: stand-up guys." The improbability of this formulation is underlined by the fact that less than 2 percent of Texans now work with ambulant cows in any capacity.

Larry McMurtry, who has spent years trying to discredit the cowboy myth in his fiction ("I've called them fascists"), manages to run four large bookstores, each of them a warehouse, in Archer City (at last, a civilized Texas School Book Depository), a town of perhaps 1,500 souls many miles from anywhere on the flatland, one of those places where if the wind drops, all the chickens fall over. He told me that anyone who walks into the stores is almost certain to be from out of town. Despite this philistinism, as he points out, the Harry Ransom Center, at the University of Texas at Austin, has one of the finest collections of literature in the world. You could see Evelyn Waugh's library, complete with its furniture, as well as the papers and manuscripts of James Joyce, D. H. Lawrence, Isaac Bashevis Singer, Robert Lowell, Graham Greene, Somerset Maugham, Tom Stoppard, John Fowles, and all twenty thousand pounds of Norman Mailer's archives. There are three first-class art museums in Fort Worth, where some say the South ends and the West begins, and the names Rothko and de Menil are almost synonymous with Houston.

Texas's other great living writer, John Graves—author of the wonderful *Goodbye to a River*—also lives way out the hell and gone, near Glen Rose. He has a respect for the grain and grit of the Texan character, and for the Calvinism that enabled those raw settlers to survive and grow in a harsh land, but now that Calvinism isn't needed for that purpose, it can be a slight pain in the ass. "I wish I lived in a world," he says softly, "where it was possible to be religious and think at the same time." A few miles down the road from his place there stands the Creation Evidence Museum: a pathetic freak show featuring organisms allegedly so complex that they must have been invented and let loose by the divine hand all in one day. . . .

Texas has a land border that is 1,254 miles in length, so appeals to the frontier spirit seldom fall on deaf ears, and by the year 2025 a majority of the state's population may be Hispanic. But then, even the word "cowboy" originally comes from "vaquero" and is a Spanish imperial idea. You can see the reaction, though, in an emerging town like Plano, just outside Dallas. Here, rows and rows of new villa-style housing, punctuated by churches, schools, and the mandatory football fields, are creating a whole new white, observant, affluent constituency. This, and the feline redistricting plan that goes along with it, is one of the building blocks of the intended future Republican majority. (Ten years ago, the Texas Democrats had both houses and the governorship; now they can only whistle at how fast the state has metamorphosed from blue to red.)

I chose Atlanta for my last stop, intending to make a side trip to the town of Kennesaw, where local law makes gun ownership mandatory. ("An armed society is a polite society," as some like to say.) But I ended up concentrating on Professor Eugene Genovese, the former Marxist from Brooklyn who with his scholar wife, Elizabeth, has moved south and become the preeminent historian of the area. I suppose I was looking for an encapsulating sentence: at all events they furnished me with one. Eugene had been praising some work on the South by the historian Eric Foner, who is a New Yorker to his fingertips, when his wife broke in to say, "It's not that good. It lacks the tragic sense."

And that was it, in a phrase. Never quite able to get over a lost past, never quite at ease with the federal government (though very much at ease with the armed forces), and just not quite large enough to impose itself on the rest of the country, the South keeps on "reviving" and redefining itself, always pushing at its limits and limitations—and always finding them.

(Vanity Fair, September 2005)

The Turkey Has Landed

⊸∞∞⊷

CONCERNING THANKSGIVING, THAT most distinctive and unique of all American holidays, there need be no resentment and no recrimination. Likewise, there need be no wearisome present-giving, no order of divine service, and no obligation to the dead. This holiday is like a free gift, or even (profane though the concept may be to some readers) a free lunch—and a very big and handsome one at that. This is the festival on which one hears that distinct and generous American voice: the one that says "Why not?" Family values are certainly involved, but even those with no family will still be invited, or will invite. The doors are not exactly left open as for a Passover seder, yet who would not be ashamed to think of a neighbor who was excluded or forgotten on such a national day?

Immigrants like me tend to mention it as their favorite. And this is paradoxical, perhaps, since it was tentative and yet ambitious immigrants who haltingly began the tradition. But these were immigrants to the Americas, not to the United States.

You can have a decent quarrel about the poor return that Native Americans received for their kindness in leading Puritans to find corn and turkeys in the course of a harsh winter. You may find yourself embroiled, as on Columbus Day, with those who detest the conquistadores or who did not get here by way of Plymouth Rock or Ellis

Island. ("Not for us it isn't," as the receptionist at Louis Farrakhan's *Final Call* once glacially told me, after I had pointed out that her boss had desired me to telephone that very day.) Even Hallowe'en is fraught, with undertones of human sacrifice and Protestant ascendancy. But Thanksgiving really comes from the time when the USA had replaced the squabbling confessional colonists, and is fine, and all-American, too.

As with so many fine things, it results from the granite jaw and the unhypocritical speech of Abraham Lincoln. It seemed to him, as it must have seemed in his composition of the Gettysburg Address, that there ought to be one day that belonged exclusively to all free citizens of a democratic republic. It need not trouble us that he spoke in April and named a regular calendar day at the end of November, any more than it need trouble us that he mentioned "God" but specified no particular religion. No nation can be without a day of its own, and who but a demagogue or a sentimentalist would have appointed a simulacrum of Easter or Passover? The Union had just been preserved from every kind of hazard and fanaticism: just be grateful. If there were to be any ceremonial or devotional moment at Thanksgiving, and I am sure that I wish that there were not, it still might not kill the spirit of the thing if Lincoln's second inaugural were to be read aloud, or at least printed on a few place mats.

Any attempt at further grandiosity would fail. To remember the terrible war that saved the Union, or the Winthropian fundamentalism about that "city on a hill," would be too strenuous. And there are other days, in any case, on which one may celebrate or commemorate these things. I myself always concentrate on the dry wisdom of Benjamin Franklin, who once proposed that the turkey instead of the eagle should be the American national bird. After all, as he noted, the eagle is an inedible and arrogant predator whereas the turkey is harmless to others, nutritious, thrifty, industrious, and profuse. Pausing only to think of the variable slogans here ("Where Turkeys Dare"; "The Turkey Has Landed"; "On Wings of Turkeys" and, by a stretch, "Legal Turkeys") I marvel to think that a nation so potentially strong could have had a Founding Father who was so irreverent. I also wish that I liked turkey. But there is always stuffing, cranberry sauce, and gravy—to be eked out by pumpkin pie, which I also wish I could pretend to relish.

Indeed, it is the sheer modesty of the occasion that partly recommends it. Everybody knows what's coming. Nobody acts as if caviar and venison are about to be served, rammed home by syllabub and fine Madeira. The whole point is that one forces down, at an odd hour of the afternoon, the sort of food that even the least discriminating diner in a restaurant would never order by choice. Perhaps false modesty is better than no modesty at all.

Never mind all that. I am quite sure (indeed, I know) that many a Thanksgiving table is set with vegetarian delights for all the family. And never mind if you think that Norman Rockwell is a great cornball as well as a considerable painter. Many people all over the world, including many members of my own great profession of journalism, almost make their livings by describing the United States as a predatory and taloned bird, swooping down on the humble dinners of others. And of course, no country would really wish to represent itself on its own coinage and emblems as a feathered, flapping, gobbling, and flightless product of evolution. Still and all, I have become one of those to whom Thanksgiving is a festival to be welcomed, and not dreaded. I once grabbed a plate of what was quite possibly turkey, but which certainly involved processed cranberry and pumpkin, in a US Army position in the desert on the frontier of Iraq. It was the worst meal—by far the worst meal—I have ever eaten. But in all directions from the chow hall, I could see Americans of every conceivable stripe and confession, cheerfully asserting their connection, in awful heat, with a fall of long ago. And this in a holiday that in no way could divide them. May this always be so, and may one give some modest thanks for it.

(*Wall Street Journal*, November 23, 2005)

Bah, Humbug

———— ⊗⊗⊗ ————

I USED TO HARBOR the quiet but fierce ambition to write just one definitive, annihilating anti-Christmas column and then find an editor sufficiently indulgent to run it every December. My model was the Thanksgiving pastiche knocked off by Art Buchwald several decades ago and recycled annually in a serious ongoing test of reader tolerance. But I have slowly come to appreciate that this hope was in vain. The thing must be done annually and afresh. Partly this is because the whole business becomes more vile and insufferable—and in new and worse ways—every twelve months. It also starts to kick in earlier each year: it was at Thanksgiving this year that, making my way through an airport, I was confronted by the leering and antlered visage of what to my disordered senses appeared to be a bloody great moose. Only as reason regained her throne did I realize that the reindeer—that plague species—were back.

Not long after I'd swallowed this bitter pill, I was invited onto *Scarborough Country* on MSNBC to debate the proposition that reindeer were an ancient symbol of Christianity and thus deserving of First Amendment protection, if not indeed of mandatory display at every mall in the land. I am told that nobody watches that show anymore—certainly I heard from almost nobody who had seen it—so I must tell you that the view taken by the host was that coniferous trees were also a symbol of Christianity, and that the Founding Fathers had endorsed this proposition. From his cue cards, he even quoted a few vaguely deistic sentences from Benjamin Franklin and George Washington, neither of them remotely Christian in tone. When I pointed out the latter, and added that Christmas trees, yule logs, and all the rest were symbols of the winter solstice holidays before any birth had been registered in the greater Bethlehem area, I was greeted by a storm of abuse, as if I had broken into the studio instead of having been entreated to come by *Scarborough*'s increasingly desperate staff. And when I added that it wasn't very Tiny Tim–like to invite a seasonal guest and then tell him to shut up, I was told that I was henceforth stricken from the *Scarborough* Rolodex. The ultimate threat: no room at the Bigmouth Inn.

This was a useful demonstration of what I have always hated about the month of December: the atmosphere of a one-party state. On all media and in all newspapers, endless invocations of the same repetitive theme. In all public places, from train stations to department stores, an insistent din of identical propaganda and identical music. The collectivization of gaiety and the compulsory infliction of joy. Time wasted on foolishness at one's children's schools. Vapid ecumenical messages from the president, who has more pressing things to do and who is constitutionally required to avoid any religious endorsements.

And yet none of this party-line unanimity is enough for the party's true hard-liners. The slogans must be exactly right. No "Happy Holidays" or even "Cool Yule" or a cheery Dickensian "Compliments of the season." No, all banners and chants must be specifically designated in honor of the birth of the Dear Leader and the authority of the Great Leader. By chance, the *New York Times* on December 19 ran a story about the difficulties encountered by Christian missionaries working among North Korean defectors, including a certain Mr. Park. One missionary was quoted as saying ruefully that "he knew he had not won over Mr. Park. He knew that Christianity reminded Mr. Park, as well as other defectors, of 'North Korean ideology.'" An interesting admission, if a bit of a stretch. Let's just say that the birth of the

Dear Leader is indeed celebrated as a miraculous one—accompanied, among other things, by heavenly portents and by birds singing in Korean—and that compulsory worship and compulsory adoration can indeed become a touch wearying to the spirit.

Our Christian enthusiasts are evidently too stupid, as well as too insecure, to appreciate this. A revealing mark of their insecurity is their rage when public places are not annually given over to religious symbolism, and now, their fresh rage when palaces of private consumption do not follow suit. The Fox News campaign against Walmart—and other outlets whose observance of the official feast day is otherwise fanatical and punctilious to a degree, but a degree that falls short of unswerving orthodoxy—is one of the most sinister as well as one of the most laughable campaigns on record. If these dolts knew anything about the real Protestant tradition, they would know that it was exactly this paganism and corruption that led Oliver Cromwell—my own favorite Protestant fundamentalist—to ban the celebration of Christmas altogether.

No believer in the First Amendment could go that far. But there are millions of well-appointed buildings all across the United States, most of them tax-exempt and some of them receiving state subventions, where anyone can go at any time and celebrate miraculous births and pregnant virgins all day and all night if they so desire. These places are known as "churches," and they can also force passersby to look at the displays and billboards they erect and to give ear to the bells that they ring. In addition, they can count on numberless radio and TV stations to beam their stuff all through the ether. If this is not sufficient, then god damn them. God damn them everyone.

(*Slate*, December 20, 2005)

A. N. Wilson:
Downhill All the Way

⊖⊕⊕⊖

THE LATE CHRISTOPHER Hill—arguably not A. N. Wilson's beau ideal as a historian—once told me a small joke in his mildly stuttering style. It seemed that the fifth or sixth husband of Barbara Hutton had been interviewed on his nuptial night, and when asked how he felt at being the latest to possess the celebrated Woolworth heiress, had replied, "Well, I know what I have g-got to d-do, but I am not quite sure how I am going to make it i-i-i-*interesting*."

Some of the same apprehensiveness may descend upon anyone who undertakes to write about the eclipse of British power in the first half of the twentieth century. The basic outlines—or, if you prefer, the essential holds and grapples and maneuvers—are tolerably well known. Death of the Old Queen in 1901; a nasty and expensive war in South Africa presaging a deadly rivalry with her vicious grandson, the kaiser; a "Great War" that bled the country white; two decades of stupidity and drift marked by fatuities such as the restoration of the gold standard and the myopic placation of unappeasable dictators; another cataclysmic war, which caused the reluctant surrender of global supremacy to the United States. Honor partly rescued by

---

Review of *After the Victorians: The Decline of Britain in the World* by A. N. Wilson

titanic standing of Winston Churchill and unexpectedly long reign of a second Elizabeth; both these wasting assets subject to sharply diminishing returns.

Wilson does not depart very much from this well-beaten track. Indeed, he more than once cites, and actually rather lamely concludes with, Dean Acheson's much quoted remark that Britain had "lost an empire and not yet found a role." That fairly banal observation, made at West Point in 1962, might have been overlooked if it had not so infuriated Churchill. It is also outside the ostensible scope of Wilson's book, which closes with the early 1950s and suggests that a trilogy (including it and its predecessor, *The Victorians*) may be in train.

I must say that I hope so. Wilson does indeed know how to make it interesting. He manages this by an adroit alternation between the macrocosmic and the microcosmic. At one point he takes us on a tour of the great British Empire Exhibition at Wembley, in 1924, with lavishly exotic pavilions provided by India and Malaya and a sturdy sculpture, in pure Canadian butter, of the Prince of Wales. (It is easy to forget that Britain ended the First World War with *more* territories under its control than it had enjoyed in 1914.) Then we are shown the 1936 funeral of the first Communist member of Parliament, an Indian Parsi named Shapurji Saklatvala; the precincts of the crematorium were still decked with red flags when the next customer's cortege arrived—containing the coffin of Rudyard Kipling. By that time the loyal and butter-sculpted Prince of Wales had mutated into the willful and mutinous King Edward VIII, whose sexual thrall to the Baltimore divorcée Wallis Simpson was to provoke the first ever abdication. (Wilson relates the last words of old King George V, father to this impetuous boy, and expresses the usual doubt that he ever asked, "How is the empire?" as he lay dying. He does not canvass the idea that the expiring monarch actually inquired, "How's the vampire?": an allusion to the designing woman who had already undermined the throne.) And he has no patience with the well-attested view that young Edward was "a selfish sybarite, a Nazi sympathizer," saying that "history" has a "babyish" need to believe this, when (as he does not mention) it was the conclusion reluctantly arrived at by the eminent royal historian Philip Ziegler.

No matter. Wilson may also be unfair to E. M. Forster, but he writes in the spirit of Forster's old maxim "Only connect." In particular, and in a very clever way, he allows us to see all the prefigurations of that rising American influence, which, slowly accreting, was to burst upon the post-1945 British as if it had come as a complete surprise. The first female to take her seat in the House of Commons (Nancy Astor) was an American. Winston Churchill's influential mother was an American. Kipling's wife was an American. Stan Laurel and Oliver Hardy, the former from the English music hall and the latter from the Deep South, are imaginatively represented by Wilson as a duo based on Henry James's Anglo-American ambiguities. And it made little difference that atom splitting, radar, and television were British discoveries, since like jazz and cinema the main uptake of all the big ideas was on the American side of the Atlantic. (The British abandoned television broadcasts as soon as the Second World War began, thus conducting the propaganda fight largely on radio: a medium dominated by an Irish-American named William Joyce, or "Lord Haw-Haw," who transmitted from Hitler's Berlin.) There is a wider Hibernian subtext to the story. The two British teak-heads responsible for the Amritsar massacre, in April 1919, and therefore for the moral end of the British dominion in India, were General Reginald Dyer and Governor Michael O'Dwyer. Both were Irish-Protestant Unionists. It was the Orange Unionists who defended them in Parliament, at a time when Ireland itself was terrorized by the Black and Tans, and it was Sir Henry Wilson—leader of the 1914 Ulster mutiny—who pronounced that if Ireland was lost, then the whole imperial game was up. Reading this book, I was suddenly put in mind of its illustrious forerunner, George Dangerfield's *The Strange Death of Liberal England*. Like Dangerfield, A. N. Wilson can grasp the encapsulating anecdote and the numinous coincidence, and capture the manner in which tragedy gibbers happily over the shoulders of the group photographed on the well-kept lawn.

Ninety-two years on, and liberals, conservatives, and Marxists can all reckon August 1914 as the month from which everything measurable is—to annex the title of Leonard Woolf's autobiography—downhill all the way. As often as Wilson counsels us against the fallacy of scanning the past through the reversed telescope of the present, he is unable to free himself from this crucial—and just—conclusion. The mechanization of warfare, the glorification of the state, the mass mobilization of peoples, the advantage given to demagogues, and the permission to engage in genocide under the color of warfare: all this would have raised the eyebrows of the most self-confident Victorian imperialist.

In counterpoint, then, to the grandiose general globalizing of "telegrams and anger," ultimatums and campaigns, wars and alarms, Wilson stresses the quiet, discreet, private, faintly annoying way in which many of the British so often managed to find the situation desperate but not serious. He spends time in the company of reform-minded rural vicars of the Church of England (one or two of them satisfyingly deranged), and with those charitable and voluntary associations that began to repair the damage inflicted by Victorian slums and the Victorian factory system. Perhaps too much aware that the usual model for this habit of "decency" and modesty is the austere figure of George Orwell, he tries too hard to be different from the norm and makes the amazing claim that *The Road to Wigan Pier* was a "treasured text" of the blackshirts. (A swift glance at the relevant footnote reveals this weird notion to be based on a private conversation with Sir Oswald Mosley's widow—an unrepentant blue-blooded Nazi bitch who most probably had not read the book and who certainly had not noticed Orwell's despair, in its pages, at the way in which some workers were stupid enough to be gulled by her husband.) Still, and at a time when Sir Oswald Mosley was being taken seriously, about seventy thousand European Jews managed to make an emergency home by crossing the Channel. Wilson mentions Popper, Pevsner, Solti, Freud, Menuhin, and Elton (and could have added Koestler and Deutscher, and also have mentioned how many were interned and maltreated), but probably captures the awkwardness best by relating the story of Eva Neurach in the clutches of a hostess.

"Where are you from?"

"Berlin."

"Ah, well, never mind."

It is almost certain that the questioner in the above case was wondering how to be civil to a German, not a Jew. But the insistent politeness and the tradition of uncomfortable hospitality still count for something. (I am told that the great hostess Sybil Colefax, finding Albert Einstein among her guests at one such soiree, was instructed to put him at his ease and began by asking, "*Did* you hear that mad old Woofles has left Pug-Wug completely flat—and run off with Binky-poo?" There is a reason why Evelyn Waugh can be regarded as a social historian of this epoch.)

The cover of the book shows the chiaroscuro photograph, ineffaceable from modern memory, of Wren's masterpiece, St. Paul's, as it was enshrouded by smoke and flame during a Nazi bombing raid. But in his discussion of the Second World War—still regarded by many British people and by even more Americans as the crisis that justified and legitimized everything—Wilson adopts a tone of skepticism that approaches sourness. In the first place, the war could have been avoided by a less selfish and supine policy during the preceding decades. In the second place, its conduct was often very close to criminal, in particular as regards the immolation of German cities and civilians. In the third place, having begun with the appeasement of Nazis and fascists, it closed with a capitulation to Stalinism and a sellout to the nascent American empire. There have been several growling ultra-Tory voices raised among British historians in the past decade to the same effect. Some of these voices are reactionary in the strict sense of the term, and nostalgic for both Joseph and Neville Chamberlain. Wilson takes the view that Britain is well shot of the colonies and believes that the social reforms of the postwar Labour government were noble in both intention and effect. That makes a nice change.

The late John Muggeridge, son of Malcolm, described to me once how he had been dispatched to Kenya in the early 1950s, and had voyaged there by way of Malta, Cyprus, and the Suez Canal Zone without ever having to carry a British passport. It is amazing to reflect both how recent all this was and how long ago it all seems. Wilson has the ability to evoke the past without condescension, and to measure its passing without sentimentality. Where this will take him with what seems like the necessary succeeding volume, I cannot easily tell. Just ahead lies the Britain of Margaret Thatcher—who had a soft spot, if not indeed a hard spot, for what she termed "Victorian values." And this must give place to the Britain of Tony Blair, who re-created social democracy by fusing it with post-Thatcherism. Both of them, in their different ways, disproved Dean Acheson, by showing that Britain had the ability to act as a medium between Washington and Brussels. Both of them also showed that some shells were left in the British postcolonial arsenal. And then there is the question—oddly unaddressed by Wilson—of the English language as a lingua franca for everything from air-traffic control to the Internet. I believe I can guess that Wilson is no friend to the American global mission. (In a rare concession to sheer or mere euphemism, he describes Chirac's and Schröder's reaction to the Iraq operation as one of "skeptical alarm.") But then, it may be Barbara Hutton who has the last word. When the *Titanic*, that triumph of British shipbuilding, was first launched, it was shown as being greater in length than even the Woolworth Building in New York—then the tallest skyscraper in the world. Within a few decades Hutton had given her mansion in London to the American embassy for use as an ambassadorial residence, easily outdoing in magnificence anything that could be offered by Carlton House Terrace. And within a few years of that my friends' parents were abandoning the traditional corner shop and country store to do what they used to despise: shop at Woolworth's. Britishness suffered great battlefield and market reverses, but it was also five-and-dimed away, and perhaps that's the detail that makes it interesting.

(*The Atlantic*, January/February 2006)

Ian Fleming: Bottoms Up

———∞∞∞———

I want to suggest that the anal anxiety of *Diamonds* is primarily important not as a textbook illustration of the Rat Man's particular obsessions, but as a surface trace of a deeper phenomenon. I'd like to argue that the Bond universe is premised on a certain obsessive-compulsive logic, but a logic that can more profitably be understood as Althusserian and ideological rather than as simply Freudian and psychological, a logic that is less about regression to infantile sexuality than about the hopes and anxieties spawned by postwar culture.

—Dennis W. Allen, "'Alimentary, Dr. Leiter': Anal Anxiety in *Diamonds Are Forever*"

T HE ABOVE IS excerpted from the essay collection *Ian Fleming & James Bond: The Cultural Politics of 007*, which was also the name of a symposium held at Indiana University in 2003. Bloomington, of all places, is the repository of the bulk of Fleming's books and papers. These, according to an excellent biography by Andrew Lycett, include *State of Excitement*, Fleming's only unpublished work—disappointingly enough, an account of a trip he made to Kuwait in 1960. (The book failed to meet with the approval of the Kuwait Oil Company, which had commissioned it but did not care for its tone. So it is not the case that Fleming invariably romanticized British postcolonialism.) Now consider this:

> The point of Felix Leiter, such a nonentity as a piece of characterization, is that he, the American, takes orders from Bond, the Britisher, and that Bond is constantly doing better than he, showing himself, not braver or more devoted, but smarter, wilier, tougher, more resourceful—the incarnation of little old England with her quiet ways and shoestring budget wiping the eye of great big global-tentacled multi-billion-dollar-appropriating America.
>
> —Kingsley Amis, *The James Bond Dossier*

I cannot think of anyone more likely to have ridiculed a "postmodern" conference on the work of Fleming and the semiotics of Bond than the author of this passage. Yet it seems that even Amis felt that Fleming's novels could not be taken at face value. Bond's triumph over Leiter in *Diamonds*—he tells him where to look inside a corpse for hidden stones—is perhaps an instance of British "guts" rather than British anality. Bond himself is almost always described, and describes himself, as "English," but in the premature *Times* obituary that is printed in the late-bloomer *You Only Live Twice*, he is described as having had a Scottish father and a Swiss mother and thus cannot be said to be English at all. Still, there is no doubt that the CIA man Leiter is made from indigestible cardboard—a sort of Jamesian foil for Bond's superior sophistication. (My own very small contribution to Bond studies has been to point out that "Leiter" was the family name of the rich American woman who married Lord Curzon, in the great age of matrimonial alliances between Churchills, Vanderbilts, and Astors, thus helping to secure his fortune and her position in society.) Other than that, Felix Leiter can indeed be read as a sort of signifier or cipher.

And "cipher" is the nom de guerre of Le Chiffre, the numbers-man racketeer of the French Communist Party and perhaps the most odiously sadistic of Fleming's villains. He features in the first of the published Bond books, *Casino Royale*, which is the only one that has not been made into a "serious" film. A farcical and noncanonical version of it was made starring Peter Sellers and David Niven, which causes one to reflect upon what might have happened had Fleming got his way and secured Niven instead of Sean Connery as the original Bond. (Role selection was not Fleming's strong suit; he invited Noël Coward, his neighbor in Jamaica, to take the part of Dr. No—picture it if you will.) Now it seems that a fresh *Casino Royale* will be made, and the new casting will give us Daniel Craig as Bond. You may have caught Mr. Craig playing a hopelessly sinister and useless South African Jew in Steven Spielberg's laughable *Munich* ("the ownly blid thit mitters to mee is *Jewish* blid"). We are, so to speak, back where we started.

My own adolescence coincided perfectly with the emergence of the somehow brilliantly named Ursula Andress from the foaming Jamaican breakers, in *Dr. No*. (Fleming gave stupid mock monikers to many of his cock-fodder heroines, from Pussy Galore to Kissy Suzuki, but Ursula Andress is a natural porn name if ever I've struck one.) One noted various things about Andress, from the knife belt around her waist to the blade hanging against her thigh, and then feverishly consulted the original text, only to discover that it adhered to a constant theme and also awarded her a boy's rear end. Concerning this decision, Coward wrote to Fleming, "I know that we are all becoming progressively more broad-minded nowadays but really, old chap, what *could* you have been thinking of?"

Anyway, for the first time in my life I had found a book that everybody else, including my pustular contemporaries, had also read. And this was very handy for the give-and-take of textual criticism. Today, however, I can be virtually certain that most Americans below a certain age know of Fleming solely, or chiefly, through the movies. It is under this guise only that the product has been bonded for universal export.

People like to condescend to the brand-name snobbery and Savile

Row (or Bond Street) affectation, but these are only the outward show of two of the books' most important elements. When Fleming started to publish his stories, Britain was only just emerging from a long period of postwar austerity and uniformity, and it was beginning to be possible to emphasize luxury and style again without having a bad conscience. This development was somewhat identified with the return of the British Conservatives to power, and helped enable Fleming to be more frankly Churchillian and pro-imperial than would have been possible a few years previously.

The second element, namely a distinctive blend of fine leather, good tailoring, and club-land confidence, was of huge importance in appealing to American Anglophilia—perhaps most especially the sort of Anglophilia that had led the United States to clone the Office of Strategic Services, and later the CIA, from the British MI5 and MI6. Fleming himself had played a supporting part in this process, visiting wartime Washington for the British Naval Intelligence Division and writing a lengthy memo on the ways in which London could be of help to "the Cousins." He was to pay another call in 1960, to meet John F. Kennedy and discuss a number of demented schemes for the elimination of Fidel Castro. (In 1961, *Life* magazine printed the boy president's list of "top ten" books, with *From Russia with Love* coming in at number nine; we have paid dearly for this juvenile taste.) In the interim, however, British imperialism had come to a humiliating halt at Suez in 1956, as a direct consequence of President Eisenhower's refusal to support the Anglo-French-Israeli invasion of Egypt. Fleming had every reason to take this personally: the British prime minister at the time, Sir Anthony Eden, had gone at least temporarily insane and been forced to take a long rest—which he did at Goldeneye, Fleming's private Jamaican retreat.

Thus, the central paradox of the classic Bond stories is that, although superficially devoted to the Anglo-American war against Communism, they are full of contempt and resentment for America and Americans. And not just political contempt, or the penis envy of a declining power for a burgeoning one, but cultural contempt as well.

And not just with cultural contempt in general, but more specifically disgust about America's plebeian interest in sex and consumerism, the two Bond staples. "Baseball, amusement arcades, hot dogs, hideously large bosoms, neon lighting" is how Tiger Tanaka mouths the anti-American trope in *You Only Live Twice*. And how does Bond react when praised by the exquisite Tatiana Romanova for his resemblance to an American film star? By barking, "For God's sake! That's the worst insult you can pay a man!" This and other revulsions from the Hollywood ethos (a similar distaste is evinced in *For Your Eyes Only*) are an irony in themselves. And notice, please, that emphasis on "hideously large bosoms." Some displacement seems to be involved here. For Fleming, it was the southern hemispheres that counted, and size mattered like hell.

I am afraid that the mention of Tatiana Romanova obliges me to record that Fleming described her otherwise peerless behind as "so hardened with exercise that it had lost the smooth downward feminine sweep, and now, round at the back and flat and hard at the sides, it jutted like a man's." Not quite like a boy's, in other words. How is one to deal with the blizzard of information on this point? From Lycett's biography we learn that the young Fleming had not only a mentor whose pseudonym was Phyllis Bottome but also a lover named Monique Panchaud de Bottomes. This might be coincidence (it could hardly be conspiracy), but in that same premature *Times* obituary, ostensibly written by "M," we are expected to believe that the newly orphaned Bond was sent to live with an aunt in the "quaintly named" Kentish hamlet of Pett Bottom. "That was just a love-pat," says the boorish Australian "Dikko" Henderson in *For Your Eyes Only*, after he's floored a Japanese chick. "What's a girl's bottom for, anyway?" Fleming himself appeared to have a ready answer to this question. As he wrote to his complaisant future wife, who seems to have shared some of his tastes, "I am the chosen instrument of the Holy Man to whip some of the devil out of you, and I must do my duty however much pain it causes me. So be prepared to drink your cocktails standing for a few days."

When one really reflects on the memorable scenes in the fiction (shall I say those that stick out?), it becomes obvious that Fleming expended much more careful thought on torture than on sex. It is true that Bond's bottom is never threatened (Coward would have put a swift stop to any of *that*), but the other menaces and taunts and practices are distinctly lascivious and lovingly rehearsed. Even Simon Raven, giving *Casino Royale* an admiring review, protested that the torture scene was essentially unpardonable.

But there is no point in being prissy about this. If Fleming had not been quite a heavy sadist and narcissist and all-around repressed pervert, we might never have got to know Rosa Klebb or Auric Goldfinger or Ernst Stavro Blofeld. And, having said that Bond was originally a figure designed to hold up the British end of the "special relationship," I ought to add that the cleverness of the series lay partly in how it saw past the confines of the Cold War. The transition probably begins after *From Russia with Love*. Who would have believed a paranoid tale about the Bulgarians shooting the pope in 1982 if it had not been for the memory of Moscow's Bulgar robots in that adventure? The stories are a kind of bridge from the period of ideological warfare to our own, where the fear of a frigid colossus or a nuclear "exchange" has been deposed by the fear of an uncorked psychopath and a "dirty bomb." However anal that last stupid expression may be (a toilet-trained bomb is perhaps more a wish than a possibility), it was Fleming who first conjured it and who reached beyond the KGB into our world of the Colombian cartel, the Russian mafia, and other "non-state actors" like al-Qaeda. "SPECTRE," I noticed recently, is an anagram of "Respect," the name of a small British party led by a power-drunk micro-megalomaniac called George Galloway, a man with a friendly connection to Saddam Hussein.

Also rather contemporary, at least from one end of the special relationship, is the cold dislike of France that keeps recurring. Le Chiffre and Goldfinger both act for the French Communists. Rosa Klebb can operate in Paris with ease, thanks to the climate of treason that pervades the place. Bond finds Paris empty and hypocritical, like a cynical whore.

"It was its heart that was gone," Fleming writes, "pawned to the tourists, pawned to the Russians and Rumanians and Bulgars, pawned to the scum of the world who had gradually taken the town over." That reflection occurs in "From a View to a Kill," published in 1960 in the short-story collection *For Your Eyes Only*, where even Castro's rebels are granted some grudging sympathy (the Caribbean then being Britain's backyard, thanks all the same, and not some polluted Yankee pond).

Fleming once confessed that he hoped to "take the story along so fast that nobody would notice the idiosyncrasies." Fat chance. His "idiosyncrasies" jut out like Tatiana Romanova's ass. What he ought to have said was that he hoped to pile on the pace and thereby hustle the reader past the point where belief has to be suspended. The smaller details, of products and appurtenances and accessories, fulfill the function of the conjuror's other hand. They distract attention from the glaring lacunae in the plots, the amazing stupidity of the supposedly mastermind villains, and the reckless disregard for his own safety that this supposedly ice-cold agent displays by falling for every lure. Another critic whose exegesis might have startled Bond's creator was Umberto Eco, who wrote:

> Fleming takes time to convey the familiar with photographic accuracy, because it is upon the familiar that he can solicit our capacity for identification. Our credulity is solicited, blandished, directed to the region of possible and desirable things. Here the narration is realistic, the attention to detail intense; for the rest, so far as the unlikely is concerned, a few pages suffice and an implicit wink of the eye.

The movie industry saw through this trick and learned, with such a big wink, how to replicate it for the masses and to make even Fleming's pulp fiction look like literature. Fleming was angling for Hollywood, however much he may have despised it.

(*The Atlantic*, April 2006)

Power Suits

B ECAUSE I AM a supporter of the armed struggle against the forces of al-Qaeda, the Taliban, and Saddam Hussein, I quite often get asked if I have become a Republican in my declining years. Never mind for now the many reactionary Republicans, from Brent Scowcroft to Patrick J. Buchanan, who are my enemies in this argument: the fact is that I have been a republican all my life. Not in the sense that I favor the reunification of Ireland—though I certainly do—but in the sense of being opposed to all forms of monarchy and absolutism. I moved to the United States a quarter of a century ago, partly to escape the British royal family (whose publicity alas followed me across the Atlantic) and partly because it was much easier to be an independent writer in a country that had a written constitution and a codified Bill of Rights. After the barbaric assault on American civil society that took place on September 11, 2001, I resolved to stop cheating on my dues and applied to become a citizen, and although my paperwork seems to have vanished into the hideous maelstrom that goes by the name "Homeland Security," I consider myself to be standing in line to take a formal oath to defend that constitution against all enemies foreign and domestic.

In January of this year I found myself involved in two legal actions, one in my country of adoption and another in my country of birth, both directed at arbitrary power. In the first instance, I was contacted by Anthony Romero, the director of the American Civil Liberties Union. He asked if I would agree to become a plaintiff in a suit against the National Security Agency (NSA) and by implication against the Justice Department. It had been disclosed that the NSA was engaging in widespread warrantless surveillance of American citizens. It seemed obvious to me (and the suit alleges) that this violated the First and Fourth Amendments to the Constitution, in that it hampered the confidentiality with which reporters and scholars and lawyers must work, in the Middle East and western Asia, and in that it was an unreasonable invasion of privacy rights. The First Amendment is how I make my living. But it is precious to me in other ways, in that it stands against any infringement of free expression. So I said yes.

I then had to fill out a questionnaire about my travels to, and contacts in, such countries as Iran, Iraq, Afghanistan, Pakistan, and Indonesia, all of which I have covered for this magazine in the past few years. One of the questions asked if I was in contact with any person or group that the United States government could regard as being associated with terrorists. I would have paused at this anyway. Most of those with whom I exchange e-mail or phone traffic in Iraq and Afghanistan are dedicated to defeating the forces of bin Ladenism. But then there was this other little matter I'd gotten myself involved with. Two men were about to step into a dock in a London court: one of them, named David Keogh, is a former official in Prime Minister Tony Blair's Cabinet Office, and the other, named Leo O'Connor, is an alleged recipient of a document from Keogh. What the document is said to show is this: that on April 16, 2004, President George Bush proposed bombing the Al Jazeera network headquarters, in Qatar, and was talked out of it only by Tony Blair. Now, I have visited those same offices and have friends there, and I sometimes appear on Al Jazeera chat shows. So it seemed that, by one definition at least, I did have contact with suspected-terrorist targets. I had given some help in Washington to a team of British reporters at the London *Daily Mirror*, which broke the story, and also exchanged information with a celebrated British lawyer, Geoffrey Robertson, who had drafted a Freedom of Information request in London, on behalf of Al Jazeera, in order to get a look at the relevant memo.

Both these actions have quite momentous implications. In the case of the first, our lawsuit alleges that President Bush has flat out broken the law: the 1978 Foreign Intelligence Surveillance Act (FISA), which set out *"the exclusive means by which* electronic surveillance . . . and the interception of domestic wire, oral and electronic communications may be conducted." (My italics.) These "exclusive means" do not include the words "by secret presidential fiat." In the second case, if the allegation is true, it means that a very important center of communications, in a neutral country friendly to the United States (and host of the U.S. Central Command), would have been blitzed. I've tried to imagine the possible effect of that in the Arab world, but can't quite manage to do so. Let's just say that it would have put a large and smoldering hole in Karen Hughes's "make nice" diplomacy. It would furthermore have raised the suspicion that the American bombing of Al Jazeera's Baghdad office, in 2003, which killed a reporter, had not been a regrettable accident.

In a way, I am already flirting with lawbreaking by ventilating these questions. Since we filed our suit, the Bush administration has issued a "white paper," and has agreed to hearings on Capitol Hill about the propriety of using the NSA against Americans. But this was not at all the first response to the revelation of the surveillance program. It was angrily announced by the White House that whoever disclosed it had violated the law and was giving aid and comfort to the enemy. A criminal inquiry has been set in motion to uncover the source of the leak. Meanwhile, in Britain, the Crown Prosecution wants to delay proceedings against Keogh and O'Connor while it seeks endorsement of a secret venue from Blair's foreign secretary, Jack Straw. (British law features an Official Secrets Act, allowing the government to decide that even public information is secret, which in the US would be a violation of the First Amendment. Another reason, it occurred to me, why I had changed countries to begin with.) In other words, do bear in mind, dear reader, that you were not even supposed to know about these arguments in the first place!

Let us be scrupulous and put the opposite case. Things have changed since 1978, when FISA became law. The distinction between "overseas" and "at home" has been eroded by transnational jihadist groups. The forces of law and order must be able to move very swiftly. The Justice Department white paper argues that Congress *did* permit the president to order warrantless surveillance when after 9/11 it granted him the Authorization for Use of Military Force (AUMF). In ruling on the Yaser Esam Hamdi case, which was that of an "enemy combatant," the Supreme Court found that the AUMF included detention in "narrow circumstances" as a "fundamental incident of waging war." The Justice Department now wants to say that electronic surveillance is also a "fundamental incident." Oh, and Abraham Lincoln suspended habeas corpus during the Civil War.

Well, the fact remains that the AUMF doesn't say a word about surveillance. And is it not the Republican Party which makes a fetish of "original intent," and opposes the discovery of hidden or novel interpretations of existing laws? Furthermore, Congress amended FISA *after* it passed the AUMF. Thus, it can't be argued that Congress intended that the AUMF supersede or override FISA. It can't be argued even if, as its critics say when they are finally forced to discuss the matter, FISA is itself unconstitutional. If Bush feels that the act unbalances the separation of powers by granting too much authority to Congress, he must ask for it to be repealed or amended, or request that the Supreme Court strike it down. Meanwhile, *it is the law of the land* and he is bound by oath to uphold and obey it. And if the Supreme Court is to be cited, then remember what it said in June 2004, when the administration wanted to hold "enemy combatants" without a hearing. It ruled that "a state of war is not a blank check for the President." In dreams begin responsibilities, and in wars begin the temptation for the rulers to arrogate extraordinary powers to themselves. Bush once appointed an attorney general, John Ashcroft, who knew so little about the United States Constitution that he announced that, in America, "we have no king but Jesus." That moronic statement was exactly two words too long.

As for the Hamdi case, involving an actual combatant and the "fundamental incident of waging war," if warrantless electronic spying on Americans is now to be defined as such a fundamental incident, then it is difficult if not impossible to say what could *not* be. Warrantless searches of offices and homes? Prior censorship of the press? This is where the Lincoln analogy becomes more relevant. Honest Abe did try unilaterally to suspend the writ of habeas corpus. But the chief justice ruled that only Congress could suspend habeas corpus, and Lincoln was forced to submit the matter to Capitol Hill. I have never heard it argued that this repressive measure actually shortened the war or hastened the Emancipation Proclamation, but it may have had the psychological effect of showing that the Union would use any weapon at its disposal. The thing to keep your eye on is this: we have already been "at war" with our nonstate enemy for as long as the Civil War went on. We are endlessly told it will be a lengthy struggle. All the more important, then, that we know what our rights and responsibilities are. The administration tries to dissolve this thought by saying, in effect, "It's an emergency. Be afraid. Trust us." What sinister poppycock. Our intelligence "community," with its multibillion-dollar secret budget, left us under open skies on 9/11. The only born-and-raised American who had infiltrated the Taliban was John Walker Lindh of Marin County. George Tenet's reaction to hearing of the Twin Towers in conflagration was to say that he wondered if it had anything to do with that guy in the flight-training school in Minnesota. For this, Bush gave him a Presidential Medal of Freedom. When the CIA wasn't generating junk intelligence over Iraq, it was leaking hostile propaganda to discredit the whole idea of "regime change" in that country. These people are not even accountable to Bush: when he "authorized" the warrantless surveillance in late 2001 he found that the NSA had already started doing it without anyone's permission. The FBI, on which tons of the resulting raw material was dumped, has stated that it was mostly useless and time wasting. It also must say something if an organization whose headquarters building still bears the name of J. Edgar Hoover (who wiretapped Martin Luther King Jr. and tried to scare him into committing suicide) has asked the question: Is this even legal? To this and other concerns, General Michael Hayden, former director of the NSA, has blandly responded, "I can say unequivocally that we have got information through this program that would not otherwise have been available." Well, presumably. That could also be said if we all had to empty our BlackBerrys into his capacious lap.

If you get yourself involved in a civil liberty lawsuit, you will invariably find that you have teamed up with people you don't like. I became a supporter of the ACLU three decades ago, when it lost a good chunk of its membership by defending the First Amendment right of the American Nazi Party to hold a parade in the Jewish suburb of Skokie, Illinois. I told Anthony Romero that he could sign me up for the suit but that I was curious to know who the other plaintiffs might be. The National Association of Criminal Defense Lawyers: fine. Members of this group complain that warrantless eavesdropping destroys attorney-client privilege and makes it almost impossible to represent defendants in far-off locations without flying to see them in person each time. The Council on American-Islamic Relations: yuck. These people produce rationalizations for Muslim fundamentalism and were the advocates for the demented crooner Yusuf Islam (formerly Cat Stevens), who has incited the murder of Salman Rushdie. Still, how mad and pathetic of Homeland Security to divert a whole transatlantic flight just because the crooner was on board. Professors Larry Diamond and Barnett Rubin, of Stanford and of New York University, respectively: good company to be in. Diamond was a member of the transitional authority in Iraq, before he quit in disillusionment, and Rubin remains an invaluable adviser to the United Nations and the government in Afghanistan. These two men have done more to fight the foe than George Tenet ever did, but they now find that old friends and contacts are reluctant to speak freely on the phone or in e-mail. This is important to me too, and to you, because though my own contribution has been slight, it is reporters like John Burns and Peter Bergen who have come up with far more valuable advance intelligence about al-Qaeda than the CIA or NSA ever has. Put a chilling effect on the investigative work of men like that and you endanger national security. At our press conference, on January 17, the three-hundredth birthday of Benjamin Franklin, I said that this was a sad but appropriate way to commemorate the man who (a) was the presiding spirit at the Constitutional Convention and (b) elucidated the emancipating power of electricity.

Another distinguished co-plaintiff is James Bamford, whose books on the NSA, *The Puzzle Palace* and *Body of Secrets*, are the main public resource for knowledge of a gigantic agency which for a long time was not even known to exist. Thanks to Bamford and others, we now know that the NSA was used to spy on American civilians throughout the Vietnam War, in order to try to prove that the antiwar and civil-rights movements were being manipulated by foreign powers. Black Panthers and Quakers were targeted without distinction, and the first writer to touch upon the fact—David Kahn, author of *The Codebreakers*—was himself placed under an extensive watch. It was this wholesale abuse of power that led to the Senate hearings convened by Senator Frank Church, of Idaho, that contributed to the proposed impeachment of Richard Nixon, and that led to the passage of FISA in the first place. The federal court in which we have filed our suit— in the Eastern District of Michigan—is the court that first held in 1972 that warrantless wiretapping of Americans for national-security purposes was unconstitutional. This ruling against Nixon was later upheld by the Supreme Court. One wonders if a Bush-dominated Court will do the same, but when my neoconservative friends complain about my undermining of the "wartime president," I have my answer ready: give this power or this right to any one president and you give it, indefinitely and unaccountably, to them all. The surveillance spreads like weeds, and there is no way to know if it is of you, or to get yourself taken off the watch list. Apparently even John Ashcroft could see this elementary point: I've heard from a friend of mine that he was opposed to a national ID card because he didn't want a future President Clinton to have that much power. In all the recent arguments over the Patriot Act and the "national-security state," one has often seen senior liberal Democrats take a powder, or join enthusiastically in the aggrandizement of police power (as they did when Bill Clinton rammed through the panicky Antiterrorism and Effective Death Penalty Act of 1996 after the Oklahoma City atrocity), whereas certain prominent conservatives, such as Grover Norquist and former congressman Bob Barr, have been consistently libertarian. As I was getting ready to sign on for the ACLU suit, I had dinner with both of those gentlemen in the interval of a conference of the National Rifle Association. Well, Bob Barr now speaks on tour for the ACLU as well, so if the fans of the Second Amendment can be mobilized to defend the First and Fourth ones, that's absolutely fine by me.

And what of the War on Terror as it applies to Al Jazeera? Stopped by a *Daily Mirror* reporter outside a Virginia church on January 8, Colin Powell (who accompanied Bush on April 16, 2004) said, "You're asking me about a two-year-old meeting that I don't remember." (When contacted by *Vanity Fair*, Powell responded, "My quote does not confirm that I was at the meeting where such a thing may have been discussed. I was at the Blair visit on 16 April, but not necessarily [at] every conversation they had that day. I don't have memcons to recover all this, but I never took seriously any such idea nor did the president.") This falls some way short of a strong denial. One might think that such a conversation would either (a) stick in the mind if it had occurred or (b) appear so unimaginable that it could be roundly and affirmatively said not to have happened at all. The first response to the Freedom of Information Act request, on 10 Downing Street writing paper, confirmed that the Cabinet Office "holds information which is relevant to your request," concerning "memos or notes that record President Bush's discussions with the prime minister about the bombing of the Al-Jazeera television station in Qatar." It then goes on to say that disclosure of the said information "would, or would be likely to, prejudice relations between the United Kingdom and any other state." The Cabinet Office has the right under law to refuse to discuss the matter at all, on grounds of national security, so it is peculiar that it should implicitly confirm the story in a letter. And, of course, if there's nothing to it, or if the president was only making a joke in very poor taste and the transcribers misunderstood, then we'll all climb down. But in that case why are two British citizens facing a trial, which the government wants to conduct in camera?

When I wanted a picture to illustrate this article, I went with a photographer to the turnoff in Virginia where a large public sign points traffic to the "George Bush Center for Intelligence: CIA." We managed to take a few shots before six police cars turned up, and large men kept their hands on their holsters while ordering us to keep our hands in plain sight. It was only with difficulty that we persuaded them they had no right to confiscate the film. We were on public land, on the Potomac Heritage Trail, under the blue skies of America and protected by the great roof of the Constitution, and were next to a sign which millions of motorists pass every year. And what was going unwatched while six carloads of troopers wasted taxpayer money in this way? In my experience, countries where undisguised photographers attract police attention are countries where the citizen is the property of the state. The duty of a true republican is to resist the banana republic, and perhaps some bananas Republicans, as well as bananas Democrats, so that the Bill of Rights survives this war as it has survived the previous ones. When Attorney General Alberto Gonzales made an appearance at Georgetown University Law Center on January 24, a group of students got up to unfurl a banner which read, "Those who would sacrifice liberty for security deserve neither." And, I might add, will get neither. The words are taken from Benjamin Franklin.

(*Vanity Fair*, April 2006)

Blood for No Oil!

W HETHER INTENTIONALLY OR not, Peter Beinart sets out
to challenge and annoy the American left from the first three
words of his title. "The good fight" is a nostalgic, hymnal term that
the mixed bag of remaining "progressives" still reserve very much for
themselves; it is most commonly used to invoke the Spanish Civil War
and, in particular, those Americans who went, under the ostensible
banner of the Abraham Lincoln Battalion but under the effective
command of the Comintern, to take part in it. And as one looks back
on it now, this episode of heroism and betrayal is remarkable for
one thing above all: it represents the only time in modern history
that American radicals were in favor of, or had a direct hand in, any
"foreign entanglement." Their highest moral exemplar, as badly as it
ended, is in fact the great exception that violates their rule.

Seeing the title, I had hoped that Beinart would open with a challenge to the myth of "premature antifascism" and would point out
that otherwise during that period the American left had made common cause with the isolationists and even, for a while, with the idea
of a formal military pact between Stalin and Hitler. Trace elements of

Review of *The Good Fight: Why Liberals—and Only Liberals—Can Win the War on Terror and Make America Great Again* by Peter Beinart

this mentality survive to our own day: both Gore Vidal and Patrick J. Buchanan still revere the figure of Charles Lindbergh, whose influence was so inadequately captured, from the traditionally wearisome New Jersey Jewish keyhole, in Philip Roth's *Plot Against America*. (The moving spirit of today's Antiwar.com, a preening figure named Justin Raimondo, is also given to paeans in favor of Lindbergh's charismatic manliness and authority.)

Instead, Beinart opens the story with the Henry Wallace campaign of 1948—the setting of another Philip Roth novel, this time *I Married a Communist*. In that year, a strategic majority of the American left worked hard for a man who would have given Eastern Europe to Stalin (and perhaps some of Western Europe, too) with the same insouciance that—until Stalin himself had been attacked—it had allowed the region to be given to Hitler. Had the Wallace campaign done as well as had been predicted, the chief domestic effect would have been to throw the election to Thomas Dewey. But as it was, the era of the tough-minded "Cold War liberal" had begun. Beinart's book locates the crucial step in this evolution at the founding of Americans for Democratic Action, or ADA, in the Willard Hotel in Washington in January 1947. Present for this event were Hubert Humphrey, Walter Reuther, Eleanor Roosevelt, Arthur Schlesinger Jr., David Dubinsky, and—Beinart's personal hero—Reinhold Niebuhr.

It is easy to summarize what attracts Beinart to this group: in a breathtaking moment of reactionary parochialism and insularity, Henry Wallace had declared against Marshall aid for Europe but supposedly in favor of civil rights and the rights of labor. By assembling a distinguished group that endorsed Marshall aid and had seen through Communism, but that took a forward position on New Deal programs and the emancipation of black Americans, the ADA had echoed Mrs. Julia Ward Howe, who in the Willard Hotel almost a century earlier had "sounded forth the trumpet that shall never call retreat." Beinart gives due credit to the unjustly forgotten Bayard Rustin, who was perhaps the true genius of the civil-rights and democratic-socialist movements, but his emphasis on Niebuhr is what truly informs the book, because this solemn old Protestant theologian provided a constant warning against American hubris.

Beinart's aim is to refashion this tradition for the war against jihadism, and to reposition American liberals as the friends of democracy and equality at home and abroad. The Truman administration presents a rough pattern of what he admires, from its desegregation of the US armed forces to its willingness to confront Communism in Greece, Turkey, and Korea while relying, where it could, on local democratic forces rather than on regional oligarchies. He seeks to represent the upward curve of domestic reform, especially the amazing burgeoning of the civil-rights movement, as intersecting nicely with "containment" overseas and the demonstrated willingness to employ force—even annihilating thermonuclear force—as well. Result: prosperity at home and "peace through strength" abroad.

This retrospective optimism is in many ways too neat. In the first place, the Allied victors in 1945 had decided to leave fascist despotism in place in Spain and Portugal, and to recruit Hitler's spies and rocket scientists, from Reinhard Gehlen to Wernher von Braun, into a new "national-security state." In the second place, there were always leftists, notably I. F. Stone, who understood that the Wallace campaign was a fellow-traveling fiasco. In the third place, there were more-centrist liberals who voiced grave concern over Washington's policy in Iran in 1953, Guatemala in 1954, Lebanon in 1958 (all these episodes are omitted by Beinart), and elsewhere, and who did not think that the Cold War was a license for imperialism. Finally, there has probably never been a more hubristic rhetoric—or practice—than during the time of the New Frontier (which so memorably featured the rhetorical skills of Schlesinger). Within a decade and a half of the Willard Hotel meeting, the Camelot darling of American liberals had risked global catastrophe over Cuba and committed the United States to the degrading role of successor to the French Empire in Indochina, all the while dragging his feet on the only idea whose time actually *had* come: Rustin's beautiful scheme for a march on Washington. There's no mystery about the rise of the New Left. John F. Kennedy was more of a sellout in terms of the ADA's guiding principles than even the most credulous liberal should have been prepared to accept.

This does not excuse those who reverted to post-Vietnam isolationism and who regarded the later advent of the "KKK" (the Khmer Rouge in Cambodia, the Ayatollah Khomeini in Iran, and the Khalq faction of Stalinism in Afghanistan) as nothing more than an invitation for America to "come home." And it has been demonstrated in more than one case that a crisis ducked by liberals will recur as an opportunity taken, or even seized, by conservatives. Without the American Right (and "vital center") there might have been no shah or Somoza to be overthrown in the first instance. Easy propaganda points can be made to the effect that the United States' ruling establishment is often the author of its own misfortunes. But this does not exempt the citizens of the country, confronted with chickens from whatever roost they may originate, from deciding whether or not these birds of ill omen should be shot down. And on this visceral point, as Beinart eventually concedes with infinite regret, the Right appears to speak with less ambiguity.

Jimmy Carter was not Henry Wallace, but Beinart's history of liberalism during the post-Vietnam years identifies the same mentality—of wishful thinking about the Evil Empire—that gave the Right its next big chance. In this narrative, the role of the ADA is superseded by the roles of Scoop Jackson and the now forgotten Congressman Dave McCurdy, who sought a "third way" in the crisis over Central America. The eventual implosion of the Soviet system makes some of these debates appear to be further away from us than they really are. (The dispute between Paul Berman and Michael Moore, the former of whom wrote a *Mother Jones* piece critical of the Sandinistas that was censored by the latter, was, however, a harbinger.) Beinart understates the importance of Ronald Reagan's abandonment of "mutual assured destruction," or MAD, a long-standing, containment-based bipartisan commitment that was suddenly (and correctly) discovered to be unstable as well as immoral. Not only did this policy shift perform well in the world of "realism," in that the decision to retool for strategic defense had a measurable influence upon Mikhail Gorbachev; it also had the effect of making liberal noises about a nuclear "freeze" seem tinny and irrelevant. The other great argument of the time—over the imposition of sanctions on South Africa—gave the Left the moral high ground for a year or two, but was eventually co-opted by Reagan and Margaret Thatcher as well.

If American liberalism had seriously wanted to regain its moral standing after the Cold War ended, the reemergence of the one-party, one-leader aggressive state, in the forms of Greater Serbia and Greater Iraq, should have provided the ideal opportunity. But although the first President Bush secured United Nations support, and Syrian and Egyptian troops, for the recovery of Kuwait, he did so without any noticeable help from the left of center, who were too fastidious about the oil issue to soil their hands. (We can now say, with almost 100 percent certainty, that if Saddam Hussein had kept Kuwait, he would have acquired the bomb.) In Bosnia, where there was no oil but there was genocide, a "New Democrat" administration was finally persuaded to take action, again without the support of the large and consistent antiwar wing of American politics, whose members moaned ceaselessly about quagmire. Most of the traditional Right was silent or hostile on this occasion, too. Those who pressed for solidarity with Bosnia included some leftists like Susan Sontag, a great part of the American Jewish community, and a few traditional hawks—but perhaps most notably (and in a case that did not involve the state interest of Israel) the emerging neoconservatives. As one who took part in this argument, I can testify that many on the pro-Bosnian Left had more or less to assure themselves that their demand for intervention was kosher, precisely because it did *not* seem to be in the immediate national-security interest of the United States. Blood for no oil!

All of this was a dismal prelude to the crisis that struck the United States in the fall of 2001. One *knew*, before that terrible day was out, what would be said by the academic and journalistic and Hollywood Left. Much of the rhetoric of that time has been forgotten (though not by me), and now those who never wanted a fight in Afghanistan in the first place are free to complain that the war with al-Qaeda in Iraq is a distraction from the struggle they opposed. But in some untranslatable manner, this two-faced position has communicated itself to a large number of American voters. These people may be as uninformed as Beinart complains they are (look how many of them believe that Saddam Hussein was behind the World Trade Center attacks), but they are not so stupid as to believe that the president invaded Iraq to avenge his daddy, or to swell the coffers of Halliburton, or to please General Sharon. Nor are they so dumb and credulous as to believe that there would be no jihadists in Iraq if it were not for the coalition presence. Fatuity of that kind—especially the last kind—is the preserve of the Democratic intelligentsia, not just of the MoveOn.org types but also of figures like Harry Reid, Barbara Boxer, and Al Gore. I am not a tremendous admirer of Senator Joseph Lieberman, but his expressed opinions make him a smaller figure in Democratic circles than was Henry Wallace in 1948. How can a Truman emerge from this galère?

In other words, the whole comparison with the ADA is hopelessly inexact. The hard-liners in 1948 were principled enough to do the Democratic Party the favor of deserting it and running their own slate. They were also, one might concede, at least intelligible in their naïveté about the USSR. A thinking person could, then at least, be brought to believe that state socialism was an improvement on monopoly capitalism, and that war was to be avoided at any price. In the present case, however, not only are the hard-liners the activist and fund-raising core of the party; they also express ambivalence about a foe that does not even pretend to share the values of the Enlightenment, and that is furthermore immune to the cruder rationality of MAD. The Soviet leadership had every reason to avoid suicide, while the Islamist fanatics dream of nothing else. In this context, Beinart's wishful and halfhearted belief that Saddam Hussein could have been contained is the one position that nobody can seriously hold. He gives himself away when he argues that a continuation of the cruel and indiscriminate sanctions could have led the Baathist regime to self-destruct. Has he even tried to imagine what Iraq would have looked like on the day that that self-destruction occurred? Let us just assume that it would not have been a Velvet Revolution. It would have more closely resembled a Rwanda or a Congo on the Gulf. Bad as things are now, they would certainly have been worse.

Thus, however ineptly it may have been phrased and implemented, the Bush administration's improvised adoption of political change in the region may bear some comparison with Reagan's repudiation of Cold War stasis. And I see no sign that the American Left and the liberals understand what it means to have become once again the party of the status quo. In his wishful and overconfident subtitle, where he asserts that *only* liberals can win this war, Beinart vainly tries to split a difference. In the first place, it is a war against a version of apocalyptic fascism, of which terrorism is only the expression. In the second place, the bulk of the liberal consensus has already demonstrated a want of spine and sinew, and ceded much ground to the freshly converted and clumsy anti-isolationist Right. Retrospect may grant us time to pass a verdict on which of these two blunders was the decisive one. Meanwhile, the rough retranslation of Beinart's title is *Hillary in 2008*—a prospect some distance short of a liberal dream.

(*The Atlantic*, May 2006)

How Uninviting

N JANUARY OF this year, I was invited by a group called the Republican Jewish Coalition to come and speak at a public meeting. The subject was the UN "oil for food" program or, to give it another name, the means by which the corruption of the United Nations had actually helped Saddam Hussein to finance many of the French, Russian, and British friends of his regime. I was eager to say more about this appalling scheme, and it didn't matter to me that I had little else in common with the group that had been kind enough to offer me a platform. A date was booked, a place arranged (an old temple in downtown DC), and I even remember telling the organizers that I also do this for a living and would expect a modest fee.

At about the time that pre-publicity for the event had gotten under way, Morton Klein of the Zionist Organization of America began to raise a stink. If I picked up the phone in those days, it was invariably to hear a reporter from the *Forward*, or some other such paper, asking me to comment on his comments. Klein didn't appreciate some of the things I had said about Israel and Israeli policy over the years. He was empurpled by the idea that a conservative Jewish group would even consider inviting me. It didn't matter to him that I wasn't even being asked to comment on Zionism, let alone on the ultra-Jabotinsky Zionist faction of which he is the bugle. The upshot was that the meeting was canceled. I received even more calls from the Republican Jewish Coalition, in which they spoke critically of Klein, alluded in the most heartfelt way to the scheduling conflict that had suddenly arisen, and assured me most warmly that the invitation still stood. And then the telephone fell mercifully silent.

I wasn't born yesterday, and I have sources of my own within Washington's Jewish community, so it didn't take that long to discover what I already knew, which was that I had not been the accidental victim of a scheduling conflict. So, we can score one for Morton Klein, and we can cancel that tiny check that I had earmarked for my favorite charity (the Patriotic Union of Kurdistan).

I think that Klein and the Republican Jewish Coalition were well within their rights. I have a perfect right, which I would defend to the death, to express my views on the question of Palestine. But I do not have a perfect right to express that opinion—which would have had to come up, even in a discussion of Iraq and the degeneration of the United Nations—at a meeting of a private group that takes the opposing view. Nor do I have an absolute right to criticize Theodor Herzl and all his works from a podium belonging to a neutral organization. Such outfits have their own right to pick and to choose and even to reconsider.

What a chance I missed to call attention to myself. I now can't open my e-mail or check my voice mail without reading or hearing about the repression visited on Professor Tony Judt of New York University. It seems that he was booked to speak at a meeting sponsored by a group called Network 20/20 at the Polish consulate in New York and had his event canceled when the relevant Polish diplomat decided that the evening might be—given Professor Judt's views on Israel—more trouble than it was worth. I now hear of a fulminating letter, signed by no fewer than 114 intellectuals, that has been published in the *New York Review of Books* (there's glory for you) in which this repression is denounced. How dare the Polish consulate refuse the heroic dissident Judt a platform! And how dare the Anti-Defamation League, or its chief spokesman Abraham Foxman (it's not quite clear who called) even telephone the Poles to complain?

I live my life without reference to Foxman. He was a leading mourner at the funeral of the fascist bigmouth Meir Kahane, and he took donations of $250,000 from the fugitive scumbag Marc Rich and did some lobbying of Bill Clinton in respect of a pardon (which caused William Safire to demand that he resign his post, which he has not). Who is such an abject sap as to require a kosher stamp from such a man? And what is the ADL, which is supposed to counter slanders against Jews, doing in the first place by taking a position on Jewish criticism of Israel? Yet the 114 signatories make indignant squeals, crediting the ADL as "an organization dedicated to promoting civil rights and public education." No doubt they believe themselves to be ironic. And so they are, inasmuch as they give literal credit to Foxman. But on what basis can they demand that criticism of Israel be granted as a right on those square feet of New York City that constitute Polish soil?

The astonishing extent of this brouhaha recalls the reception accorded to the John Mearsheimer–Stephen Walt critique of Jewish-American influence on US foreign policy. And the two episodes are, in fact, somewhat related. Once again, absolutely conventional attacks on Israeli and US policy are presented as heroically original. Once again, it is insinuated that the bravery of those making the point is such as to draw down the Iron Heel. Once again, no distinction is made between private organizations and the public sphere. Mearsheimer and Walt ended up complaining of persecution because they got a rude notice from Alan Dershowitz! Such self-pity.

Professor Judt has a podium of his very own, at the Remarque Institute at New York University. He once invited me to speak there. He would not have invited me if I were a Kahane supporter and, though I defend the right of the Kach Party to hold its own meetings, I would protest if it were allowed to use the Remarque Institute for this purpose. This distinction seems worth making, at a time when free expression has much deadlier enemies who succeeded, for example, in preventing any of the editors who signed the Judt letter, as well as the magazine in which their letter appears, from publishing the Danish cartoons. To do that would have taken some nerve. This protest does not.

(*Slate*, October 23, 2006)

Look Who's Cutting and Running Now

---⊛⊛⊛---

A CCORDING TO THE Associated Press, Henry Kissinger made it official Sunday morning in London, when he told a BBC interviewer that military victory was not possible in Iraq. Actually, what he said was this:

> If you mean by "military victory" an Iraqi government that can be established and whose writ runs across the whole country, that gets the civil war under control and sectarian violence under control in a time period that the political processes of the democracies will support, I don't believe that is possible.

There are a couple of qualifications in there, and what Kissinger is describing is really more the definition of a political victory than a military one, but say what you will about our Henry, he wasn't born yesterday. He must have known that the question would come up, what his answer would be, and what the ensuing AP headline ("Kissinger: Iraq Military Win Impossible") would look like.

Taken together with the dismissal of Donald Rumsfeld, the nomination of Robert Gates, and the holy awe with which the findings of the Iraq Study Group are now expected, this means that the Bush administration, or large parts of it, is now cutting if not actually running, and it is looking for partners in the process. (You have to admit that it was clever of the president to make it appear that Rumsfeld had been fired by the electorate rather than by him.) It seems that Kissinger has been giving his "realist" advice even to the supposedly most hawkish member of the administration, namely the vice president, and at a dinner in honor of the president-elect of Mexico a few nights ago, I saw him mixing easily with such ISG elders as former Rep. Lee Hamilton. Members of this wing or tendency were all over the *New York Times* on Sunday as well, imputing near-ethereal qualities of leadership to Robert Gates, so a sort of self-reinforcing feedback loop appears to be in place.

The summa of wisdom in these circles is the need for consultation with Iraq's immediate neighbors in Syria and Iran. Given that these two regimes have recently succeeded in destroying the other most hopeful democratic experiment in the region—the brief emergence of a self-determined Lebanon that was free of foreign occupation—and are busily engaged in promoting their own version of sectarian mayhem there, through the trusty medium of Hezbollah, it looks as if a distinctly unsentimental process is under way.

This will present few difficulties to Baker, who supported the Syrian near-annexation of Lebanon. In order to recruit the Baathist regime of Hafez al-Assad to his coalition of the cynical against Saddam in the Kuwait war, Baker and Bush Sr. both acquiesced in the obliteration of Lebanese sovereignty. "I believe in talking to your enemies," said Baker last month—invoking what is certainly a principle of diplomacy. In this instance, however, it will surely seem to him to be more like talking to old friends—who just happen to be supplying the sinews of war to those who kill American soldiers and Iraqi civilians. Is it likely that they will stop doing this once they become convinced that an American withdrawal is only a matter of time?

At around the same time he made this statement, Baker was quoted as saying, with great self-satisfaction, that nobody ever asks him any more about the decision to leave Saddam Hussein in power in 1991.

It's interesting to know that he still feels himself invested in that grand bargain of realpolitik, which, contrary to what he may think, has not by any means been forgotten. It's also interesting in shedding light on the sort of conversations he has been having in Baghdad. For millions of Iraqis, the betrayal of their uprising against Saddam in 1991 is something that they can never forget. They tend to bring it up, too, and to fear a repetition of it. This apprehension about another sellout is especially strong among the Shiite and Kurdish elements who together make up a majority of the population, but it seems from its public reports so far that the ISG has not visited the Kurdish north of the country. If Baker thinks that the episode is a closed subject, it shows us something of what the quality of his "listening" must be like.

In 1991, for those who keep insisting on the importance of sending enough troops, there were half a million already-triumphant coalition soldiers on the scene. Iraq was stuffed with weapons of mass destruction, just waiting to be discovered by the inspectors of UNSCOM. The mass graves were fresh. The strength of sectarian militias was slight. The influence of Iran, still recovering from the devastating aggression of Saddam Hussein, was limited. Syria was—let's give Baker his due—"on side." The Iraqi Baathists were demoralized by the sheer speed and ignominy of their eviction from Kuwait and completely isolated even from their usual protectors in Moscow, Paris, and Beijing. There would never have been a better opportunity to "address the root cause" and to remove a dictator who was a permanent menace to his subjects, his neighbors, and the world beyond. Instead, he was shamefully confirmed in power and a miserable twelve-year period of sanctions helped him to enrich himself and to create the immiserated, uneducated, unemployed underclass that is now one of the "root causes" of a new social breakdown in Iraq. It seems a bit much that the man principally responsible for all this should be so pleased with himself and that he should be hailed on all sides as the very model of the statesmanship we now need.

(*Slate*, November 20, 2006)

Oriana Fallaci and the
Art of the Interview

HERE IS AN excerpt from an interview with what our media culture calls a "world leader":

Dan Rather: Mr. President, I hope you will take this question in the spirit in which it's asked. First of all, I regret that I do not speak Arabic. Do you speak any . . . any English at all?
Saddam Hussein (through translator): Have some coffee.
Rather: I have coffee.
Hussein (through translator): Americans like coffee.
Rather: That's true. And this American likes coffee.

And here is another interview with another "world leader":

Oriana Fallaci: When I try to talk about you, here in Tehran, people lock themselves in a fearful silence. They don't even dare pronounce your name, Majesty. Why is that?
The Shah: Out of an excess of respect, I suppose.
Fallaci: I'd like to ask you: if I were an Iranian instead of an Italian, and lived here and thought as I do and wrote as I do,

I mean if I were to criticize you, would you throw me in jail?
The Shah: Probably.

The difference here is not just in the quality of the answers given by the two homicidal dictators. It is in the quality of the questions. Mr. Rather (who is in mid-interview in one of Saddam's palaces and who already knows that his subject doesn't speak English and uses only his own interpreters) begins to ask a question, half apologizes for doing so, and is then completely unhorsed by an irrelevant remark about coffee. It's unclear whether he ever returned to the question that he hoped would be taken in the spirit in which it was asked, so we will never know what that "spirit" was. And at no point in the interview, which was in February 2003, did Rather ask Saddam Hussein about his somewhat, shall we say, spotty record on human rights. It was enough that he had secured what the networks call "the big get." After that, the interviewee could spout all the boilerplate he liked, and CBS would hold the megaphone by which this was transmitted to the world:

> **Rather:** Are you afraid of being killed or captured?
> **Hussein:** Whatever Allah decides. We are believers. We believe in what he decides. There is no value for any life without imam, without faith. The believer still believes that what God decides is acceptable. . . . Nothing is going to change the will of God.
> **Rather:** But don't my research notes say that you are a secularist?

Actually, I made up that last question. Dan Rather just sat through the preceding answer and went on to the next question on his list, which was about Osama bin Laden. Perhaps there was someone telling him to move things along a bit. At least he never began a question by asking, "Mr. President, how does it feel . . ."

Whereas when the supposedly secular Shah also began speaking as if the opposite were the case, burbling about his deep religious faith and his personal encounters—"not in a dream, in reality"—with the Prophet Ali, Oriana Fallaci was openly skeptical:

Fallaci: Majesty, I don't understand you at all. We had got off to such a good start, and instead now . . . this business of visions, of apparitions.

(Subsequently she asked His Imperial Majesty—no doubt with a wary eye on the exit—"Did you have these visions only as a child, or have you also had them later as an adult?")

With Oriana Fallaci's demise at seventy-seven from a host of cancers, in September, in her beloved Florence, there also died something of the art of the interview. Her absolutely heroic period was that of the 1970s, probably the last chance we had of staving off the complete triumph of celebrity culture. Throughout that decade, she scoured the globe, badgering the famous and the powerful and the self-important until they agreed to talk with her, and then reducing them to human scale. Facing Colonel Qaddafi in Libya, she bluntly asked him, "Do you know you are so unloved and unliked?" And she didn't spare figures who enjoyed more general approval, either. As a warm-up with Lech Wałęsa, she put Poland's leading anti-Communist at his ease by inquiring, "Has anyone ever told you that you resemble Stalin? I mean physically. Yes, same nose, same profile, same features, same mustache. And same height, I believe, same size." Henry Kissinger, then at the apogee of his near-hypnotic control over the media, described his encounter with her as the most disastrous conversation he had ever had. It's easy to see why. This well-cushioned man who had always been the client of powerful patrons ascribed his success to the following:

The main point arises from the fact that I've always acted alone. Americans like that immensely.

Americans like the cowboy who leads the wagon train by riding ahead alone on his horse, the cowboy who rides all alone into the town, the village, with his horse and nothing else. Maybe even without a pistol, since he doesn't shoot. He acts, that's all, by being in the right place at the right time. In short, a Western. . . . This amazing, romantic character suits me precisely because to be alone has always been part of my style or, if you like, my technique.

Neither Kissinger nor "Americans" in general liked this passage when it appeared in all its full-blown absurdity in late 1972. In fact, Kissinger disliked it so much that he claimed to have been misquoted and distorted. (Always watch out, by the way, when a politician or star claims to have been "quoted out of context." A quotation is by definition an excerpt from context.) In this case, though, Oriana was able to produce the tape, a transcript of which she later reprinted in a book. And there it is for all to read, with Kissinger raving on and on about the uncanny similarities between himself and Henry Fonda. The book is called *Interview with History*.

That title didn't suffer from an excess of modesty, but then, neither did its author. People began to sneer and gossip, saying that Oriana was just a confrontational bitch who used her femininity to get results, and who goaded men into saying incriminating things. I remember having it whispered to me that she would leave the transcript of the answers untouched but rephrase her original questions so that they seemed more penetrating than they had really been. As it happens, I found an opportunity to check that last rumor. During her interview with President Makarios, of Cyprus, who was also a Greek Orthodox patriarch, she had asked him straight-out if he was overfond of women, and more or less got him to admit that his silence in response to her direct questioning was a confession. (The paragraphs from *Interview with History* here are too long to quote, but show a brilliantly incisive line of interrogation.) Many Greek Cypriots of my acquaintance were scandalized, and quite certain that their beloved leader would never have spoken that way. I knew the old boy slightly, and took the chance to ask him if he had read the relevant chapter. "Oh yes," he said, with perfect gravity. "It is just as I remember it."

Occasionally, Oriana's interviews actually influenced history, or at the least the pace and rhythm of events. Interviewing Pakistan's leader

Zulfikar Ali Bhutto just after the war with India over Bangladesh, she induced him to say what he really thought of his opposite number in India, Mrs. Indira Gandhi ("a diligent drudge of a schoolgirl, a woman devoid of initiative and imagination . . . She should have half her father's talent!"). Demanding a full copy of the text, Mrs. Gandhi thereupon declined to attend the proposed signing of a peace agreement with Pakistan. Bhutto had to pursue Oriana, through a diplomatic envoy, all the way to Addis Ababa, to which she had journeyed to interview Emperor Haile Selassie. Bhutto's ambassador begged her to disown the Gandhi parts, and hysterically claimed that the lives of 600 million people were at stake if she did not. One of the hardest things to resist, for reporters and journalists, is the appeal to the world-shaking importance of their work and the need for them to be "responsible." Oriana declined to oblige, and Mr. Bhutto duly had to eat his plate of crow. Future "access" to the powerful meant absolutely nothing to her: she acted as if she had one chance to make the record and so did they.

Perhaps only one Western journalist ever managed to interview Ayatollah Khomeini twice. And from those long discussions we learned an enormous amount about the nature of the adamant theocracy that he was bent upon instituting. The second session was an achievement in itself, since Oriana had terminated the first one by wrenching off the all-enveloping chador she had been compelled to wear and calling it a "stupid, medieval rag." She told me that after this moment of drama she had been taken aside by Khomeini's son, who confided in her that it had been the only time in his life that he had seen his father laugh.

Do you really remember any recent interview with a major politician? Usually, the only thing that stands out in the mind is some stupid gaffe or piece of rambling incoherence. And if you go and check the original, it generally turns out that this was prompted by a dull or rambling question. Try reading the next transcript of a presidential "news conference," and see which makes you whimper more: the chief executive's train-wreck syntax or the lame and contrived promptings from the press. Oriana's questions were tautly phrased and persistent.

She researched her subjects minutely before going to see them, and each one of her published transcripts was preceded by an essay of several pages in length concerning the politics and the mentality of the interviewee. She proceeded, as Jeeves used to phrase it, from an appreciation of "the psychology of the individual." Thus, a provocative or impudent question from her would not be a vulgar attempt to shock but a well-timed challenge, usually after a lot of listening, and often taking the form of a statement. (To Yasir Arafat: "Conclusion: you don't at all want the peace that everyone is hoping for.")

The commonest and easiest way of explaining the decay of interviewing is to attribute it to the short-term and showbiz values of TV. But there's no innate reason why this should be true. At the dawn of the television age, John Freeman—a former cabinet minister and diplomat, and editor of the *New Statesman*—established an inquisitorial style probably borrowed in part from Ed Murrow, and provided astonishing glimpses of hitherto reclusive public figures like Evelyn Waugh. Television allows points to be pressed and repeated: the BBC's Jeremy Paxman once put the same question a dozen times to a Tory politician who was being evasive. It also brought us the huge advantage of the close-up, which did immense damage to shifty types like Richard Nixon.

Indeed, there is a whole new play by Peter Morgan (writer of *The Queen*) based on the transcript of the first post-Watergate interview that Nixon "granted," which was to David Frost. At the time, Frost was much attacked for trading easy questions in return for access (and also for paying Nixon $600,000—more than $2 million today—plus a percentage of the profits for the privilege; this led to a secondary grilling of Frost himself, by Mike Wallace of *60 Minutes*). However, despite its deference, the interview did elicit a sort of grudging acknowledgment of wrongdoing from Tricky Dick, plus the unforgettable and highly modern claim that "when the president does it, that means that it's not illegal."

Over time, however, politicians learn the business, too, and television interviews become just another part of the "spin" process. (They also become shorter, and more routine, and the test of success becomes the avoidance of any "gaffes.") Poetic justice occasionally kicks in. Edward Kennedy obviously could not believe his luck when he drew Barbara Walters for his first televised "grilling" after Chappaquiddick—she started by asking him how he'd managed to cope—but he had no idea how bad he was going to look when Roger Mudd asked him in 1979 the equally soft question about why he wanted to be president.

As someone who has been interviewed quite a lot on-screen, I have started to notice a few unspoken rules of the game. Most interviewers know that you positively want to be on their shows, either to promote a book or to explain yourself, or just to avoid having to shout back at the TV. So Charlie Rose, for example, knows you won't dry up when he opens by saying, very firmly, "Your book. Why now?" (or many more words to that effect). Larry King is, like Sam Donaldson, a master of asking a soft question in an apparently interrogative way. ("So—you got the big advance. Movie rights up the wazoo. Married to a babe everybody loves. Top of your game. What's with that?") You soon start to notice when the station breaks are coming—a perfect way of dissolving any tension that may be building up—though Rose isn't subject to this and can, and sometimes does, decide to surprise you by running long. The most unsettling technique is the simplest: Tim Russert's matter-of-fact, research-backed question, asked in the mildest tone; or Brian Lamb's complete composure, which I have only once seen disturbed, when I was on with fellow guest Richard Brookhiser. ("You had cancer?" "Yes." "Where?" "In the testicles." . . . "Nebraska—you're on the line.") And of course there's the guilty companionship of the green room, where rivals forgather to remove makeup and more or less behave as if they all know they'll be back sometime next week. This is why a real TV event, like Clinton's tantrum with Chris Wallace, is so extremely rare. And in such cases, it's almost always the interviewee who is making the difference, by departing from the script. The most searching interviewer of all was William F. Buckley in the days of *Firing Line*. If you left the show's set wishing you had done a better job as a guest, it was all your own fault. You had had your chance. But then, this was explicitly billed as ideological combat.

An additional reason for the decline of the interview is the increasing ability of leaders and celebrities to condition the way in which they are questioned. "When you were around Oriana, you sensed that something big was going on," I was told by Ben Bradlee, who had been one of the first editors to see the importance of her material. "Now, a lot of people get interviewed who don't deserve to be interviewed. And editors don't assign enough interviews of the sort that can stand by themselves." Even when Gary Condit was apparently at his most vulnerable, in the late summer of 2001, he was able to pick and choose among ravenous networks (and to make, wisely in my opinion, the selection of Connie Chung as his fearless interrogator). And then people who become too good at the job get turned down for it and are refused by the subject's nervous PR people: this happened in Washington to our very own Marjorie Williams, who was just too incisive for her own good. (It has probably happened to Ali G as well, for some of the same reasons.) There came a time when leaders would no longer submit to the risks of a sit-down with Fallaci. She diverted her energies, with some success, into the channel of fiction. And, more and more, she made it her business to point out what she had been picking up in the course of her voyages—that Islamism was on the march. There's something almost premonitory about her novel *Inshallah*, which was inspired by the first Muslim suicide bombers in Beirut, in 1983. And as she drew nearer to death she decided that she wanted to be interviewed herself, and to be the Cassandra who warned of the wrath to come.

For all that, she hated doing any listening and was extremely bad at submitting to questions. I went to meet her last April in New York, where she kept a little brownstone, and was more or less told to my face that I might well be the last man on earth she would talk to. By then she had twelve different tumors and had been asked, rather reassuringly, by one of her doctors if she had any idea why she was still alive. To this she had an answer. She carried on living in order to utter rebukes to Islamists, and to make these rebukes as abusive and frontal as possible. Gone was the rather rawboned-looking young woman who had once had her share of romantic involvement with "third world" and leftist guerrilla fighters. Instead, a tiny, emaciated, black-clad Italian lady (who really did exclaim "Mamma mia!" at intervals) ranged exhaustingly around her tiny kitchen, cooking me the fattiest sausage I have ever eaten and declaiming that the Muslim immigrants to Europe were the advance guard of a new Islamic conquest. The "sons of Allah breed like rats"—this was the least of what she said in a famous polemic entitled *The Rage and the Pride*, written in a blaze of fury after September 11, 2001, and propelled onto the Italian bestseller list. It got her part of what she wanted after the long and depressing retirement caused by her illness. She became notorious all over again, was the subject of lawsuits from outraged groups who wanted to silence her, and managed to dominate the front pages. When someone becomes obsessed with the hygiene and reproduction of another group, it can be a bad sign: Oriana's conversation (actually there was no conversation, since she scarcely drew breath) was thick with obscenities. I shall put them in Italian—*brutto stronzo, vaffanculo*—and omit some others. As to those who disagreed with her, or who did not see the danger as she did, well, they were no more than *cretini* and *disgraciatti*. It was like standing in a wind tunnel of cloacal abuse. Another bad sign was that she had started to refer to herself as "Fallaci."

All her life she had denounced clericalism and fundamentalism in every form, yet now her loathing and disgust for Islam had driven her into the embrace of the church. She had, she told me, been given one of the first private audiences with the new pope, whom she referred to as "Ratzinger." "He is adorable! He agrees with me—but completely!" But beyond assuring me that his holiness was in her corner, she would tell me nothing of their conversation. Four months later, almost at the exact moment when Oriana was dying, the pope did deliver himself of the celebrated speech in which he flailed on about the medieval objections to Islam and managed to set off a furor that moved us a little closer to a real clash of civilizations. This time, though, we did not have the Fallaci version of his views, or the pleasure of seeing him have to explain or defend himself to her. She managed a final "big get," and then kept it all to herself.

(*Vanity Fair*, December 2006)

Imperial Follies

─────◦◦◦◦─────

FIFTY WINTERS AGO, Russian tanks were demolishing buildings in Budapest, and British warplanes were bombing Cairo International Airport. The coincidence of these two crimes and disasters made a fool out of the nascent United Nations, gave birth to the New Left, put an end to European colonialism, curtain-raised the fall of Communism in 1989, and confirmed the United States as the postwar superpower. In retrospect, the twin episodes of hubris seem almost irrational. Yet hubris has its reasons, too, and they are worth examining.

"If a particular cause, like the accidental result of a battle, has ruined a state," wrote Montesquieu in considering the role of chance and contingency in the Roman case, "there was a general cause that made the downfall of this state ensue from a single battle." Though this insight may verge on the tautologous, it is nonetheless superior to the view—pungently expressed by one of the pupils in Alan Bennett's triumphant success *The History Boys*—that history itself is no more than "one fucking thing after another." The powder train had been laid across Europe before the random event at Sarajevo, and might

Review of *Failed Illusions: Moscow, Washington, Budapest, and the 1956 Hungarian Revolt* by Charles Gati; *Twelve Days: The Story of the 1956 Hungarian Revolution* by Victor Sebestyen; and *Ends of British Imperialism: The Scramble for Empire, Suez, and Decolonization* by Wm. Roger Louis

almost as easily have been ignited by the confrontation at Agadir in Morocco a few years earlier. If the Confederacy had not been so hubristic as to fire on Fort Sumter, it certainly was hubristic enough to be doomed to make a comparably fatal mistake.

Perhaps this view necessarily applies better to endings than to beginnings: one does not have the same sense of certainty concerning, for example, the open question of which European people would or could have been the first to subjugate and settle the Americas. Hegel's famous remark about the owl of Minerva—which takes wing only at dusk, and which thus enables one to mark only the closure of a period—is for this reason much over-employed. But the crepuscular theory of history is no less serviceable for being something of a cliché. When General de Gaulle was asked why he was so reluctant to recognize Communist rule in Eastern Europe as permanent, he responded, *"Parce que l'avenir dure longtemps."*

Once it is pitilessly conceded that the future has a big future, certain once-epochal events immediately become more manageable and intelligible. In the fall of 1956, one undoubtedly saw the closing moments of two very imposing systems. One of them, the Soviet empire in Eastern Europe, was ironically almost Rasputin-like in surviving the evidently mortal wound and staggering on for several more decades. The other, the British Empire in the eastern Mediterranean and Near East, had already outlived a number of apparently terminal moments but after Suez, expired almost at once. The "verdict" of history was still the same in both cases and was apparent to some clear-sighted people at the time.

It is not often pointed out that in 1956, both the Russian and British empires had recently undergone the psychic experience of another sort of *fin de régime*, with the resignation of Winston Churchill and the death of Joseph Stalin. Their successors, Sir Anthony Eden and Nikita Khrushchev, had more to prove—and more to fear from invidious comparison—than either might have liked to admit. As these books demonstrate, both leaders felt compelled to act in ways, and in circumstances, in which they were as much the prisoners of events as the masters of them. And sometimes they were acutely aware of the fact. Most people tend to think of Soviet actions in Eastern Europe, for example, as the outcome of petrified bureaucratic thinking that was inclined to reach for repression as the first resort. And so it was in practice. But Victor Sebestyen's illuminating book shows a surprising degree of self-awareness in the Kremlin, which understood—subjectively, so to speak—that its Hungarian puppets were unloved and incompetent, and might draw the Red Army into a moral and political trap:

Under [Mátyás] Rákosi's stewardship Hungary's economy was a disaster, unease was growing, the jails were full to overflowing, the courts were handing out sentences of a severity that could not be justified and Rákosi's personality cult was appearing more and more ridiculous.

When the local Stalinists were summoned in 1953 from Budapest to a crisis meeting in Moscow, it was in order to be told that they were a disgrace to Communism. No less an authority than Lavrenty Beria attacked the excesses of the Hungarian secret police (which must have stung a bit), while Georgy Malenkov, according to Soviet archives, announced sternly:

We, all of us here on our side, are deeply appalled at your high-handed and domineering style. It has led to . . . countless mistakes and crimes and driven Hungary to the brink of catastrophe.

In May 1955, the Soviet Union agreed to evacuate its troops from neighboring Austria, on the grounds that they were no longer needed nor (to put it mildly) wanted in that country. At almost exactly this time, the British Conservatives, recognizing that the end of dominion in India logically reduced their dependence on Suez, had also made the essential concession by evacuating the Canal Zone and admitting that their period of direct rule in Egypt was at an end. Yet in October 1956, the Red Army was a hated invader on the streets of Budapest, and not long afterward, British soldiers were wading back ashore at Port Said. How came such cruel follies to be committed?

The short answer is that neither imperium could face the idea of being replaced by an inimical local government. Hungary had "joined" the Warsaw Pact on the day before the Red Army agreed to pull out of Austria, and Britain hoped to retain indirect control of the Suez Canal by means of a system of alliances with local Arab elites. The patriotism of the Budapest reform-Communists, and the nationalism of the Nasserists, threatened to remove both countries completely from the larger orbits that had held them in place. Superpower self-pity also played a role: Russia and Britain had taken large casualties in living memory in order to rescue Hungary and Egypt from Nazism. And at the back of the minds of both Khrushchev and Eden—the hardened inner-party survivor and the suave patrician diplomatist, both of them political veterans of that same war—there palpably lurked the queasy feeling that their mighty predecessors would never have let things get so far out of hand.

Had they been fully rational, both leaders would have felt constrained by the possible reaction of the Eisenhower administration. Wm. Roger Louis, in his incomparable set of essays on Suez, quotes directly from the letters and messages that the president sent to Churchill and then to Eden, making it unmistakably plain that any unilateral British action would immediately forfeit all American support. Meanwhile, CIA-sponsored radio stations were beaming incendiary broadcasts into Hungary, promising aid in the event of an armed resistance to Soviet rule. Yet both the Russian and British governments went ahead as if these and other considerations were irrelevant. In view of the so-called special relationship between the United States and Britain, it is remarkable in retrospect that it was the British who were more severely punished by Washington: Dwight Eisenhower coldly withdrew American support for the pound, while the American promises to Hungary proved to be chiefly rhetorical. The discrepancy is explained by Eisenhower's strong feeling that Eden had lied to him about his intentions. "Anthony," he demanded in an acrid transatlantic telephone call, "have you gone out of your mind?"

The answer to this, much disputed by modern historians, was probably yes: Eden had undergone a botched operation which had nicked his bile duct and was suffering from what might politely have been called "stress." Such are the truly unpredictable factors for which Montesquieu was attempting to allow. But the French and Israeli governments, which colluded with Britain in the attack, were not led by men in personal crisis, and they were also told by Washington to get out of Egypt at once or face the consequences. Secretary of State John Foster Dulles in particular had made the decision that no matter how much America's junior allies stressed the Russian threat to the Middle East, America was more endangered by the association with "colonialism."

The biggest losers in all this were the people of Hungary. In spite of all the brave talk about the "rollback" of Stalin's gains in Eastern Europe, the Eisenhower administration seems to have quite cynically decided to exploit the Russian intervention for propaganda purposes, while quite consciously doing nothing that could hamper the Soviet design. Victor Sebestyen and Charles Gati both cite Vice President Richard Nixon actually putting the policy into words at a National Security Council meeting: "It wouldn't be an unmixed evil, from the point of view of the US interest, if the Soviet armed fist were to come down hard again on the Soviet bloc." Malign neglect might have been excusable as realpolitik—the two superpowers had only recently entered the H-bomb era—but the parallel CIA program of hypocritically encouraging rebellion via Radio Free Europe was unconscionable and has never been forgiven. One especially deplorable element in CIA propaganda was the repeated lie that Hungarian prime minister Imre Nagy had requested the return of the Red Army. That falsification greatly increased the difficulties faced by this courageous if hesitant man, and ultimately made it easier for the hard-liners to have him hanged.

The British Cabinet, ostensibly America's chief Cold War ally, never even discussed Hungary. It was this self-centered indifference, perhaps more than anything else, that animated the great campaign against the Suez adventure launched by Aneurin Bevan, the Labour Party's spokesman on foreign affairs. Not only had Eden acted outside international law, said this most eloquent of the advocates for democratic socialism, and lied about his collusion with France and Israel; he had increased the isolation and misery of the Hungarians at just the time when they most needed their friends. This was in some ways the finest hour of the left in the Cold War, and it meant that the tens of thousands of people who deserted the Communist parties that October felt they had somewhere to go. Meanwhile, the abject failure of the United Nations even to comment on events in Budapest until it was too late cannot be blamed solely on Henry Cabot Lodge's decision, taken in concert with Eisenhower and Dulles, to downplay the issue. "There is only one motto worse than 'my country right or wrong,'" as Bevan once phrased it, "and that is 'the United Nations right or wrong.'" This is not the only lesson that the intervening half century has taught us.

(*The Atlantic*, December 2006)

Clive James: The Omnivore

---∞∞∞---

I OPENED THIS BOOK, which despite its subtitle is a series of mini-profiles promising a rich and varied salad of brief lives and long reputations, only to nearly slam it shut again when I read Clive James thanking an editor for rescuing him from a confusion between Louis Malle and Miloš Forman—"a conspicuous instance of the embarrassing phenomenon known to clinical psychologists as the Malle-Forman malformation." How could anyone, embarking on such a project, be so arch and so ingratiating?

Yet perhaps the joke, such as it is, was on me. Clive James knows very well that there is huge confusion and insecurity as to which Mann was which, and as to the differences between, say, the Frankfurt School and the Vienna Circle, and part of his objective is to show—disarmingly, in the result—how long he himself took to acquire any confidence in these matters. A certain amount of evolution is required to produce the omnivore. I once heard Susan Sontag, in conversation with Umberto Eco, define the polymath as one "who is interested in everything, and in nothing else." A trifle annoying and complacent as

---

Review of *Cultural Amnesia: Necessary Memories From History and the Arts* by Clive James

that was, it nonetheless raised the question of how a polymath—or omnivore—should learn to discriminate.

Although in choice of subjects James oscillates as far in one direction as Coco Chanel and as far in the other as Czesław Miłosz, he doesn't waste very much time in giving us his principle of selection. It is of the sort that might have been employed by Isaiah Berlin, or the editors of the old *Partisan Review*. To qualify for his admiration, you must have witnessed for liberal principles in a time of trial. To earn his disapprobation, you need to have said something so wickedly stupid that (to paraphrase Orwell) only an intellectual would be daft enough to fall for it. Most of the candidates are therefore drawn from the gaunt gallery of the twentieth century, with a strong emphasis on its hellish midpoint: the locust years in which the "European tidal waves," as James phrases it in writing about Manès Sperber, "collided." Even those few who evade this verdict by the grace of early birth, like Hegel and Proust, are renewed in its retrospective light. If a single motto could distill the whole, it might be the one furnished by the Italian prosecutor Virginio Rognoni, who took on the Red Brigades in the 1980s without resorting overmuch to police-state tactics and said: "In whichever way a democratic system might be sick, terrorism does not heal it; it kills it. Democracy is healed with democracy."

Such a platitude excites few intellectuals. In fact it bores and disgusts so many of them that they prefer to deal in high-sounding justifications for violence. Thus another way of summarizing James's ambition might be to say that he tries to glamorize the uninspiring—tries to show how tough and shapely were the commonsense formulations of Raymond Aron, for example, when set against the seductive, panoptic bloviations of Jean-Paul Sartre. This might appear to be too easy a task—how much nerve does it really take to defend the vital center?—but James succeeds in it by trying to comb out all centrist clichés, and by caring almost as much about language as it is possible to do.

Alasdair MacIntyre once wrote an essay called "How to Write about Lenin—and How Not To," in which he said that the one unpardonable historical sin was that of being patronizing. If you could not or would not care to imagine what conditions were like in 1905 or 1917, then it might be best if you kept your virginal judgments to yourself.

On the whole, James passes this test. He can see why, as a German nationalist, Ernst Jünger might have been soft on Hitler, which means that he can see where Jünger went wrong. He grants that Fidel Castro possessed charisma and then wasted it. Instead of simply saying that Leszek Kołakowski got most things right about Poland and about Communism, he says the following about his *Main Currents of Marxism*:

> [The hook extends] from Marx's own lifetime to those crucial years after Stalin's death when the dream, somehow deprived of energy by the subtraction of its nightmare element, was already showing signs of coming to an end, in Europe at least.

This sentence does a lot of work, especially in its second clause, while that coda about Europe (somewhat inelegantly tacked on, perhaps) shows that James revisited the aperçu and thought about it in the light of Chile and South Africa.

He has a gift for noticing and highlighting the telling phrase. Albert Camus's observation, in *The Rebel*, that "tyrants conduct monologues above a million solitudes" allows James a useful meditation on the role of sheer tedium in the apparatus of totalitarianism. Indeed, several of the miniature portraits here are occasions for tangential reflections. Heinrich Heine provides an excuse for discussing the terrifying rise of celebrity culture. William Hazlitt spurs an excellent piece on the importance (and rarity) of generosity among literary rivals—where a paragraph on Auden and Yeats wouldn't have come amiss. Reflections on Georg Christoph Lichtenberg detour into some notes on the disappointments of modern pornography. A treatment of Evelyn Waugh becomes a learned disquisition on the use of the dangling modifier by, among others, Anthony Powell.

There are also occasional repetitions: James (whose Australian father was a casualty of the Pacific War) thrice attacks Gore Vidal for his belief that Franklin Roosevelt deliberately provoked Pearl Harbor, but in the process makes a useful point by describing Japan's modern right wing as "recidivist"—a far better term than the more common "revisionist." There are some oddities: Beatrix Potter is upbraided for concealing the awful truth about bacon in *The Tale of Pigling Bland*, whereas any schoolboy knows that she could be positively ghoulish about human and other carnivorousness—see especially *The Tale of Mr. Tod*, but also *Peter Rabbit*. Of H. L. Mencken it is said, very acutely, that "a guardian angel riding in his forehead made sure that the stuff from his brain's bilges didn't get through from his secret diaries to the public page." (The word "usually" might have been forgivable here.)

In attempting to do this anthology justice, I am running the risk of making it sound more eclectic than it really is. If James could have been born in another time and place, he would have chosen Mitteleuropa in the first third of the twentieth century—that drowned world and lost bohemia of Jewish savants and painters and café-philosophers. It is men like Peter Altenberg and Karl Kraus whom he envies, while of course never ceasing to wonder (as we all must) how he himself would have shaped up when the Nazis came. Another of his gold standards is the Russian and French literary opposition, leavened with a good sprinkling of those—like Robert Brasillach—whose talents led them to identify with the overdogs.

A unifying principle of the collection is its feminism. James believes that this is a good cause in its own right, and also a useful negation of the ideological mind-set, since "feminism is a claim for impartial justice, and all ideologies deny that such a term has meaning." He celebrates and mourns Anna Akhmatova and Nadezhda Mandelstam— I wish he had included Rosa Luxemburg—and highlights less well known heroines such as Heda Kovály, Ricarda Huch, and Sophie Scholl, flawless ornament of the White Rose resistance circle in Hitler's Germany. The book is dedicated to Scholl's memory, and to the living examples of Ayaan Hirsi Ali, Aung San Suu Kyi, and Ingrid Betancourt. Men who maltreated or exploited women, or who took them for granted, are invariably awarded a chivalrous drubbing—Rainer Maria Rilke being given a deservedly hard time in this respect. And James clearly wants us to understand that his historical examples are meant to be contemporary and relevant, in that today's Islamist totalitarianism has given us all the warning—precisely by its contempt for women—that we could possibly need.

One of James's charms as a critic is that he genuinely seems to enjoy praising people. (An early collection of his poems was actually titled *Fan-Mail.*) But in order to appear ungrudging, he is sometimes hyperbolic, and therefore unconvincing: Is it really apt to write of Camus that "the Gods poured success on him but it could only darken his trench coat: it never soaked him to the skin"? Or of Flaubert that "he searched the far past, and lo! He found a new dawn"?

Yet much may be forgiven a man who can begin a paragraph by saying, "It will be argued that Heinrich Heine was not Greta Garbo," or who can admit that for years he has been authoritatively mispronouncing the name "Degas" and the word "empyrean." If you open *Cultural Amnesia* in the hope of getting a bluffer's guide to the intellectuals, you will be disappointed; but if you read it as an account of how an educator has himself been self-educated, you will be rewarded well enough.

(*The Atlantic*, April 2007)

Gertrude Bell:
The Woman Who Made Iraq

———— ✇ ————

O N THE COVER of this book is an arresting photograph taken
in front of the Sphinx in March 1921, on the last day of the
Cairo conference on the Middle East. It shows Gertrude Bell astride a
camel, flanked by Winston Churchill and T. E. Lawrence. She wears a
look of some assurance and satisfaction, perhaps because—apart from
having spent far more time on camelback than either man—she has
just assisted at the birth of a new country, which is to be called Iraq.

The picture is especially apt because Bell spent a good part of her
life sandwiched between Churchill and Lawrence. If Churchill had
not committed the Allies to the hideous expedition to Gallipoli, she
would probably have married a young man—imperishably named Dick
Doughty-Wylie—who lost his life on that arid and thorny peninsula.
And if the Turks had not triumphed at Gallipoli, the British would
not have had to resort to raising an Arab revolt against them and
staffing it with idealistic Arabists of uncertain temperament. Finally, if
Churchill as a postwar colonial secretary had not been forced to make
economies and to find Arab leaders to whom Britain could surrender
responsibility, there would have been no Iraq.

Review of *Gertrude Bell: Queen of the Desert, Shaper of Nations* by Georgina Howell

As Georgina Howell puts it in this excitingly informative book, those idealistic Arabists of Britain's hastily formed "Arab Bureau" were objectively committed to living a lie. They knew that the promises given to the Arab tribes—self-determination at war's end if you join us against the Turks—were made in order to be broken. The dishonesty was famously too much for Lawrence, who became morose and inward and changed his name to Shaw. But it was not too much for Gertrude Bell, who was determined that some part of the promise be kept, and who helped change Mesopotamia's name to Iraq.

Once more we are confronted with the old question: What is it that turns certain specimens of the most insular people into natural internationalists? Bell was born into a family of ironmasters in the north of England, liberal and free-trade in their politics, and though the family firm had its vicissitudes, she never had to be concerned about money. Her life pre-1914 (the war is the only watershed that matters in considering her generation) was spent partly in doing things young girls don't normally do, such as Alpine mountaineering and desert archaeology, and partly in adopting causes one might not expect, such as that of the Anti-Suffrage League. As it happened, the First World War involved so many women on the "home front" that it made the post-1918 extension of the franchise almost automatic. The war also forced Bell to realize that she would probably never lose her virginity, which she simultaneously wanted, and dreaded, to be rid of. Her beau ideal lay in a shallow grave on the Dardanelles: she had missed her opportunity and wouldn't settle for a lesser lover. It's usually men who volunteer to go off on a desert mission at this point, but by late 1915 Gertrude was in Cairo as the first woman officer (known as "Major Miss Bell") ever to be employed by British military intelligence.

She was given this distinction because her extraordinary prewar travels and researches in Arabia Deserta had suddenly acquired strategic importance. In the film version of *The English Patient*, some British soldiers are scrutinizing a map when one asks, "But can we get through those mountains?" Another replies, "The Bell maps show a way," to which the response comes, "Let's hope he was right." This is a pardonable mistake, perhaps, because even now it is extraordinary to read of the solitary woman who explored and charted a great swath of Arabia, from remotest Syria to the waters of the Persian Gulf, just when Wilhelmine Germany was planning a Berlin-to-Baghdad railway. John Buchan and Erskine Childers both wrote important fiction about the impending clash of civilizations, but if anyone's work should have been titled *The Riddle of the Sands*, it is Gertrude Bell's.

Reading about Bell, one is struck not just by her ability to master the Arabic language and to revere and appreciate the history and culture of the Arabs, but by her political acuity. Where others saw only squabbles between nomads, she was able to discern the emergence of two great rival forces—the Wahhabis of Ibn Saud and the Hashemites of Faisal—and she stored away the knowledge for future reference. Georgina Howell occasionally overdoes the speculative and the fanciful, writing "she must have" when she lacks precise information, but she also considers questions other narratives tend to skip, such as, What does an Englishwoman in the desert, surrounded by inquisitive and hostile Turks, do when it is imperative that she relieve herself? (The answer: Take care to have a stout Arab servant who will interpose his body, then reward and nurture him for the rest of his life.) The title of the book may seem exorbitant in its flattery—and depressing in its echo of poor, mad Lady Hester Stanhope—but Bell's bearing was such that many of the desert dwellers truly believed a queen had come to visit them.

Bell's own more pragmatic search was for a credible king. Mesopotamia—-or the former Ottoman vilayets of Basra, Baghdad, and Mosul—had rid itself of the Turks by 1918, more as a consequence of the arrival of British and Indian troops than as a result of local efforts. The new colonial authorities borrowed a term—*"Al Iraq,"* or "the Iraq," from the verb meaning "to be deeply rooted"—that Arabs had formerly used to describe the southern portion of the territory. Much else about their rule was provisional and improvised. Bell saw the truth of a Baghdad newspaper's observation that London had promised an Arab government with British advisers, but had imposed a British government with Arab advisers. Her immediate superior, A. T. Wilson, believed in strict British imperial control. The colonial leadership in India, which tended to think of Delhi as the capital through which relations with the Gulf states were maintained, was also staunchly opposed to any sentimental talk of Arab independence. As if to further fragment the jigsaw of difficulties, the British government issued the Balfour Declaration into this milieu, awarding a national home in Palestine to the Zionist movement, and the new Bolshevik regime in Russia had the brilliant idea of publishing the terms of the Sykes-Picot Agreement, which had fallen into its hands. The disclosure of this covert wartime pact between czarist Russia and the British and French empires to carve up the region had the effect of hugely increasing Arab suspicion of British intentions. It also had the effect of spurring President Wilson to issue his Fourteen Points, which proposed a grant of self-determination to all colonial subjects. But at the subsequent Paris peace talks, the Arabs and the Kurds, along with the Armenians, were to be the orphans of this process. Even the imperialist A. T. Wilson found himself sympathizing with Bell at that dismal conclave:

> The very existence of a Shi'ah majority in Iraq was blandly denied as a figment of my imagination by one "expert" with an international reputation, and Miss Bell and I found it impossible to convince either the Military or the Foreign Office Delegations that Kurds in the Mosul vilayet were numerous and likely to be troublesome, [or] that Ibn Saud was a power seriously to be reckoned with.

These are not the only echoes that come resounding down the years. Official British policy hoped to please all parties and square all circles, with just a hint of traditional divide-and-rule. Bell believed that a state could be created on the foundation of mutual respect, and she was rather partial to the Kurds and the Shiites. She was also very critical of the Zionist idea, which she thought could only increase Arab antipathy and endanger the large Jewish community in Baghdad. As to the prejudices of Sir Mark Sykes, coauthor of the secret deal with France and Russia, she had acquired an early warning. They had met in Haifa as early as 1905, where he had appalled her with his talk of Arabs as "animals" who were "cowardly," "diseased," and "idle." She had also been several steps ahead of him on an expedition to the Druze fastnesses of Lebanon and Syria, and he always attributed her head start to foul play. As he complained fairly comprehensively in a letter to his wife: "Confound the silly chattering windbag of conceited, gushing, flat-chested, man-woman, globetrotting, rump-wagging, blethering ass!" There seems to have been a hint of fascination in the midst of this disgust. If so, it would have fit with the general predilections of the British, who were fixated on androgyny in the most alarming way. (Their slang word for Arabs was "Frocks," a means of feminizing the colonial subject that was not quite congruent with the manly skills they were otherwise demanding from the desert warriors.)

Determined to disprove and outlast the Sykeses of the world, Bell made Baghdad her permanent home, helped to organize elections and write a constitution, drew some rather wobbly borders with Saudi Arabia and Kuwait, founded the Iraqi national museum, and wrote a study, "A Review of the Civil Administration of Mesopotamia," that compares well with the best of the Victorian "blue books." She also nurtured and cajoled King Faisal, who founded a constitutional monarchy that lasted from 1921 until 1958—impressive by regional standards. (Faisal was of course a Sunni Arab; the Kurds and the Shiites had both proved too turbulent to be trusted with stewardship.) So, was all her effort at nation building a romantic waste? T. E. Lawrence, who was perhaps envious, partly thought so. After learning of her death, he wrote:

That Irak [sic] state is a fine monument; even if it only lasts a few more years, as I often fear and sometimes hope. It seems such a very doubtful benefit—government—to give a people who have long done without.

That might stand as a cynical judgment for the ages, but one can still think of Gertrude Bell in the same company as Wilfred Blunt, R. B. Cunninghame Graham, Edward Thompson, and indeed Lawrence himself—English people who thought other peoples, too, deserved their place in the sun.

(The Atlantic, June 2007)

Physician, Heal Thyself

———— ✦✦✦ ————

MAKE ANY PRESUMPTION of innocence that you like, and it still looks as if the latest cell of religious would-be murderers in Britain is made up of members of the medical profession. When I was growing up, the expression "Doctors' Plot" was a chilling one, expressing the paranoia of Stalin about his Jewish physicians and their evil conspiracy; a paranoia that was on the verge of unleashing an official pogrom in Moscow before the old brute succumbed to death by natural causes just in time. Now it seems that there really was a doctors' plot in London and Glasgow and that its members were so hungry for death that they rushed from one aborted crime scene to another in their eagerness to take the lives of strangers.

The normal human reaction to this is one of profound shock, because of the Hippocratic principles that are supposed to draw certain people toward the noble practice and high calling of medicine. Not only does one want to be able to count on this in the case of any physician consulted by oneself, but one also has the slight expectation that a doctor involved in politics will tend to be actuated by humanitarian motives. Certainly, this used to be true on the left: one of the most powerful magnets drawing members of the middle class toward socialism used to be the experience of doctors in the slums, forced to confront the raw injustice and maldistribution that dominated the life-and-death question of health care. The hero of Graham Greene's *Stamboul Train* is such a one, impelled into action by the realization that his patients cannot afford the care they desperately need. Mao Zedong wrote a paean to the Canadian physician Norman Bethune, inventor of the battlefield blood transfusion, who gave up a promising career to help the revolutionary forces in the Spanish and Chinese civil wars. Salvador Allende in Chile, Vassos Lyssarides in Cyprus—these are only among the better-known names of party leaders who won the admiration of the poor by trying to practice what they preached in Hippocratic terms.

Medicine is hierarchic as a profession but democratic in essence: in principle, a doctor may not refuse to treat anyone and must always use his or her best efforts to save life and ward off disease. When we read of doctors who cheat their patients, or who poison them in order to get their property or just for the fun of it, we feel outraged more, perhaps, than we would feel if a lawyer had tried to fleece a client. It seems a deeper betrayal. A doctor as a perpetrator of random murder is a nightmarish figure who has violated a trust.

Yet the dark side of the medical profession is also well-known to folklore. Messrs. Burke and Hare, not always willing to wait for corpses to sell to an anatomy professor, killed to provide the cadavers. A columnist in the *Financial Times* recently mentioned the names of Josef Mengele and Che Guevara, two physicians who were capable of extreme cruelty. I didn't think the comparison was fair: Mengele was a sadist in his capacity as a doctor; while Guevara, willing enough to slay what he thought of as the class enemy, did not prostitute his gifts as a doctor in order to do so. Nonetheless, the nasty fact must be faced: torture regimes have always been able to find doctors to advise on torture and even to participate in it, and the experience of Nazism taught us that the profession contains enough perverts who desire the license to conduct ghastly experiments on human subjects and (as with H. G. Wells's Dr. Moreau) satisfy an obscene curiosity as to how far they can go. Mengele is not the only evidence that such depraved characters also relish the idea of "practicing" on women and even children.

Still, the aberrant and the sadistic don't seem to explain the resort to murder in the present case. Nothing was to be gained by it from an experimental point of view, and the opportunities for a gloating vivisection are slim when your bag of instruments is a car full of propane and nails. So, we must look elsewhere for the explanation. Why have doctors apparently become killers in this instance? That's easy. *Because of religion.*

You may recall the case of Dr. Baruch Goldstein. On February 25, 1994, this Israeli army physician stalked into the so-called Cave of the Patriarchs in Hebron, unslung his automatic weapon, and fired into the crowd of Muslim worshippers, killing twenty-nine people of all ages and both sexes before being killed himself. It took no time at all to establish that Goldstein, no mere loner or psycho, had given ample warning of his character and intentions. Army sources reported that he had consistently refused to treat Arab or Druze or any other "Gentile" patients, citing as his authority the halachic law that excuses a pious Jew from coming to the aid of a non-Jew. (The whole appalling story is told in chapter 6 of *Jewish Fundamentalism in Israel*, by Israel Shahak and Norton Mezvinsky.) In Goldstein's view, Hippocratic precepts were overridden by Orthodox teaching, and there were a number of rabbis ready to support his stand on the matter. There were also a number of rabbis who decided to consecrate his tomb as a shrine to a brave Jewish martyr, and the children of ultra-Orthodox settlers were seen wearing buttons reading, "Dr. Goldstein cured Israel's ills." Now it seems that an Iraqi physician, in the old and famous university town of Cambridge, was so diseased by his own faith that he advocated even the murder of rival Muslims and showed videos of decapitation to housemates who were so profane as to play musical instruments.

Remember that Stalinism itself was self-defined as "a great experiment" on the human being and that fascists loved to say that they were cutting out the tumors of society and extirpating the "bacilli" that caused disorders in (another revealing phrase) "the body politic." Even our metaphors of healing can be turned into horrible negations. What is more probable than that the oldest and latest form of totalitarianism, religious mania, will come to infect doctors as well?

(*Slate*, July 9, 2007)

Edmund Wilson:
Literary Companion

⁓⊶⊷⁓

IN A BEAUTIFULLY turned reminiscence of Alexander Woollcott
published in 1943, and originally intended as a defense of that great
critic against an ungenerous obituarist, Edmund Wilson managed to
spin what he admitted was a slight acquaintance into a charming portrait of a man and of a moment—the moment being the time when
both men's parents were connected with a Fourierist socialist community in Red Bank, New Jersey. Recollections of Woollcott the man
of the theater, intercut with reflections on the arcana of the American
left, combine to make a fine profile and a nice period piece: journalism at its best. What caught and held me, though, was an episode in
the 1930s, when Wilson, fresh from reporting on the labor front for
the *New Republic*, was invited to call on Woollcott at Sutton Place:

> As soon as I entered the room, he cried out, without any other
> greeting: "You've gotten very fat!" It was his way of disarming,
> I thought, any horror I might have felt at his own pudding-like
> rotundity, which had trebled since I had seen him last.

Review of *Literary Essays and Reviews of the 1920s & 30s* and *Literary Essays and
Reviews of the 1930s & 40s* by Edmund Wilson

This, and other aspects of the evening, make clear that Wilson understood why Woollcott's personality didn't appeal to everybody. But the preemptive strike on the question of girth also made me realize that there must have been a time when Edmund Wilson was thin.

This absolutely negated the picture that my mind's eye had been conditioned to summon. Wilson's prose, if not precisely rotund, was astonishingly *solid*. One cannot turn the pages of this heavy and handsome set, produced by the Library of America, without a sense of his mass and weight and gravitas. He was the sort of man who, as people used to say, "got up" a subject. The modern and vulgar way of phrasing this is to say that so-and-so reads a book "so you don't have to." Wilson, though, presumed a certain amount of knowledge in his readers, kept them well-supplied with allusions and cross-references, and undertook to help them fill in blanks in their education. An autodidact himself, he seems to have hoped to be the cause of autodidacticism in others.

An excellent instance of Wilson as a sort of co-reader, tutor, and literary adviser comes in his successive discussions of *Finnegans Wake*. In an essay originally included in *The Wound and the Bow*, titled "The Dream of H. C. Earwicker," he guides his audience through the extraordinary density and intricacy of the slumber life of James Joyce's snoring pub keeper. He furnishes handholds and issues both exhortations and admonitions: readers are told, in effect, that there will be passages of extreme difficulty and complexity (and of plain longueur), but they are simultaneously assured that the effort will be rewarding and worthwhile. Footnotes are provided, to point them to a collection of essays published by *Transition* magazine in Paris, which may help to supply a "key." A learned reference is made to part 3, chapter 3 of Max Eastman's *The Literary Mind*, which, when consulted, discloses Joyce's rather daunting ambition: a desire that his readers would devote their entire lives to the scrutiny of his work. Almost as if stiffening himself to accept this challenge, Wilson writes:

Just as Joyce in *Ulysses* laid the *Odyssey* under requisition to help provide a structure for his Material—material which, once it had begun to gush from the rock of Joyce's sealed personality at the blow of the Aaron's rod of free association, threatened to rise and submerge the artist like the flood which the sorcerer's apprentice let loose by his bedeviled broom; so in the face of an even more formidable danger, he has here brought in the historical theory of the eighteenth-century philosopher, Giambattista Vico, to help him to organize *Finnegans Wake*.

At first one is inclined to think that Wilson has become infected by the gorgeous prolixity of his subject, then impelled to invoke that old *New Yorker* injunction ("Block That Metaphor!"), and only then to suspect that he might be doing it on purpose. And notice the introduction of Vico, whose work served as a kind of template for *To the Finland Station*, Wilson's grand study of teleology and messianism.

In a subsequent essay, "A Guide to Finnegans Wake," published in August 1944, Wilson again enlisted his readers in the grand attempt to master the Joycean. This time a new codex, *A Skeleton Key to Finnegans Wake*, written by Joseph Campbell and Henry Morton Robinson, was the spark to his enthusiasm. After advising us that it is better to come to the subject by way of Virgil, Dante, and Milton, he added that the best course of action is to acquire the original, plus "the Campbell-Robinson key," and

> prepare to have them around for years . . . Joyce worked on it through seventeen years, and it is equivalent to about seventeen books by the ordinary gifted writer.

Having thoroughly challenged his audience in this forbidding yet exciting way (and I recommend heartily that anyone hesitating over Joyce follow Wilson's counsel), he averred that the coauthors of the guide merited "a citation from the Republic of Letters."

Now, when is the last time that you saw *that* expression in print? Or that you came across a reviewer who tried to make your reading life more exacting rather than less? It is not easy to imagine Mr. Wilson (he almost invariably alluded to other authors as "Mr.," "Mrs.," or "Miss") sending in his annual recommendation for the summer "beach bag," let alone responding to the even more rebarbative notion that people should be more likely to buy and enjoy books at Christmas. His famous preprinted postcard, which he sent out to supplicants of all kinds, showed him massively indifferent to the petty seductions of literary celebrity:

> Mr. Edmund Wilson regrets that it is impossible for him to: Read manuscripts, write articles or books to order, write forewords or introductions, make statements for publicity purposes, do any kind of editorial work, judge literary contests, give interviews, take part in writers' conferences, answer questionnaires, contribute to or take part in symposiums or "panels" of any kind, contribute manuscripts for sales, donate copies of his books to libraries, autograph works for strangers, allow his name to be used on letterheads, supply personal information about himself, or supply opinions on literary or other subjects.

But if this gives the impression of a sort of Jamesian loftiness, then the idea is counteracted by Wilson's decision to engage with popular fiction. His contempt for the slovenly and disgraceful habit of "reading" detective stories—especially the dismal pulp produced by Dorothy L. Sayers—was offset by an admiration for Sir Arthur Conan Doyle, and by his readiness to respond to the many readers who wrote in to disagree with him.

Anyone who has ever tried to digest *The Da Vinci Code*, for example, or the Left Behind series, will know that bad writing, aimed at a subliterate audience, is actually much more difficult to read than anything by Borges or Kundera. But a certain populism, perhaps, inhibits critics from saying so. I borrow from Jacobo Timerman's wonderful remark on scanning the Cuban Communist daily *Granma* ("a degradation of the act of reading"), and I make a bet that the Left Behind books repose, unfinished, on the shelf along with the seldom-opened family Bible. And I draw confidence from Wilson's admirable pugnacity in "Who Cares Who Killed Roger Ackroyd?" In discussing one of the tales of Margery Allingham, he stated baldly, "The story and the writing both showed a surface so wooden and dead that I could not keep my mind on the page." He defied his correspondents to disagree with him, and many shamefacedly did admit that they, too, found the stuff bad almost beyond endurance, yet clung to it as a pathetic addiction. Generous as (almost) always—he did take a decided whack at the now-forgotten critic Bernard DeVoto ("I hadn't quite realized before, though I had noted his own rather messy style, to what degree he was insensitive to writing")—Wilson did show that he could tell gold from dross by praising Raymond Chandler, before ending the essay in this fashion:

> Friends, we represent a minority, but Literature is on our side. With so many fine books to be read, so much to be studied and known, there is no need to bore ourselves with this rubbish.

As with the "Republic of Letters," Wilson was unashamed to capitalize what was worth upholding and defending. The citizens of that putative republic, those who trusted and corresponded with him, knew that they had a stern but staunch friend who might rebuke and reward them in the same conversation. And this companion thought that there *was* such a thing as taste, and that it was not entirely relative.

One test of *un homme sérieux* is that it is possible to learn from him even when one radically disagrees with him. Wilson seems to me to underestimate the importance of Kafka in an almost worrying way (worrying because it shows a want of sympathy with those who just *knew* about the coming totalitarianism), yet I confess I had never thought of Kafka as having been so much influenced by Flaubert. When writing about Ronald Firbank, Wilson seems almost elephantine in his mass. Often somewhat out of sympathy with the English school—and again sometimes for self-imposed political reasons—he was very early and acute in getting much of the point of Evelyn Waugh.

He was rightly rather critical of *Brideshead Revisited*, and it makes me whimper when I see how closely he read the novel, and how coldly he isolated unpardonable sentences such as "Still the clouds gathered and did not break." Nonetheless, he predicted a big success for the book and, in discussing it and its successor *The Loved One*, managed to be both coolly secular and sympathetic, pointing out that Waugh was actually rather afraid of the consequences of his own Catholicism. An American critic might have chosen to resent the easy shots that Waugh took at Los Angeles and "Whispering Glades"; Wilson contented himself with indulgently pointing out that Waugh's church practiced a far more fantastic and ornamental denial of death than any Californian mortician.

Naturally, much of Wilson's political material has dated. (He was one of those who combined socialism with snobbery by saying that "the radio and motor industries" prospered only by "selling these articles to many people who didn't need them." One wonders whom he had in mind.) And the argument about, say, Herbert Croly's *The Promise of American Life* has long since cooled. But anyone wishing to revisit the intellectual and literary passions of the period will be well advised to do so in the company of someone who could be a Virgil as well as recommend the reading of him. Edmund Wilson came as close as anybody has to making the labor of criticism into an art.

(*The Atlantic*, September 2007)

On the Limits of
Self-improvement, Part I

Of Vice and Men

Begin professional report and opinion here

Insofar as we are able to be objective, here follows a brief physical review of the subject, Christopher Eric Hitchens, at the time of this writing enjoying his fifty-ninth summer. Obstacles to the continuance of such enjoyment may be listed in no especial order as follows.

The subject has good genes on both sides of his family and has been mercilessly exploiting this inherited advantage for some decades. An initial review of his facial features, as glimpsed in the shaving mirror, reveals relatively few lines or wrinkles and only a respectable minimum of secondary or tertiary chins. However, this may be because the skin is so tightly stretched by the generally porpoise-like condition of the body when considered—which with a shudder it must be—as a whole. Moreover, the fabled blue eyes and long, curled eyelashes (for some years the toast of both sexes on five continents) are now somewhat obscured by the ravages of rosacea and blepharitis, which on certain days lend a flaky aspect to the picture and at other times give the regrettable impression of a visage that is actually crumbling to powder like a dandruffed scalp. It may be for this reason that the subject prefers to undertake the morning shave through a cloud of blue cigarette smoke that wreathes the scene in the fumes of illusion. (N.B.: This would not altogether account for the subject's habit of smoking in the shower.)

The fanglike teeth are what is sometimes called "British": sturdy, if unevenly spaced, and have turned an alarming shade of yellow and brown, attributable perhaps to strong coffee as well as to nicotine, Pinot Noir, and other potations.

Proceeding south and passing over an almost vanished neck that cannot bear the strain of a fastened top button or the constriction of a tie, we come to a thickly furred chest that, together with a layer of flab, allows the subject to face winter conditions with an almost ursine insouciance. The upper part of this chest, however, has slid deplorably down to the mezzanine floor, and it is our opinion that without his extraordinary genital endowment the subject would have a hard time finding the damn thing, let alone glimpsing it from above.

Matters are hardly improved on the lower slopes, which feature a somewhat grotesque combination of plump thighs and skinny shins, the arduous descent culminating in feet which are at once much too short and a good deal too chunky. This combination, of ratlike claws and pachydermatous-size insteps, causes the subject to be very cautious about where, and indeed when, he takes off his shoes. There have been unconfirmed reports of popular protest whenever and wherever he does this. Nor do his hands, at the same time very small and very puffy, give any support to the view that the human species does not have a common ancestor with the less advanced species of ape. The nails on the hands are gnawed, and the nails on the feet are clawlike and beginning to curl in a Howard Hughes fashion (perhaps because the subject displays such a marked reluctance to involve himself in any activity that may involve bending).

Viewed from the front when clothed, the subject resembles a burst horsehair sofa cushion or (in the opinion of one of us) a condom hastily stuffed with an old sock. The side perspective is that of an avocado pear and, on certain mornings, an avocado pear that retains nothing of nutritious value but its tinge of alligator green. (N.B.: The bumps and scales of this famous delicacy are sometimes visible and palpable as well.) Of the rear view, all that need be said is that it conforms to the preceding, though with considerably less excuse as well as with mercifully less fur. Seen from directly above, the subject has a little more protective cover than some males of his age, but this threatens to become a pile of tobacco-colored strands clumsily coated onto an admittedly large skull. At all times, the subject gives off a scent that resembles that of an illegal assembly, either of people or of materials, in the hog wallows of Tennessee or in the more remote and primitive islands of Scotland. He becomes defensive, and sometimes aggressive, when asked about the source of this effluvium. It is considered by me, and by the rest of this committee, and by the subject's few remaining friends and surviving family, a medical mystery that he can still perform what he persists in referring to as his "job."

Initial response of subject

Well, I mean to say, I don't consider myself especially vain, but it was something of a shocker and a facer to read all that at once. I'd noticed a touch of decline here and there, but one puts these things down to Anno Domini and the acquirement of seniority. A bit of a stomach gives a chap a position in society. A glass of refreshment, in my view, never hurt anybody. This walking business is overrated: I mastered the art of doing it when I was quite small, and in any case, what are taxis for? Smoking is a vice, I will admit, but one has to have a hobby. Nonetheless, when my friends at this magazine formed up and said they would pay good money to stop having to look at me in my current shape, I agreed to a course of rehabilitation. There now exists a whole micro-economy dedicated to the proposition that a makeover is feasible, or in other words to disprove Scott Fitzgerald's dictum that there are no second acts in American lives. Objectives:

to drop down from the current 185 pounds, to improve the "tone" of the skin and muscles, to wheeze less, to enhance the hunched and round-shouldered posture, to give some thought to the hair and fur questions (more emphasis perhaps in the right places and less in the wrong ones), to sharpen up the tailoring, to lessen the booze intake, and to make the smile, which currently looks like a handful of mixed nuts, a little less scary to children.

Step one was for me to be dispatched to a spa. We chose one of the very best: the Four Seasons Biltmore resort, in Santa Barbara, California. Air like wine, gorgeous beaches, lush vegetation, and a legendary hotel with the nicest staff imaginable. The friendly people at the fitness clinic took one look at me and decided, first, on the "Executive Distress Treatment." At least, that's what my disordered senses told me they had recommended. However, it turned out to be the Executive De-Stress Treatment, during which I was massaged with hot stones all along my neck and back by a young lady who didn't turn a hair when she got to step two, which was "reflexology" applied to my leprous and scaly upper and lower paws. I can't give you a very comprehensive account of this, because it had the effect of making me fall into a refreshing sleep. I woke briefly from blissful repose to find a new female face taking the second shift, which was a Gentlemen's Facial, involving hot towels enveloping the features, followed by a treatment with "non-perfumed and non-greasy lotions." Off I went again to sleep, and came round to find myself alone, like a pink salmon on a slab, with "Greensleeves" playing softly on the stereo. I'm bound to say I don't usually wake up feeling this good.

I should then, of course, have discovered that I was locked in and that my evening meal of oatmeal, prunes, and mineral water would shortly be served. But no, I was free to go. Now, I don't know about you, but with me a feeling of fitness and well-being always lends extra zest to the cocktail hour. And what's a cocktail without a smoke? And what else gives you a better appetite for dinner? The Bella Vista restaurant at the Biltmore is justly renowned, and I thought that perhaps if I tried the tasting menu Chef Martin Frost had prepared for me, with just a little morsel for each course . . . And a meal without wine is like a day without sunshine, as they say in France. And so the long night wore on agreeably enough.

In the morning, none too early, I descended to the beach to begin my program of yoga stretching. It was not thought advisable that I do this by myself—muscles become like mussels at my stage of life, and if not stretched carefully will either lose their elasticity or else snap with a sudden "pop" that I have already once, and disconcertingly, heard as I made the mistake of running for the phone. (Why did I do that?) I thus had the exhausting experience of watching my yoga instructor, the divine Madeline McCuskey, as she showed me the moves. Even regarding her in this way was a workout of a kind. Not to be outdone by some tempestuous and tawny Californian, I attempted to balance and extend myself in the same way, only to find that I was seized by the sensation that I might die or go mad at any moment.

I was soon back at the spa, this time for a more rigorous detoxifying experience. A different young lady painted me a more delicate shade of green than my usual coloring in the a.m. and then slowly wrapped me in foil and linen. This was less like being a salmon on a slab, more like being a steamed Chilean sea bass in the hands of a capable sous chef. I was told, as the heat built up in the seaweed, that the natural green came from marine algae that were very rich in nutrients and that the coating would "draw toxins" out of my system, as well as revitalize my muscles and generally relieve tension. This time I stayed awake, felt my pores opening all right and even briefly heard them screaming, suppressed the feeling that I was about to be garnished, or served on a bed of arugula with a lemon wedge in my mouth, and realized that it had been quite a long time since I had had a smoke or a drink. This was surely progress in itself! A greatly daring session on the treadmill and with the weights was to follow, and by the time that was over I felt that I had really earned my lunch, into which I tucked with a gusto of browsing and sluicing that still had a vague feeling of conscience lurking behind it. I then punished myself by booking an eighty-minute Fitness Scrub and Massage, this time to be administered by a grown man, where I was pitilessly raked with almond meal and subsequently endured a serious pummeling and probing that identified my sloped and hunched shoulders as the main source of my generally sorry posture.

The trouble with bad habits is that they are mutually reinforcing. And, just as a bank won't lend you money unless you are too rich to need it, exercise is a pastime only for those who are already slender and physically fit. It just isn't so much fun when you have a marked tendency to wheeze and throw up, and a cannonball of a belly sloshing around inside the baggy garments. In my case, most of my bad habits are connected with the only way I know to make a living. In order to keep reading and writing, I need the junky energy that scotch can provide, and the intense short-term concentration that nicotine can help supply. To be crouched over a book or a keyboard, with these conditions of mingled reverie and alertness, is my highest happiness. (Upon having visited the doctor, Jean-Paul Sartre was offered the following alternative: give up cigarettes and carry on into a quiet old age and a normal death, or keep smoking and have his toes cut off. Then his feet. Then his legs. Assessing his prospects, Sartre told Simone de Beauvoir he "wanted to think it over." He actually did retire his gaspers, but only briefly. Later that year, asked to name the most important thing in his life, he replied, "Everything. Living. Smoking.")

Thus I soon evolved a routine at the Biltmore. A facial, followed by a cocktail and a well-chosen lunch, succeeded by a nap, followed by a brief workout, followed by a massage or wrap, some reading and writing, and then a thoughtfully selected dinner. The rooms and public areas didn't permit smoking, but room service was able to reach my ashtray-furnished patio with creditable speed. I suppose one could easily enough add seaweed and algae and mud (and, on one occasion, another tincture of green in the shape of an Avocado-Citrus Body Wrap, which at least gave me a new and better way of looking like an overripe pear) to one's list of regular addictions. It would be like going to confession in between an exhausting program of sins. You will be glad to hear, however, that I high-mindedly declined the Chardonnay-Clay Body Wrap: it savored too much of yet another method of taking in booze, through the pores. Instead, I opted for a punishing session on the Biltmore's immaculate croquet lawn. As the dolphins and seals gamboled off the beach, and as Chef Frost wielded his skillet with never diminishing brilliance, I felt that I could be very content to go on leading this life, but that each detox only sharpened the appetite for further treats, and that, all things considered, I couldn't afford the weight gain. I also had to admit what I have long secretly known, which is that I positively like stress, arrange to inflict it on myself, and sheer awkwardly away from anybody who tries to promise me a more soothed or relaxed existence. Bad habits have brought me this far: why change such a tried-and-true formula?

I also take the view that it's a mistake to try to look younger than one is, and that the face in particular ought to be the register of a properly lived life. I don't want to look as if I have been piloting the Concorde without a windshield, and I can't imagine whom I would be fooling if I did. However, this did leave the kippered lungs and the grisly teeth, and the liver and various other viscera, leading a life of their own in a kind of balloon that annoyingly preceded me into the dining room. Who was to be boss here? Was it worth getting any new clothes until this question of mastery had been decided? If the war with my outer carapace was to be won, and I was to remain a decisive minister of the interior whose orders could expect to be obeyed, it was clear that the struggle would have to be carried to a new and higher level.

(*Vanity Fair*, October 2007)

On the Limits of
Self-improvement, Part II

Vice and Versa

I N MY SQUANDERED youth I was a friend of Ian Hamilton, the biographer of Robert Lowell and J. D. Salinger and a justly renowned figure in London's bohemia. His literary magazine the *New Review* was published from a barstool in a Soho pub called the Pillars of Hercules, and editorial meetings would commence promptly at opening time. One day, there came through the door a failed poet with an equally heroic reputation for dissipation. To Ian's undisguised surprise, he declined the offer of a hand-steadying cocktail. "No," he announced dramatically. "I just don't want to do it anymore. I don't like having blackouts and waking up on rubbish dumps. I don't like having no money and no friends, smelling bad and throwing up randomly. I don't like wetting myself and getting impotent." His voice rising and cracking slightly, he concluded by avowing that he also didn't like being repellently fat, getting the shakes and amnesia, losing his teeth and gums, and suffering from premature baldness. A brief and significant silence followed this display of unmanly emotion. Then

Ian, fixing him with a stern look, responded evenly by saying, "Well, none of us likes it."

For a long time, I was a member of the Hamilton faction. (After all, is one a man or a mouse?) But Ian is gone now, and well before his time, too. His example was in my mind when I embarked on a course of treatment to see if I could become, as it were, born again. T. S. Eliot's Prufrock measured out his life in coffee spoons; I sometimes wish I could say the same, but the truth is that the calibrations have been somewhat more toxic, and that caffeine has been the least of it. They say that you can tell a lot about an animal by examining its teeth. Please look, if you can, at the "before" picture of my dentition.

My keystone addiction is to cigarettes, without which cocktails and caffeine (and food) are meaningless. So the first appointment was with a smoke ender. I took a one-on-one seminar with a senior practitioner of the Allen Carr method: a tough-minded and eloquent Ulsterman named Damian O'Hara. The Allen Carr system is this: you turn up and (in O'Hara's words) "smoke your face off" for about five hours, while a motivational speaker takes you relentlessly through the evils of the habit and the "pluses of quitting." At the conclusion of this, you are invited to light one last cigarette and then hand over your paraphernalia before leaving as a free man. O'Hara was terrifically good and I have known some hard cases who quit by using this method, but there was a problem. Sit me down across a table with an ashtray and a bottle on it, and cue the other person to make an argument, and I am programmed by the practice of a lifetime to take a contrary position. The better he phrased it, the harder I worked to resist his case and to think of counterarguments. Thus: "Cigarettes are the only drug that doesn't give you a high." Well, what's that bliss I get when I have just lit one with the first cocktail of the day? Eh? "Smoking doesn't really ward off boredom and stress; it only appears to do so, and it actually increases stress." Well, appearing to do so isn't bad, as illusions go, and if I find that a smoke and a drink help to make other people even seem less boring, then to that extent I have found an ally for life. Plus which, stress works for me and I wouldn't be without it.

About all the downsides—the shame of being conned by the tobacco companies, the disgrace of being an addict, the suspension of one's reasoning faculties in the face of self-destruction—I already knew. And there was a faint something about some of the terminology ("empowerment," for example) that smacked a little too much of a self-esteem program. Anyway, I left my pack and my lighter in O'Hara's care and for a couple of days didn't smoke and didn't much miss it, either. But then I hit a difficult patch in an essay I was writing, and turned again to the little friend that never deserts me.

A bit nettled by the rapidity of my own capitulation, I tried again a month or two later at a place called New Life, in Manhattan, which practices a sort of laser acupuncture. Simple enough: you lie in a reclining chair while a laser is applied painlessly to various points on your features, and are meanwhile reminded in a soothing voice of all the good reasons to give the damn stuff up. Again, though, there was something Goody Two-shoes about it: at the end I was asked to sign a bright little card that congratulated me on becoming "a champion." Something in me evidently resists, or wants to resist, joining any good-behavior club that will have me as a member. That evening I had dinner at an organic restaurant where everything was made out of vegetation, just to see how that would feel without a cigarette, and drank about three pints of cold sake to make up for it. Didn't light up until well past midnight.

Incidentally, and to give you a brief report on food intake, I have found it relatively easy to ingest smaller portions of leaner and better nosh, such as mercury-sodden swordfish. But here's what causes me to laugh in a hollow manner: almost every diet guide that I have been shown contains a stipulation about the "size matters" element of the platter. Your chunk of fish or lamb or lean steak should not be larger than a cigarette pack or a deck of cards. That's a terrific way to wean a guy who will go to Las Vegas to make an idiot of himself at the blackjack tables where they bring you free booze as long as you lose, all the while making detours to the nearby Indian reservation where they sell smokes by the ton.

The other problem with giving up a habit is that you don't exactly get to see the results, or not anything like fast enough. (I quit smoking once for several months and felt essentially no different, except for the absence of that parrot-cage feeling in my mouth.) Whereas with modern American dentistry it is simply amazing to see what transformation can be wrought in a single day. I presented myself at the office of Drs. Gregg Lituchy and Marc Lowenberg one afternoon, and as the sun faded over the splendors of Central Park South, my fangs took on the luster that the sky was slowly relinquishing.

I am a proud child of the National Health Service in England and remember feeling rather hurt when, while reading Gore Vidal's novel *The Judgment of Paris* many years ago, I came upon a character who was described as having "British teeth." As Dr. Lituchy readied me with a series of numbing injections, his partner came by to have a look. He wanted to see with his own eyes, he said, that my teeth really were as "British" as they looked in the "before" photograph. I duly beamed for him, and he reeled back briefly. Having become a citizen last April, I felt as if this procedure was part of my new passport to Americanization. How reassuring it was to see the picture of a gleaming Christy Turlington in the office's glossy press clippings, and to reflect that soon I could dazzle just like her. But the clever thing about this treatment (known as JK Veneers) is that it takes away the stains and the shame, without making you look like a game-show host or a candidate claiming that he likes being back in Iowa.

It's not easy to report on six hours of enforced idleness in a chair. I clicked my way through Dr. Lituchy's massively accoutred Sonos sound system, moving from Bob Dylan through Paul Simon and then—as the screech of the drill began to mount to a crescendo—the Rolling Stones' *Steel Wheels*. A foot masseur was thoughtfully provided to alleviate the tedium. But gallows humor is inseparable from dentistry: at one point I heard the good doctor say, as he plowed through the layers of plaque and tartar, "Good news. I've found some of your teeth." When it was over, and my pearls as white as snow, I looked more British in one way, since my numb and swollen lips resembled those of a bulldog, and I felt helpless because I couldn't hold a cigarette in my mouth or, for the rest of the evening, swallow a drink without a bib to catch the dribbles.

This sense of a reversion to childhood was enormously increased the following morning, when I arrived at the studio of the renowned "J Sisters," the seven girls from Brazil who have pioneered the waxing technique that bears their country's name. The salon caters mainly to women: there was a picture of Christy Turlington on the wall, and I wondered briefly if, rather than wish to be like Christy Turlington, I secretly wanted to be Christy Turlington. (My old friend Simon Hoggart has written that it's harder to become an ex-smoker than it is to have a sex change.) This thought was rudely dispelled by what followed.

The male version of the wax is officially called a *sunga*, which is the name for the Brazilian boys' bikini. I regret to inform you that the colloquial term for the business is "sack, back, and crack." I went into a cubicle which contained two vats of ominously molten wax and was instructed to call out when I had disrobed and covered my midsection with a small towel. Then in came Janea Padilha, the actual creator of the procedure. She whipped away the exiguous drapery and, instead of emitting the gasp or whistle that I had expected, asked briskly if I wanted any "shaping." Excuse me? What was the idea? A heart shape or some tiger stripes, perhaps, on the landing strip? I disdained anything so feminine and coolly asked her to *sunga* away.

Here's what happens. You have to spread your knees as far apart as they will go, while keeping your feet together. In this "wide stance" position, which is disconcertingly like waiting to have your Pampers changed, you are painted with hot wax, to which strips are successively attached and then torn away. Not once, but many, many times. I had no idea it would be so excruciating. The combined effect was like being tortured for information that you do not possess, with intervals for a (incidentally very costly) sandpaper hand job. The thing is that, in order to rip, you have to grip. A point of leverage is required: a place that can be firmly gripped and pulled while the skin is tautened.

Ms. Turlington doesn't have this problem. The businesslike Senhora Padilha daubed away, took a purchase on the only available handhold, and then wrenched and wrenched again. The impression of being a huge baby was enhanced by the blizzards of talcum powder that followed each searing application. I swear that several times she soothingly said that I was being a brave little boy. . . . Meanwhile, everything in the general area was fighting to retract itself inside my body.

Small talk is difficult under such grueling conditions, but I am ruthlessly professional and managed to keep my end up, so to speak. "What sort of men come here?" "Those who are preparing for hemorrhoid operations." Oh, great. "And those from Wall Street who sit too much and get their behinds irritated." Uh-huh. "Also many who are urged by their wives and their fiancées." You don't say. I also gather, though this wasn't part of the pitch, that male porn stars get the wax in order to enhance their profile on video. By this stage, I thought I could tell we were drawing agonizingly near to the close, but I was wrong. Boy, was I ever wrong.

You ladies will know what I mean by the stirrup position, which I was now unceremoniously instructed to assume. That's to say, I braced one leg up while Ms. Padilha braced the other. And she does this for a living. To be Dr. Lituchy and to spend every day up to your elbows in other people's oral cavities would be tough enough. But this . . . And wait: surely you can't be serious about putting . . . Oh Jesus. I was overwhelmed by a sudden access of lava-like agony, accompanied by the vertiginous sensation that there was no there there. Stunned into silence, I listened slack-jawed as she told of her plans to expand into the London market, and to fly to Dubai to demonstrate her technique. To call this a "growth industry" might be a slight mistake: the J Sisters will not rest until every blade has been torn from every crevice. Tomorrow, the world. But today, your humble servant. And my only question was: "Where's the rest of me?" We did not take a "before" picture, so with your indulgence I shall not share the "after" one. The total effect, I may tell you, is somewhat bizarre. The furry pelt that is my chest stretches southward over the protuberant savanna that is my stomach, and then turns into a desert region. Below the waist, a waste. I suppose I could have had the whole torso denuded, but then I would have looked even more like a porpoise than I already do.

My divine editor and friend Aimee Bell had sweetly come along to lend moral support, which turned out to be the only kind I didn't need. She told me later, over a healing and sustaining lunch, that the J Sisters staff had been surprised by my failure to yelp or cry out, so I suppose I can be prouder of my British reserve than I was of my British teeth. And I have a new nickname for my porn-ready but paradoxically still-wincing courting tackle: "Smooth Operator." How long, I ask myself idly, will this last?

Il faut souffrir pour être belle, as the French say. Without suffering, no beauty. As I look back on my long and arduous struggle to make myself over, and on my dismaying recent glimpses of lost babyhood, I am more than ever sure that it's enough to be born once, and to take one's chances, and to grow old disgracefully.

(*Vanity Fair*, December 2007)

On the Limits of
Self-improvement, Part III

Mission Accomplished

IT COULD BE argued that those who seek to make themselves over
into a finer state of health and physique and fitness should not put
off the job until they are in their fifty-ninth summer. As against that
comes the piercing realization that, if you have actually made it this
far and want to continue featuring in the great soap opera of your
own existence, you had better take some swift remedial steps. It was
all summed up quite neatly by whoever first said that if he'd known
he was going to live this long he'd have taken better care of himself.

Then there's the question of whether you want to feel good (or
better) or whether you want to look good (or at least a bit better).
Having tried everything from body wraps to Brazilian bikini waxes,
I rather suddenly became persuaded that all cosmetic questions had
become eclipsed by the need to survive in the very first place. In short,
I became obsessed with the imminence of my own demise.

Even as I was sampling the luxury spas and the follicular torture
chambers of the nation, I was doing an extended promotional tour
for a book of mine that for one whole week was number one on the

bestseller list. The tour became a biggish deal, and I spent quite some time on the road with my young friend Cary Goldstein, prince of publicists as well as a highly gifted commissioning editor. He got me from airport to airport and from studio to studio, and in the intervals could match me pretty well as a drinker and smoker, while utterly outclassing me in his strange, hypnotic appeal to women. Fueled with scotch and above all with nicotine—an Irish newspaper described me in this period as taking "rare oxygen breaks"—I managed a series of epic eight-day weeks on the road, and the grand memory of it will always linger. Except that I became abruptly and horribly convinced that there would be no fond memory upon which to dwell. A voice began to speak insistently inside my skull: *You aren't going to live to spend a dime of these royalties.* As if to ram the same point home, the foul taste in my mouth from cigarettes, which already called for brushing my teeth and rinsing my gums several times a day just to gain some relief from the squalor of it, began to feel more and more corpse-like. I was thinking about death *all the time.*

So I am grateful to my colleagues at *Vanity Fair* for the witty "tough love" initiative that began this process. I quite understand that their main motive was not to have to go on looking at me the way I was, but the application of cosmetic and camouflage also had some unintended consequences. For instance, having acquired a new set of gleaming white gnashers from Dr. Gregg Lituchy, I had an incentive not to turn them as yellow and brown as their predecessors had been. I signed up for a couple of antismoking procedures, at the magazine's expense, in the vague hope of kicking my worst habit, and felt the usual self-hatred and irritation when I was back to smoking within a few days, if not hours, of having quit.

However, I think that the Allen Carr antismoking course must have "worked" subliminally, because a few weeks after resuming smoking (and thus having a grinning death's-head as my hourly companion) I woke up one October morning in Madison, Wisconsin, where I'd gone to do a book signing, and knew that I was going to throw my smokes into the loo and my lighter and matches out of the window.

Which I thereupon did. The following day, I was back in Washington and being interviewed for the "Lunch with the FT" feature that the fine *Financial Times* runs every weekend. All the conditions for a relapse were perfect: my interviewer was a smoker, the day was lovely enough to permit us to sit outside with ashtrays on the table, the food was the rich and spicy and perfect cuisine of the Bombay Club, off Lafayette Square. And I didn't even ask for a puff. I was so proud of having this fact reported in the *FT* that I left the paper lying around where my antismoking daughter—whose complaints had also tipped the scale—might see it.

But now welcome to the world of the unintended or unforeseen consequence. I have or had another bad habit—that of biting my fingernails—that is even older and more deep-rooted than my nicotine dependency. I've been chewing away since I was eight, in other words. But once Dr. Lituchy had whitened and straightened and bonded my teeth, I no longer had the crooked and jagged snaggle-fangs that enabled me to get a purchase on my fingertips and to work the jaws in that nice crisp and crunchy action that makes all the difference. All of a sudden I was buying nail files at the pharmacy and buffing away at oval extremities that for the first time in half a century looked as if they belonged to a human. (Tiring of this rather feminine activity, I now go to a gay Vietnamese manicurist in my hood and fight to keep the expression "hand job" out of my mind as he fusses away over my paw-like mitts.)

Anyway, just as there are uncovenanted side benefits to major dental work, so there are things about quitting the smoking habit for which nobody prepares you. Did I have any idea that I would indulge in long, drooling—nay, dribbling—lascivious dreams in which I was still wreathed in fragrant blue fumes? I'm embarrassed to say that almost no nocturnal reverie has ever been so vivid or so actual: had the damn ciggies come to mean that much to me? I would wake with the complete and guilty conviction that I had sinned in word and deed while I was asleep. (In bold contrast, the morning mouth felt much better.)

Then there's the short-term memory loss. I might have been due for this anyway at my age, but my recall for names and faces and facts, and for things from early education such as historical dates and verses of poetry, had been holding up pretty well. Abruptly I was suffering intermittently from what a friend once called "CRAFT syndrome." (The acronym represents the words "Can't Remember a Fucking Thing.") A visage would loom up at a party, or a literary reference would be on the tip of my tongue, and my recognition of the first or recollection of the second would dissolve like a ghost at cockcrow. This was bad enough in itself, but I also began to realize that I *cared* less. What the hell will it matter in a few decades whether I can put a name to this face, or an author to this snatch of verse? Along with the mild loss of function, in other words, came an access of the blues. My friend Darryl Pinckney put it very well and very bleakly when I told him that I was being visited as never before by low-level depression and mild but persistent anxiety. "That's to be expected," he said. "You are in mourning. Maybe even grief."

The Allen Carr seminar had taught me to tell myself that quitting the habit was not losing a friend but rather slaying an enemy, and I had tried hard to remember this mantra. But one doesn't get over a love-hate relationship with mere platitudes. All I can say for sure is that—while my terrors now are minor when compared with the miseries of a year ago—the old terrors were then, whereas the current angst is now.

From the heavy to the light: my colleagues in the looks department at *VF* decided that my hair could use some work, too. The problem here is that of a tobacco-colored top, more or less doing the job of covering the domed scalp while suffering lately from some forehead encroachment. And very fine: unmanageably so, in fact, with a double crown that makes it near impossible to style. Wash it, run a brush and hand through it, and the day can begin. Two efforts have been made to improve on this. My wife's hairdresser, Dennis Roche, who cuts and blow-dries Georgetown, recommended a "Brazilian keratin treatment." (I had an immediate flashback to the ladies from Brazil as they waxed and ripped my groin.) And it was decided that I should have my locks sculpted by none other than the great Frédéric Fekkai.

The keratin hair-repair treatment, originating in Brazil like so many things in the world of body fur, is now being popularized by rug stars like Roche and Peter Coppola. It essentially shrink-wraps your hair and leaves it both thicker and (if your problem is unruly curliness) straighter, which is odd since the principal ingredient is derived from sheep's wool. There's no big deal; it's sort of painted on and then left to dry for about twenty minutes, with the result that my hair doesn't frizz out when the weather turns humid, can be combed or brushed in such a way as to lie flat and in general stay put, and doesn't look as if I've been trying anything fancy. So, two thumbs up to that.

But nothing in life goes smoothly or consistently. Not long after the first hair enhancement, and on the morning of my appointment with Fekkai, I woke up to discover that my face had swollen to approximately twice its normal size. It wasn't even a regular and consistent swelling, either: one side had ballooned out as if I'd been kicked by a mule, while below my chin was dangling a sort of goiter or wattle or dewlap. Thanks a *lot*! Nothing makes one look more immediately aged than an extra swag of flesh over the Adam's apple, let alone a bloat around the cheek, and in an hour I was due at a salon which was positively rife with youth and beauty.

Everyone was very nice about it, pretending not to notice that the frog prince was getting his turn in the Fekkai chair. My trusty photographer even murmured something consoling about "photoshopping." I was given, with an absolute minimum of fuss, a very close and skillful shave of the rudely expanded facial area, and then the most deft and swift shaping and trimming of the hair that I've ever had. A pity that everything in my self-improvement program was visibly pulling in two directions at once, and that my next appointment would be with an ENT specialist, who, oddly enough, would make me pay through the proboscis. (The pills he gave me made the swellings go away, but a month or so later a good bit of the heaviness under the chin reappeared, and seems now as if it has decided to take up permanent residence. I'm glad it likes the look of things.)

Finally to the most vexed question of all. Exercise. When you are still smoking, this doesn't really come up. A nice long walk? I'd rather have a cigarette. A visit to the gym? Some other time. What about a nice game of tennis? Are you by any chance *joking*? I have half a pack to get through. The only thing that could conceivably interest me would be a late-night snack, perhaps *avec* cocktails and wine, so as to give me a reason to open a fresh carton. And then, let conversation begin! Now that this is all in my past, what about something to fill the void?

I have often thought that when I do die it will be of sheer boredom, and the awful thing about growing older is that you begin to notice how every day consists of more and more subtracted from less and less. All right then, that rules out joining an exercise club. The sheer time spent getting there and back is bad enough, without the warm-ups and other horrors, and the encouraging chats with trainers and fellow members and all the rest of it. (I used to try to deduct the cost of a Washington, DC, club membership from my taxes, on the journalistic basis that so many of the other members were faced with indictment, but even so the zest for regular attendance soon left me.)

Then I started to hear about the ROM. This device—the initials stand for "Range of Motion"—was the perfect "no excuses" invention for slothful mammals. It promised to give you a workout in just four minutes. No: it was better than that. It insisted that you never give it *more* than four minutes. The catch was that it cost well over $14,000, but, hey, remember that great slogan for Stella Artois beer— "Reassuringly expensive"—and think of all the club subscriptions and travel time you will save over a lifetime (if you can pardon that expression). In return for the outlay, you receive a silver-and-black Harley-Davidson of a machine that acts as a standing reproach to your sloth and flab. I got one and put it in my office, so that I can't get from the door to my desk, or from my desk to the drinks cabinet, or from either to the bathroom and shower, without having to pass the glinting ROM. Lazy as I am, I am simply unable to persuade myself that I can't part with four minutes every day. Also, I need to make that money back.

The thing is constructed and balanced around a heavy steel wheel that is moved by a series of chains. The hardest way to move the wheel is with your feet, on the rear pedals. The second hardest way is with your arms, using the metal oars at the front. At first I thought that there must be some snake oil involved, but I have since met several good trainers who use the machine mainly or exclusively at their gyms. At the worst, you get your heart rate right up and break a decent sweat. At the best, you lose weight in the bargain. As a compromise, you can look thinner without getting any lighter. This is because—wouldn't you know it?—muscle weighs more than fat. In fact, the ROM people warn you that you may gain a few pounds in the first few months of use. The best I can say is that, even though I had just given up smoking, I didn't add any poundage to my 190 starting weight. And, which is the second best to shedding for real, I did start to receive a few kind remarks on how I looked thinner. I'll take what I can get. (And I wish I knew, and maybe someone can tell me, why my scales almost always show me about a fifth of a pound heavier *after* my shower than before.)

So this is the scorecard after almost a year of effort. Weight: the same, only slightly better distributed. Life expectancy: presumably somewhat increased, but who's to say? Smile: no longer frightening to children. Hair and skin: looking less as if harvested from a battlefield cadaver. Nails: a credit to the male sex. Ennui, weltschmerz, general bourgeois blues: more palpable and resulting from virtue rather than vice (which somehow makes them worse and harder to bear) but arguably less severe. Overall verdict: some of this you can try at home and some of it you certainly should.

(Vanity Fair, September 2008)

Ayaan Hirsi Ali:
The Price of Freedom

--------⟨∞⟩--------

IF ANY COUNTRY has enjoyed a long reputation for peaceful and democratic consensus combined with civic fortitude, that country is the Netherlands. It was one of the special countries of the Enlightenment, providing refuge for the family of Baruch Spinoza and for the heterodox Pierre Bayle and René Descartes. It overcame Catholic-Protestant fratricide with a unique form of coexistence, put up a spirited resistance to Nazi occupation, evolved a constitutional form of monarchy, and managed to make a fairly generous settlement with its former colonies and their inhabitants.

In the last few years, two episodes have hideously sullied this image. The first smirching was the conduct of the Dutch contingent in Bosnia, who in July 1995 abandoned the population of the UN-protected "safe haven" at Srebrenica and enabled the worst massacre of civilians on European soil since World War II. Dutch officers were photographed hoisting champagne glasses with the sadistic goons of Ratko Mladic's militia before leaving the helpless Muslim population to a fate that anyone could have predicted.

Those of us who protested at this slaughter of Europe's Muslims are also obliged to register outrage, I think, at the Dutch state's latest betrayal. On October 1, having leaked its intention in advance to the press, the Christian-Democrat administration of Jan Peter Balkenende announced that it would no longer guarantee the protection of Ayaan Hirsi Ali.

To give a brief backstory, it will be remembered that Hirsi Ali, a refugee from genital mutilation, forced marriage, and civil war in her native Somalia, was a member of the Dutch parliament. She collaborated with Theo van Gogh on a film—*Submission*—that highlighted the maltreatment of Muslim immigrant women living in Holland. Van Gogh was murdered on an Amsterdam street in November 2004; a note pinned to his body with a knife proved to be a threat to make Hirsi Ali the next victim. Placed inside a protective bubble by the authorities, she was later evicted from her home after neighbors complained that she was endangering their safety and then subjected to a crude attempt to deprive her of her citizenship. Resolving not to stay where she was not wanted, Hirsi Ali moved to the United States, where she was offered a place by the American Enterprise Institute in Washington, DC, and where the Dutch government undertook to continue to provide her with security. This promise it no longer finds it convenient to keep. The ostensible reason for the climb-down is the cost, which involves a basic 2 million euros (not very much for a state), which can admittedly sometimes be higher if Hirsi Ali has to travel.

The Dutch parliament debates this question later this week, and I hope that its embassies hear from people who don't regard this as an "internal affair" of the Netherlands. If a prominent elected politician of a Western country can be left undefended against highly credible threats from Islamist death squads, what price all of our easy babble about not "appeasing terrorists"? Especially disgraceful is the Dutch government's irresponsible decision to announce to these death squads, without even notifying Hirsi Ali, that after a given date she would be unprotected and easy game. (Lest I inadvertently strengthen this deplorable impression, let me swiftly add that at present she is under close guard in the United States.)

Suppose the narrow and parochial view prevails in Holland, then I think that we in America should welcome the chance to accept the responsibility ourselves. Ayaan Hirsi Ali has become a symbol of the resistance, by many women from the Muslim world, to gender apartheid, "honor" killing, genital mutilation, and other horrors of clerical repression. She has been a very clear and courageous voice against the ongoing attack on our civilization mounted by exactly the same forces. Her recent memoir, *Infidel* (which I recommend highly, and to which, I ought to say, I am contributing a preface in its paperback edition), is an account of an extremely arduous journey from something very like chattel slavery to a full mental and intellectual emancipation from theocracy. It is a road that we must, and for our own sake as well, be willing to help others to travel.

For a while, her security in America was provided by members of the elite Dutch squad that is responsible for the protection of the Dutch royal family and Dutch politicians. The US government requested that this be discontinued, for the perfectly understandable reason that foreign policemen should not be operating on American soil. The job has now been subcontracted, and was until recently underwritten by The Hague. If The Hague defaults, then does the "war on terror" administration take no interest in protecting the life of one of the finest enemies, and one of the most prominent targets, of the terrorists? Hirsi Ali has been accepted for permanent residence in the United States, and would, I think, like to become a citizen. That's an honor. If she was the CEO of Heineken or the president of Royal Dutch Shell, and was subject to death threats while on US soil, I have the distinct feeling that the forces of law and order would require no prompting to consider her safety a high priority.

A last resort would be to set up a trust or fund by voluntary subscription and continue to pay for her security that way. Perhaps some of the readers of this column would consider kicking in or know someone who was about to make an unwise campaign contribution that could be diverted to a better end? If so, do please watch this space and be prepared to write to your congressional representatives, or to the Dutch ambassador, in the meantime. We keep hearing that not enough sacrifices are demanded of us, and many people wonder what they can do to forward the struggle against barbarism and intimidation. So, now's your chance.

(*Slate*, October 8, 2007)

Arthur Schlesinger:
The Courtier

---ᴑᴡᴄ---

O N   T H E   L A S T   recorded occasion on which Arthur Schlesinger
spoke with his hero John Fitzgerald Kennedy, the two men were
flying from Washington to Amherst for a presidential address on "the
place of arts in a democracy"—a speech on which Schlesinger had
brought his agreeable skills and easy fluency to bear:

> We chatted about the Eisenhower reminiscences on the way
> up. The President commented on their self-righteousness.
> "Apparently he never did anything wrong," he said. "When we
> come to writing the memoirs of this administration, we'll do
> it differently."

When I reached this passage, which occurs at about the 200-page
mark, I was so astonished that I put the book down for a moment.
Obviously a journal must be true both to itself and to the day on which
it was written, and there is little evidence that Schlesinger succumbed
to any yearning to improve matters in hindsight. But it was as though
he had stumbled on the truth and then picked himself up as if nothing

Review of *Journals: 1952–2000* by Arthur Schlesinger Jr.

had happened. The annoying legend and imagery of "Camelot" may not be exactly Schlesinger's fault (he actually expresses distaste for the Theodore White cliché), but he doesn't hesitate to compare the Kennedys' accession to power with the transition from Plantagenet to York—which is an odd way of historicizing the Eisenhower-Nixon period as well as the Kennedy interlude—and in countless other ways subordinates his dignity as a historian to the requirements of the courtier and even the apologist.

Yet these journals are quite disconcertingly good. For one thing, they are extremely illuminating, if often unconsciously so, in showing the diminishing returns to which the New Deal faction became subject in the postwar and Cold War periods. For another, they are humorous and often even witty, and show an eye for the telling detail and the encapsulating anecdote.

Most of all, they demonstrate how messy and approximate is the business of statecraft. Here, I remind you, is the empurpled way in which Schlesinger wrote about JFK's comportment during the Cuba crisis in *A Thousand Days*:

> It was this combination of toughness and restraint, of will, nerve and wisdom, so brilliantly controlled, so matchlessly calibrated, that dazzled the world.

But page through the entries for October 1962 in this journal and you will discover an administration hectically improvising, ill-served by the "intelligence" services, alternating and oscillating, and uneasily aware that it is being outpointed by the boorish Khrushchev. If anyone emerges as cool and wise as well as smart, it is Averell Harriman. When writing about the more slow-motion confrontation with the Dixiecrats who did not want James Meredith to register at the University of Mississippi, Schlesinger the diarist shows us a president who dealt with such political bosses as if he, too, were merely another state governor trying persuasion. (Kennedy could be tougher when he had to be: Schlesinger was in the room when the Leader of the Free

World complained to Martin Luther King and A. Philip Randolph that Sheriff "Bull" Connor "has done more for civil rights than almost anybody else," and that proposing a March on Washington was like forcing him to negotiate at gunpoint.)

Thus we learn again that what people set down day to day is of greater value than what they try to synthesize retrospectively into a grand sweep or theory. I do not think that Schlesinger would want his previous hero Adlai Stevenson to pass into history as a vain and weak and narcissistic type, but this is the impression that inexorably builds by way of a series of well-drawn miniature encounters. How can some people argue so confidently that Indochina was Johnson's war rather than Kennedy's when Schlesinger quotes LBJ, in December 1963, still holding "to his earlier views" and asking Mike Forrestal, "Don't you think that the situation in Vietnam is more hopeless today than it has ever been before?"

Coming down a bit in the scale of grandeur: Did Isaiah Berlin really describe Evangeline Bruce as "a bloody bore"? (If so, the bell tolls here for decades of the Georgetown "special relationship" smart set.) And were Schlesinger and Bobby Kennedy really "engaged in mock competition" for the fragrant Marilyn Monroe after the JFK birthday rally at Madison Square Garden in May 1962? There is a sort of sublime naïveté in the way Schlesinger records his Galahad's doings: things that are now notorious are not so much airbrushed as unnoticed. Not a mention of the steep decline in the state of Kennedy's health and his marriage is allowed, and the name of Judith Campbell Exner, to give only one instance, is nowhere in the narrative at all.

Partisanship cannot be a complete explanation of this, nor can innocence. As the journals go on, and as American politics learns somehow to live without the Kennedys, Schlesinger learns to see through certain Democrats, even certain occupants of the White House. I would not have known, without reading the fascinating pages about the election of 1980, just how much Schlesinger and his circle had come to despise Jimmy Carter and to hope, in effect, for the election of Ronald Reagan. (It turns out that George McGovern, and every member of his family, had voted for Gerald Ford in 1976 to avert the horrible possibility of a Carter White House. In 1980, Schlesinger himself was for the witless Christian fundamentalist John Anderson—anyone but the cornball from Plains, Georgia, and his awful sidekick Zbigniew Brzezinski.)

Admittedly, much of this comes to us filtered through a dull blizzard of dinners and cocktails at Le Cirque and the Century Club and the Council on Foreign Relations, with a floating cast of vanden Heuvels and Plimptons and Styrons and Mailers. Every now and then, Schlesinger meets someone from outside his familiar charmed circle, like Mick Jagger or Abbie Hoffman, and emits a quasi-senescent whinny of astonishment that such people can talk and walk, but I never said he was another "Chips" Channon. The best running gag—every good diarist has one—starts in the spring of 1980, when Richard Nixon moves to East 65th Street in Manhattan, just over Schlesinger's garden fence, and provides some comic relief that draws the sting from the failure of Teddy Kennedy's grotesque campaign against Carter. From one such entry:

> Very few [Nixon] sightings . . . though when I throw open the curtains in the morning, around 7 o'clock, a fire is usually blazing in his fireplace. Lest he get too much moral credit for rising so early it should be noted that the Nixons seem to dine around 6 o'clock, an hour or so before we start pre-prandial drinking, and the house is generally dark by 9. Not New York hours.

Schlesinger had written the Kennedy campaign's anti-biography of Nixon for the election of 1960, and had come to the view that he was

> the greatest shit in 20th century American politics (the "20th century" bit is pure scholarly caution; I cannot at the moment think of anyone in the 19th century quite meeting Nixon's combination of sanctimoniousness and squalor).

He is quite rightly indignant at the way in which Nixon "ended" US participation in the Vietnam War in 1972, on terms no better than had been available in 1969 but after a hideous waste of life. Yet for Nixon's sinuous enabler in all this Schlesinger has nothing but praise. Henry Kissinger is continually recruited as a social partner, dinner guest, and general sage. In one 1982 entry, Schlesinger lavishes compliments on him for his memoirs and for his humanizing portrait of Nixon. Amusingly, Kissinger demurs and says that he regards Nixon as a poisonous manipulator. Again, it isn't obvious that Schlesinger understands that the irony, from a fellow member of the presidential-sycophants club, is at his expense. The exchange contains an anecdote well worth repeating. At Anwar Sadat's funeral, Ford had expressed disgust at Nixon's behavior and told Kissinger: "Sometimes I wish I had never pardoned that son of a bitch." Who would have thought that the hapless Ford administration would be so much the beneficiary of a Schlesinger memoir?

There is a disappointing absence of rancor here. Like Will Rogers, Schlesinger seems never to meet anyone for whom he can't find a good word. (I should declare an interest and say that I feature on a short "enemies list" of his, which otherwise consists of Gore Vidal, Conor Cruise O'Brien, Joan Didion, and John Gregory Dunne. He is very genial and lenient toward all of us, except Didion, and even she is forgiven when he meets her properly and finds that she has unsuspected qualities.) Such affability may be admirable, but it does slow things down a bit. Indeed, Schlesinger's good manners are almost masochistic. Of Vidal, he writes: "At least he knows me, which in a way legitimizes his right to attack me." Self-deprecation could do no more; still, one might ask for a little more gin in the martini.

Like Fabrizio in *The Charterhouse of Parma*, who could never work out whether he had been present for the Battle of Waterloo, Schlesinger gives us keyhole-size insights into events in which he was a participant. He omits all mention of his participation in the CIA-funded Congress for Cultural Freedom, and in the famous controversy over the covert funding of the magazine *Encounter*. (This seems to me to be mildly scandalous.) His slim record of the 1956 presidential campaign fails even to touch upon the Suez invasion and the Hungarian Revolution. He spares us any real account of November 22, 1963, and when in Chicago for the 1968 Democratic Convention, contents himself with recording that he once managed to get Teddy Kennedy on the phone after the line had been busy. This must have seemed important at the time, though the senator's subsequent remarks hardly seem worth preserving.

Denouncing Harriman for endorsing the detested Carter, Schlesinger commits another of his accidental innocences and writes:

> I know his penchant for staying in with Democratic Presidents, and with potential winners; but at eighty-eight he need not go out of his way to keep on good terms with power.

Schlesinger was then sixty-two. By the time he turned eighty-one, he was willing to make a fool of himself in public by testifying to Congress on Bill Clinton's behalf, saying that "gentlemen always lie about their sex lives"; Clinton was by no stretch of the definition a gentleman and was lying not about sex (which is done to protect the reputation of the woman) but about the women (which was done to defame them and to protect nobody but himself). Interestingly, the journals demonstrate that Schlesinger guessed right in private about Clinton's squalid mendacity; yet this did not prevent him from adopting a frankly partisan line, or from complaining to his diary that he was not often enough invited to the Clinton White House.

In a sentimental entry for Christmas 1983, he reflects that he might have written more books were it not for the demands of his children, but that he cannot regret the choice he made. This wistfulness is charming but self-deceptive: Schlesinger might have written not just more books but better ones (as we know from the quality of *The Age of Jackson* and *The Disuniting of America*) if he had not squandered so much time and energy being a compulsive socialite and an insecure *valet du pouvoir*.

(*The Atlantic*, December 2007)

Paul Scott:
Victoria's Secret

THERE ARE NOT as many theories about the fall of the British Empire as there once were about the eclipse of its Roman predecessor, but one of the micro-theories has always appealed to me more than any of the macro-explanations. And it concerns India. For the first century or so of British dominion over the subcontinent, the men of the East India Company more or less took their chances. They made and lost reputations, and established or overthrew regional domains, and their massive speculations led to gain or ruin or (as in the instance of Warren Hastings) both. Meanwhile, they were encouraged to pick up the custom of the country, acquire a bit of the lingo, and develop a taste for "native" food, but—this in a bit of a whisper—be very careful about the local women. Things in that sensitive quarter could be arranged, but only with the most exquisite discretion.

Thus the British developed a sort of modus vivendi that lasted until the trauma of 1857: the first Indian armed insurrection (still known as "the Mutiny" because it occurred among those the British had themselves trained and organized). Then came the stern rectitude of direct

---

Review of *The Raj Quartet: The Jewel in the Crown, The Day of the Scorpion, The Towers of Silence, A Division of the Spoils* by Paul Scott

rule from London, replacing the improvised jollities and deal-making of "John Company," as the old racket had come to be affectionately known. And in the wake of this came the dreaded memsahib: the wife and companion and helpmeet of the officer, the district commissioner, the civil servant, and the judge. She was unlikely to tolerate the pretty housemaid or the indulgent cook. Worse, she was herself in need of protection against even a misdirected or insolent native glance. To protect white womanhood, the British erected a wall between themselves and those they ruled. They marked off cantonments, rigidly inscribing them on the map. They built country clubs and Anglican churches where ladies could go, under strict escort, and be unmolested. They invented a telling term—*chi-chi*—to define, and to explain away, the number of children and indeed adults who looked as if they might have had English fathers and Indian mothers or (even more troubling) the reverse. Gradually, the British withdrew into a private and costive and repressed universe where eventually they could say, as the angry policeman Ronald Merrick does in *The Day of the Scorpion*, the second volume of Paul Scott's *The Raj Quartet*: "We don't rule this country any more. We preside over it."

In this anecdotal theory, the decline of the British Raj can be attributed to the subtle influence of the female, to the male need to protect her (and thus fence her in), and to the related male need to fight for her honor and to punish with exceptional severity anybody who seems to impugn it. And so we may note with interest that it took one English homosexual, and one English bisexual, to unravel the erotic ambiguities of empire. "After all," says the district collector Turton in E. M. Forster's *A Passage to India*, "it's our women who make everything more difficult out here." And Paul Scott accepted that he had little choice but to follow the track that Forster had laid down.

I choose the word "track" with care, since the railway network was (apart from Lord Macaulay's education system) the most enduring achievement of the British Raj: the most proudly flourished emblem of the unity and punctuality it brought to the nation, as well as the speediest possible method of annexing Indian capital and shipping it to the ports of Bombay, Madras, and Calcutta in order to fuel the English Industrial Revolution. The Indian railways feature by name in *Bhowani Junction*, one of the most gripping of John Masters's Anglo-Indian novels, and their imagery appears to have oppressed Paul Scott. According to Scott's brilliant biographer Hilary Spurling, whose introduction to this handsome two-volume Everyman edition is a jewel in itself, Scott felt that "Forster loomed over literary India like a train terminus beyond which no other novelist could be permitted to travel by the critics." When Scott deliberately chose a rape as his central event—as it had been in Forster's *Passage*—we can see that he ultimately resolved to face the comparison and attempt to transcend it. To borrow the language of "cultural studies," he did so by exploring the interactions of race, class, and gender, as Orwell had tried to do in *Burmese Days*, while not forgetting the politics.

In the last of Scott's tetralogy (*A Division of the Spoils*), we meet a certain Captain Purvis, who represents the new, brusque British postwar consensus about India, namely that it was and is

> "a wasted asset, a place irrevocably ruined by the interaction of a conservative and tradition-bound population and an indolent, bone-headed and utterly uneducated administration, an elit- ist bureaucracy so out of touch with the social and economic thinking of even just the past hundred years that you honestly wonder where they've come from . . . The most sensible thing for us to do is get rid of it fast to the first bidder before it becomes an intolerable burden."

This no doubt partly represents Scott's own view, or the view he took as a liberal-minded young officer watching the scenery being dismantled after the defeat of Japan and before the division of the spoils into India and Pakistan. It was obviously high time for the Brit- ish to leave. Yet there is one last train to be caught, the one stopped in the desert in 1947 by a Hindu mob, who drag a Muslim from the carriage and do him to death beside the tracks. The train resumes its journey, bearing its complement of British officials away from the distressing scene. Sergeant Guy Perron, who has listened to Purvis's rational rant and who has quarrels of his own with the authorities (and whom I think we are to see as the Scott figure in the story), is hit hard as he watches the former rulers make good their escape, and finds something unpleasantly "greasy and evasive" in the snaking movement of the train that carries them away. The ensuing awful bloodbath of partition took place principally at the railway stations and on the trains, but by then the British could claim that they had washed their hands rather than stained them.

Scott's work on India, which is really a quintet given the coda *Staying On*, is tense and beautiful in a way that Forster's is not, because it understands that Fabian utilitarianism has its limits, too. The novels also possess a dimension of historical irony, because they understand that the British stayed too long *and* left too soon. The date on which it became evident that the game was up is a date that every Indian still knows: April 13, 1919. Maddened by a report of a mob attack on (yes, it had to be) an Englishwoman, Brigadier General Reginald Dyer ordered his soldiers to fire into a crowd in the public square in the northern city of Amritsar. That event was the Boston Massacre or the Lexington and Concord of the Indian revolution. From then on, it was a matter not of whether the British would quit, but of when. Scott understands this so well that he makes the name of that Amritsar square—Jallianwallah—a totem that recurs throughout the books.

But there remains a question of, if you like, etiquette. How exactly *do* you behave when you want to leave and know you have to leave but don't want to do so in an unseemly rush? Moreover, how do you conduct yourself when Japanese imperialism makes a sudden bid for mastery in Asia, which means that British rule will be succeeded not by English-trained Indian democrats and liberals, but by Hirohito's Co-Prosperity Sphere? These are difficulties that Forster never had to confront. (The Amritsar events took place years after the visit to India that inspired his landmark novel.) Scott's account begins at the precise moment, in 1942, when the British have made the grotesque mistake of declaring war on India's behalf, without consultation, and when Mahatma Gandhi has announced that they must "quit India" and leave her "to God or to anarchy" (in the circumstances of growing Hindu-Muslim fratricide, something of a false antithesis). Depressed by Gandhi's failure to take the Japanese threat seriously, the old missionary lady Edwina Crane removes his picture from her wall, revealing:

> the upright oblong patch of paler distemper, all that was left to Miss Crane of the Mahatma's spectacled, smiling image, the image of a man she had put her faith in, but had now transferred to Mr. Nehru and Mr. Rajagopalachari who obviously understood the different degrees of tyranny men could exercise and, if there had to be a preference, probably preferred to live a while longer with the imperial degree in order not only to avoid submitting to but to resist the totalitarian.

And of course it is Miss Crane, trying to help, who is viciously manhandled by the rioters. And of course it is Daphne Manners, the gawky girl who defies convention so much as to have an affair with an Indian boy, who is gang-raped during the same disorders. Adela Quested in *A Passage to India* is making up her hysterical allegation about what happened in the Marabar Caves, but Daphne is so eager to shield her genuine Indian lover that she refuses to testify about the real rapists who came upon them when they were lying together. And the boyfriend, who is charged with the rape and sent to prison, is himself sexually assaulted by Ronald Merrick during the course of his interrogation. Forster never dared attempt this level of complexity, or indeed of realism.

The ramifications of a small but cruel injustice allow Scott to test the whole fabric of decaying British India. Gradually, we come to understand that the British have betrayed their own promise—of

impartial, unifying, and modernizing administration—and are resorting to divide-and-rule tactics. These are best described by Daphne's
boyfriend, Hari Kumar, who notices

> the extent to which the English now seem to depend upon the
> divisions in Indian political opinion perpetuating their own rule
> at least until after the war . . . They prefer Muslims to Hindus
> (because of the closer affinity that exists between God and Allah
> than exists between God and the Brahma), are constitution-
> ally predisposed to Indian princes, emotionally affected by the
> thought of untouchables, and mad keen about the peasants who
> look on any raj as God.

Poor Daphne, less political and more intuitive, sees where things
have gone wrong in a different way:

> Perhaps at one time there was a moral as well as a physical
> force at work. But the moral thing had gone sour. Has gone
> sour. Our faces reflect the sourness. The women look worse
> than the men because consciousness of physical superiority is
> unnatural to us. A white man in India can feel physically superior
> without unsexing himself. But what happens to a woman if she
> tells herself that ninety-nine per cent of the men she sees are
> not men at all, but creatures of an inferior species whose color
> is their main distinguishing mark?

Daphne's great-aunt, Lady Ethel Manners, the widow of a former
governor, is outraged by Lord Mountbatten's hasty agreement to
partition:

> The creation of Pakistan is our crowning failure. I can't bear
> it. . . . Our only justification for two hundred years of power was
> unification. But we've divided one composite nation into two.

The Raj Quartet, as these excerpts help to make plain, is not so much about India as it is about the British. To understand how they betrayed their own mission in the subcontinent is to understand, in Scott's words, how "in Ranpur, and in places like Ranpur, the British came to the end of themselves as they were."

(*The Atlantic*, January/February 2008)

The Case against Hillary Clinton

⎯⎯⎯∞⎯⎯⎯

S EEING THE NAME "Hillary" in a headline last week—a headline
about a life that had involved real achievement—I felt a mouse
stirring in the attic of my memory. Eventually, I was able to recall how
the two Hillarys had once been mentionable in the same breath. On a
first-lady goodwill tour of Asia in April 1995—the kind of banal trip
that she now claims as part of her foreign-policy "experience"—Mrs.
Clinton had been in Nepal and been briefly introduced to the late Sir
Edmund Hillary, conqueror of Mount Everest. Ever ready to milk the
moment, she announced that her mother had actually named her for
this famous and intrepid explorer. The claim "worked" well enough
to be repeated at other stops and even showed up in Bill Clinton's
memoirs almost a decade later, as one more instance of the gutsy
tradition that undergirds the junior senator from New York.

Sen. Clinton was born in 1947, and Sir Edmund Hillary and his
partner Tenzing Norgay did not ascend Mount Everest until 1953,
so the story was self-evidently untrue and eventually yielded to fact-
checking. Indeed, a spokeswoman for Sen. Clinton named Jennifer
Hanley phrased it like this in a statement in October 2006, conceding
that the tale was untrue but nonetheless charming: "It was a sweet
family story her mother shared to inspire greatness in her daughter,
to great results I might add."

Perfect. It worked, in other words, having been coined long *after* Sir Edmund became a bankable celebrity, but now its usefulness is exhausted and its untruth can safely be blamed on Mummy. Yet isn't it all—all of it, every single episode and detail of the Clinton saga—exactly like that? And isn't some of it a little bit more serious? For Sen. Clinton, something is true if it validates the myth of her striving and her "greatness" (her overweening ambition in other words) and only ceases to be true when it no longer serves that limitless purpose. And we are all supposed to applaud the skill and the barefaced bravado with which this is done. In the New Hampshire primary in 1992, she knowingly lied about her husband's uncontainable sex life and put him eternally in her debt. This is now thought of, and referred to in print, purely as a smart move on her part. In the Iowa caucuses of 2008, he returns the favor by telling a huge lie about his own record on the war in Iraq, falsely asserting that he was opposed to the intervention from the very start. This is thought of, and referred to in print, as purely a tactical mistake on his part: trying too hard to help the spouse. The happy couple has now united on an equally mendacious account of what they thought about Iraq and when they thought it. What would it take to break this cheap little spell and make us wake up and inquire what on earth we are doing when we make the Clinton family drama—*yet again*—a central part of our own politics?

What do you have to forget or overlook in order to desire that this dysfunctional clan once more occupies the White House and is again in a position to rent the Lincoln Bedroom to campaign donors and to employ the Oval Office as a massage parlor? You have to be able to forget, first, what happened to those who complained, or who told the truth, last time. It's often said, by people trying to show how grown-up and unshocked they are, that all Clinton did to get himself impeached was lie about sex. That's not really true. What he actually lied about, in the perjury that also got him disbarred, was the *women*. And what this involved was a steady campaign of defamation, backed up by private dicks (you should excuse the expression) and salaried government employees, against women who I believe were telling the truth. In my opinion, Gennifer Flowers was telling the truth; so was Monica Lewinsky, and so was Kathleen Willey, and so, lest we forget, was Juanita Broaddrick, the woman who says she was *raped* by Bill Clinton. (For the full background on this, see the chapter "Is There a Rapist in the Oval Office?" in the paperback version of my book *No One Left to Lie To*. This essay, I may modestly say, has never been challenged by anybody in the fabled Clinton "rapid response" team.) Yet one constantly reads that both Clintons, including the female who helped intensify the slanders against her mistreated sisters, are excellent on women's "issues."

One also hears a great deal about how this awful joint tenure of the executive mansion was a good thing in that it conferred "experience" on the despised and much-deceived wife. Well, the main "experience" involved the comprehensive fouling-up of the nation's health-care arrangements, so as to make them considerably worse than they had been before and to create an opening for the worst-of-all-worlds option of the so-called HMO, combining as it did the maximum of capitalist gouging with the maximum of socialistic bureaucracy. This abysmal outcome, forgiven for no reason that I can perceive, was the individual responsibility of the woman who now seems to think it entitles her to the presidency. But there was another "experience," this time a collaborative one, that is even more significant.

During the Senate debate on the intervention in Iraq, Sen. Clinton made considerable use of her background and "experience" to argue that, yes, Saddam Hussein was indeed a threat. She did not argue so much from the position adopted by the Bush administration as she emphasized the stand taken, by both her husband and Al Gore, when they were in office, to the effect that another and final confrontation with the Baathist regime was more or less inevitable. Now, it does not especially matter whether you agree or agreed with her about this (as I, for once, do and did). What does matter is that she has since altered her position and attempted, with her husband's help, to make people forget that she ever held it. And this, on a grave matter of national honor and security, merely to influence her short-term standing in the

Iowa caucuses. Surely that on its own should be sufficient to disqualify her from consideration? Indifferent to truth, willing to use police-state tactics and vulgar libels against inconvenient witnesses, hopeless on health care, and flippant and fast and loose with national security: the case against Hillary Clinton for president is open-and-shut. Of course, against all these considerations you might prefer the newly fashionable and more media-weighty notion that if you don't show her enough appreciation, and after all she's done for us, she may cry.

(*Slate*, January 14, 2008)

The Tall Tale of Tuzla

⎯⎯⎯ ⌘⌘⌘ ⎯⎯⎯

T HE PUNISHMENT VISITED on Sen. Hillary Clinton for her flagrant, hysterical, repetitive, pathological lying about her visit to Bosnia should be much heavier than it has yet been and should be exacted for much more than just the lying itself. There are two kinds of deliberate and premeditated deceit, commonly known as "suggestio falsi" and "suppressio veri." (Neither of them is covered by the additionally lying claim of having "misspoken.") The first involves what seems to be most obvious in the present case: the putting forward of a bogus or misleading account of events. But the second, and often the more serious, means that the liar in question has also attempted to bury or to obscure something that actually *is* true. Let us examine how Sen. Clinton has managed to commit both of these offenses to veracity and decency and how in doing so she has rivaled, if not indeed surpassed, the disbarred and perjured hack who is her husband and tutor.

I remember disembarking at the Sarajevo airport in the summer of 1992 after an agonizing flight on a UN relief plane that had had to "corkscrew" its downward approach in order to avoid Serbian flak and ground fire. As I hunched over to scuttle the distance to the terminal, a mortar shell fell as close to me as I ever want any mortar shell to fall. The vicious noise it made is with me still. And so is the shock I felt at seeing a civilized and multicultural European city bombarded round the clock by an ethnoreligious militia under the command of fascistic barbarians. I didn't like the Clinton candidacy even then, but I have to report that many Bosnians were enthused by Bill Clinton's pledge, during that ghastly summer, to abandon the hypocritical and sordid neutrality of the George H. W. Bush/James Baker regime and to come to the defense of the victims of ethnic cleansing.

I am recalling these two things for a reason. First, and even though I admit that I did once later misidentify a building in Sarajevo from a set of photographs, I can tell you for an absolute certainty that it would be quite impossible to imagine that one had undergone that experience at the airport if one actually had not. Yet Sen. Clinton, given repeated chances to modify her absurd claim to have oper-ated under fire while in the company of her then-sixteen-year-old daughter and a USO entertainment troupe, kept up a stone-faced and self-loving insistence that, yes, she *had* exposed herself to sniper fire in the cause of gaining moral credit and, perhaps to be banked for the future, national-security "experience." This must mean either (a) that she lies without conscience or reflection; or (b) that she is subject to fantasies of an illusory past; or (c) both of the above. Any of the foregoing would constitute a disqualification for the presidency of the United States.

Yet this is only to underline the YouTube version of events and the farcical or stupid or Howard Wolfson (take your pick) aspects of the story. But here is the historical rather than personal aspect, which is what you should keep your eye on. Note the date of Sen. Clinton's visit to Tuzla. She went there in March 1996. By that time, the critical and tragic phase of the Bosnia war was effectively over, as was the greater part of her husband's first term. What had happened in the interim? In particular, what had happened to the 1992 promise, four years earlier, that genocide in Bosnia would be opposed by a Clinton administration?

(*Slate*, March 31, 2008)

V. S. Naipaul:
Cruel and Unusual

⊗⊗⊗

W HILE RECENTLY REREADING *The Enigma of Arrival,* considered by many to be Sir Vidia Naipaul's masterpiece, I was
struck all over again by the breathtakingly observant operations of his
eye and brain. In a novel that is so plainly autobiographical as to be
scarcely classified as fiction, he describes the atmosphere and context
of his home on Salisbury Plain in Wiltshire, and the many obvious
contrasts—as well as surprising comparisons—it affords to his native
Trinidad. One comes to know the lives and characters of all the workers and servants on the landed estate of which the author's cottage is
a peripheral part, and when he introduces other real-life characters,
such as the novelist Anthony Powell and the reclusive 1920s survivor
Stephen Tennant, Naipaul's landlord, there is no attempt at disguise;
many are given their real first names. So great was my absorption in
Sir Vidia's descriptions of the grain and contour of southern England,
and the habits and vernacular of its people, that an immensely salient
detail escaped me until I was almost closing the book. The narrator's
domestic arrangements are often touched upon, as are his everyday

---

Review of *The World Is What It Is: The Authorized Biography of V. S. Naipaul* by
Patrick French

encounters with other human beings. But he is evidently a bachelor, or at any rate a person living on his own—whereas for the entire period of Naipaul's residence in Wiltshire, as for many decades of his life, he was married to the late Patricia Hale.

It isn't very profitable to inquire whether she might have felt hurt by this kind of literary neglect, indeed airbrushing. The reception of Patrick French's astonishing (and astonishingly *authorized*) biography has already focused very considerably on the ways in which Naipaul maltreated his wife, not only through his extensive resort to the services of prostitutes and his long-running affair with another woman, but through what might be called a sustained assault on her self-respect:

> Vidia's unconscious hope may have been that if he were sufficiently horrible to Pat, she might disappear. Alone in her room at the cottage, she dutifully recorded his insults. . . . "He has not enjoyed making love to me since 1967 [the entry is for 1973]"; "You know you are the only woman I know who has no skill. Vanessa paints, Tristram's wife paints, Antonia, Marigold Johnson" . . . Even when she was alone, Pat felt she had failed her husband. After going up to London to watch a play with Antonia, Francis and Julian Jebb, she concluded that while she was there she had "lived up to Vidia's dictum: 'You don't behave like a writer's wife. You behave like the wife of a clerk who has risen above her station.'"

And Naipaul himself loftily handed this diary to Patrick French. In 1982, he had been asked for a piece of autobiography, by Richard Locke at the revived *Vanity Fair*. His running the idea past his wife produced the following diary entry on her part:

> Last night I spoke of him letting me know the morning, nay the afternoon after our marriage, that he didn't really want to be married to me. Yes, he said, he wanted to ask my permission

to write about that. . . . Would anyone, I asked, enjoy reading about that? I put in my usual plea: fiction & comedy . . . I am very low. But then perhaps it is my own fault.

One feels quite pierced with pity at reading those last eight words, indicative of perhaps some sort of masochism or self-abnegation. If so, it is perfectly matched by the interstellar coldness of her husband's attitude. Speaking to French about the way his wife had reacted to his giving an interview about his years as "a great prostitute man," he says with magnificent offhandedness:

Shortly after that she became ill again, and people say that this cancer business can come with great distress and grief. . . . I think she had all the relapses and everything after that. All the remission ended . . . It could be said that I had killed her. It could be said. I feel a little bit that way.

He plainly believed that it would be useful if his biographer were able to tidy up that loose end.

I feel justified in reproducing so much of this painful material because it undoubtedly assists us in forming a picture of the many repressions and reticences that have allowed Naipaul to continue canalizing his experiences into works both of fiction and reportage. With the aid of this exhaustive and efficient biography, one can make some more-educated surmises about the connection between Naipaul's rigidly maintained exterior and the many layers of insecurity—perhaps better say the many varieties of insecurity—that underlie it. It was shrewd and intelligent of French to take the opening sentence from *A Bend in the River*—"The world is what it is; men who are nothing, who allow themselves to become nothing, have no place in it"—and describe it as "terrifying," then annex it for his title.

There were many times when the transformation of Vidyadhar Surajprasad into first the nicknamed Trinidadian youth "Vido" and then into V. S. Naipaul and eventually Sir Vidia could have been aborted, and one senses Naipaul's disdain for any sort of weakness, allied to the conviction that it is this very disdain that has enabled him to survive. The trope can be detected in that telling jeer to his wife about rising "above her station," and also as early as another quasi-autobiographical novel, *A House for Mr. Biswas*:

> Contempt, quick, deep, inclusive, became part of his nature. It
> led to inadequacies, to self-awareness and a lasting loneliness.
> But it made him unassailable.

Naipaul might not have escaped his family: a struggling clan of Indians with more Brahmanism in their aspirations than in their actual background, transported by the British from India to Trinidad. He might, having managed a scholarship to Oxford, have succumbed to the isolation and prejudice that he felt there—and that he was to register even more keenly when rooming in London at a time when black and brown faces were fairly rare. That he was able to transcend all this and become a figure in English society, as well as one of the acknowledged masters of its prose, is plainly felt by him to be best celebrated as a triumph of the will.

With the baggage of being dark-skinned in Britain, though, came the less obvious problem of having been lighter-skinned than most of his fellow Trinidadians. French demonstrates some expertise in handling this contradiction. Almost all Indians in Trinidad (in common with their kinfolk in the other Caribbean and African states where there is an Indian diaspora) were at some point made to feel (a) patronized by the English and (b) threatened by the demands of the black majority. In this crucible is formed the young Naipaul, who writes home from Oxford to Seepersad Naipaul, his beloved and writerly father and mentor, to say: "I want to come top of my group. I have got to show these people that I can beat them at their own language." But the same context produces the Naipaul who very freely employs the word "nigger," a vulgar term that has no place in any elevated or discriminating vocabulary.

Here I feel I must say a word or two in defense of Paul Theroux. It is now a decade since he brought out his book *Sir Vidia's Shadow*, in which (as he has since phrased it) he depicted his former friend as "a grouch, a skinflint, tantrum-prone, with race on the brain." At the time, many critics characterized this as an envious vendetta, and the pressure of libel lawyers was enough to attenuate many of Theroux's observations, which in retrospect appear understated. "I wanted to write about his cruelty to his wife, his crazed domination of his mistress that lasted almost 25 years, his screaming fits, his depressions." Well, now that has been done, and published by Naipaul's own publisher, and assisted by his own hand and voice.

To me, the most extraordinary thing is the chiaroscuro. To immerse oneself in *The Enigma of Arrival*, say, is to experience the deep, slow calm that comes over its narrator as he paces the ancient chalky downland of Salisbury Plain, takes the measure of the seasons and the wildlife, familiarizes himself with the habits of the local rustics, and makes leisured comparisons between the agricultural rhythms of England and those of his Caribbean homeland. Yet to read Theroux or French is to uncover a sordid rural slum that is essentially an emotional master-slave concentration camp built for two. It's as if Blandings Castle were to become the setting for *Straw Dogs*.

"He wanted to be an Englishman," reports Naipaul's Oxford tutor, Peter Bayley. Well, no shame in that, I hope. (Indeed, Bayley was rather impressed by the young Vidia's precocious grasp of authors as venerable as Milton and as recent as Orwell.) However, and as the friends of T. S. Eliot also used to notice, there can be—perhaps especially with Anglophiles—the problem of trying too hard. One wears a top hat on the wrong occasion, as Eliot was wont to do, or behaves with exaggerated grandeur in a fine tearoom, as Naipaul did in Oxford, or affects to know more (and discloses that one actually knows less) about matters such as Camelot and Trafalgar, as he does in *The Enigma of Arrival*. And sometimes this haughtiness and defensiveness take the form of extreme revulsion against the great unwashed, as when, in travel books like *An Area of Darkness* and novels like *Guerrillas* and journalistic reports like those from Argentina, a near obsession with excrement and sodomy is disclosed. Oh, you know—Brahman fastidiousness, his defenders used to murmur. I am not so sure that this alibi will work any longer.

The supreme need of the arriviste is to be able to disown and forget those who have helped him so far. But this isn't always so easy. If Pat Hale had really turned into a frump or a shrew or a bore, or taken to attacking the cooking sherry when company called, Naipaul's treatment of her might perhaps be more understandable. But French leaves me in no doubt that Naipaul hated her because he had depended upon her, and because she had sacrificed everything to help him both as a person and as a writer, and to be consecrated to his work and his success. He used her as an unpaid editor and amanuensis, and then spurned her because he resented her knowledge of his weaker moments. There will always be those—I am one of them—who are determined not to have authors and writers judged by their private or personal shortcomings. But there is a limit, and this is a biography as well as a critical study, and I think I know what French wants us to understand when he says, reporting a literary-financial spat toward the end of the book: "Never one to forgive a past favor, the man without loyalties threatened to break his links with the *New York Review.*"

In these pages some years ago, I mentioned another alarming example of Naipaul's willingness to tread on the hands that had helped steady the ladder on which he rose. The brave Pakistani writer Ahmed Rashid, who did so much to alert us to the dangers of the Taliban, and who guided Naipaul around Lahore and even introduced him to his second wife, was rewarded by being lampooned and sneered at as a failed guerrilla in the pages of *Beyond Belief.* Patrick French can add only a little more to this dismal tale, because he apparently agreed to end the story with the death of Pat and the very rapid promotion of the next wife into the matrimonial home. Thus, and by means of a rather abrupt terminus that may signal authorial relief, we are spared the full story of Naipaul's later flirtation with the Hindu-chauvinist party the BJP, and his enthusiasm for the notorious pogrom at the Babri mosque in Ayodhya. Apparently, when Indians become arrogant overdogs and bullies, Naipaul likes them all the better. "Don't feel that I want to reform the human race," he once wrote from Oxford. "I am free of the emancipatory fire." Well, whoever thought otherwise? What we find in these pages, however, is the transition from the conservative and the lover of tradition into something that is often wrongly confused with it: the reactionary and the triumphalist. Let me remind you how Naipaul could be at his best, even if it did involve evoking the rivalry between Africans and Indians. His novella *In a Free State* includes a moment when well-tailored African politicians and bureaucrats sit in a bar. "They hadn't paid for the suits they wore; in some cases they had had the drapers deported." That's very nearly spot-on. Reviewing the book in 1970, Nadine Gordimer said that Naipaul was "past master of the difficult art of making you laugh and then feel shame at your laughter." Such ironic lightness seems, and is, a long time ago.

Two small portraits in contrast could have been more fully and usefully rendered by French. In Naipaul's earlier and slightly more generous days, when he benefited from the solidarity on offer from the BBC's Caribbean service and its network of struggling writers, he used to concede a debt to his fellow Trinidadian C. L. R. James, who as well as being the world's authority on the game of cricket was the author of *The Black Jacobins*, a seismic history of the Haitian revolution of 1791. Indeed, Naipaul's first collection of local-color Port of Spain stories, *Miguel Street*, clearly owes something to James's *Minty Alley*, a book published in 1936 that also influenced Naipaul's journalist father. The character of Lebrun in *A Way in the World*, who is depicted in a half-admiring and half-fearful way as a prophet of black power, is also rooted in a portrait of James. One wishes that French had stepped aside for a second and said something about James's place in regional and literary history.

It would also have been nice to have a little more justice done to Naipaul's younger brother, Shiva. He was felled by a heart attack in 1985, at the age of forty, leaving all who had known him with an aching feeling that we had had the best still to come. In a rather sketchy account—which does include the useful term "Naipauline"—French vaguely praises Shiva's book *North of South* but fails to give due recognition to one of the great tragicomic novels of our day, his *Fireflies*. I mention these comparisons because both of these authors, too, had to confront the colonial and postcolonial condition and were obliged to make their way in a foreign land and negotiate the difficulties of racism and social insecurity; and they managed to do so without saying or doing anything hateful. Their humanism and internationalism, far from being insipid, suggest that if Sir Vidia ever did want to excuse his own callousness—a prospect that seems extremely distant—he would not now be able to plead that his fault lay in his stars rather than in himself.

(*The Atlantic*, November 2008)

No Regrets

YES, YES. I was on the downtown streets of Washington bright and early, mingling with the bright-eyed and the wide-eyed. Yes, by all means I was there on the Mall Sunday afternoon, feeling no more moist than the next person but not much less moist, either (and getting a strange lump in the throat at the rendition of—funny how these things work—"American Pie"). And yes, that was me at the ball given by *The Root*, making a mild fool of myself as I boogied chubbily on down to the strains of Biz Markie, DJ to the capital's black elite.

I wouldn't reconsider my vote for Barack Hussein Obama, in other words, and when he takes the oath, I hope to have a ringside seat. I already know something about "the speech" and its Lincolnian tropes. (If you want your own understated preview, take a look at what he said to the crowd in Baltimore Saturday, as his whistle-stop train made its way from Philadelphia to DC's Union Station.) But on the last day of his presidency, I want to say why I still do not wish that Al Gore had beaten George W. Bush in 2000 or that John Kerry had emerged the victor in 2004.

In Oliver Stone's not very good but surprisingly well-received film *W.*, there is an unnoticed omission, or rather there is an event that does not occur on-screen. The crashing of two airliners into two large skyscrapers isn't shown (and is only once and very indirectly referred to). This cannot be because it wouldn't have been of any help in making Bush look bad; it's pretty generally agreed that he acted erratically that day and made the worst speech of his presidency in the evening, and why would Stone miss the chance of restaging *My Pet Goat*?

The answer, I am reasonably certain, is that it is the events of September 11, 2001, that explain the transformation of George Bush from a rather lazy small-government conservative into an interventionist, in almost every sense, politician. The unfortunate thing about this analysis, from the liberal point of view, is that it leaves such little room for speculation about his oedipal relationship with his father, his thwarted revenge fantasies about Saddam Hussein, his dry-drunk alcoholism, and all the rest of it. (And, since Laura Bush in the film is even more desirable than the lovely first lady in person, we are left yet again to wonder how such a dolt was able to woo and to win such a honey.)

We are never invited to ask ourselves what would have happened if the Democrats had been in power that fall. But it might be worth speculating for a second. The Antiterrorism and Effective Death Penalty Act, rushed through both houses by Bill Clinton after the relative pinprick of the Oklahoma City bombing, was correctly described by the American Civil Liberties Union as the worst possible setback for the cause of citizens' rights. Given that precedent and multiplying it for the sake of proportion, I think we can be pretty sure that "wiretapping" and "waterboarding" would have become household words, perhaps even more quickly than they did, and that we might even have heard a few more liberal defenses of the practice. I don't know if Gore-Lieberman would have thought of using Guantanamo Bay, but that, of course, raises the interesting question—now to be faced by a new administration—of where exactly you *do* keep such actually or potentially dangerous customers, especially since you are not supposed to "rendition" them. There would have been a nasty prison somewhere or a lot of prisoners un-taken on the battlefield, you can depend on that.

We might have avoided the Iraq war, even though both Bill Clinton and Al Gore had repeatedly and publicly said that another and conclusive round with Saddam Hussein was, given his flagrant defiance of all the relevant UN resolutions, unavoidably in our future. And the inconvenient downside to avoiding the Iraq intervention is that a choke point of the world economy would still be controlled by a psychopathic crime family that kept a staff of WMD experts on hand and that paid for jihadist suicide bombers around the region. In his farewell interviews, President Bush hasn't been able to find much to say for himself on this point, but I think it's a certainty that historians will not conclude that the removal of Saddam Hussein was something that the international community ought to have postponed any further. (Indeed, if there is a disgrace, it is that previous administrations left the responsibility undischarged.)

The obvious failures—in particular the increasing arrogance and insanity of the dictatorships of Iran and North Korea—are at least failures in their own terms: failure to live up to the original rhetoric and failure to mesh human rights imperatives with geostrategic and security ones. Again, it's not clear to me how any alternative administration would have behaved. And the collapse of our financial system has its roots in a long-ago attempt, not disgraceful in and of itself, to put home ownership within reach even of the least affluent. So the old question "compared to what?" does not allow too much glibness.

Inescapable as it is, "compared to what?" isn't much of a defense. And nor has this column been intended exactly as a defense, either. It's just that there's an element of hubris in all this current hope-mongering and that I am beginning to be a little bit afraid to think of what Wednesday morning will feel like.

(*Slate*, January 19, 2009)

Barack Obama: Cool Cat

I HAVE A SMALL wish of my own in this season of public and private
Utopias. It is that the emergence—or should I say ascendance?—of
Barack Hussein Obama will allow the reentry into circulation of an
old linguistic coinage. Exploited perhaps to greatest effect by James
Baldwin, the word I have in mind is "cat." Some of you will be old
enough to remember it in real time, before the lugubrious and nerve-
racking days when people never knew from one moment to the next
what expression would put them in the wrong: the days of "Negro"
and "colored" and "black" and "African American" and "people of
color." After all of this strenuous and heated and boring discourse, does
not the very mien of our new president suggest something lithe and
laid-back, agile but rested, cool but not *too* cool? A "cat" also, in jazz
vernacular, can be a white person, just as Obama, in some non–*Plessy v.
Ferguson* ways, can be. I think it might be rather nice to have a feline
for president, even if only after enduring so many dogs. (Think, for
one thing, of the kitten-like grace of those daughters.) The metaphor
also puts us in mind of a useful cliché, which is that cats have nine
lives—and an ability to land noiselessly and painlessly on their feet.

Review of *The Case Against Barack Obama* by David Freddoso; *The Audacity of
Hope* by Barack Obama; and *Dreams from My Father* by Barack Obama

Toward the beginning of his second book, *The Audacity of Hope*, Obama displays the modesty that is one of his many engaging qualities, attributing his victory in his very first US Senate race (all the way back in 2004) to "my almost spooky good fortune." This understates matters to a huge degree. The front-runner in the original contest for the Democratic nomination in that race, a man named Blair Hull, who had spent $28.7 million of his own money, was hit by news reports that his second wife had sought a protection order during an ugly divorce some years before. Not only did his commanding lead in the polls evaporate, but he had already lost the advice and services of the gifted political consultant David Axelrod, who joined the Obama camp. Meanwhile, the Republican primary had resulted in a victory for the personable Jack Ryan, whose early campaign showed distinct promise. Ryan was also to be unhorsed by earlier divorce accusations from his former wife, the actress Jeri Ryan, who accused the GOP standard-bearer of forcing her to go to S&M clubs and have sex in public. (You know how that upsets the family-values constituency.) Obliged to find another candidate at short notice, the Illinois GOP made the appalling and condescending mistake of selecting Alan Keyes, a highly volatile and extremely right-wing black man who had run for office almost everywhere *but* Illinois, and who promptly decided to accuse Obama of being insufficiently African American because none of his ancestors had been slaves! In the course of the campaign, for good measure, Obama was chosen to give the keynote address at the Democratic convention, with, as he sweetly phrases it, "seventeen minutes of unfiltered, uninterrupted air-time on national television."

Nor does this exhaust the story of his luck—the quality that, you will remember, was considered by Napoléon to be the most essential ingredient of good generalship. Hillary Clinton, when seeking an avenue back into national politics, might have tried to return by way of her native Illinois. But that eventuality was precluded by the offer, from a senior member of the Black Caucus, of an uncontested nomination in New York. John Edwards's marital difficulties might have come to light a little earlier, but as it happened, he stayed in the 2008 race long enough to beat Clinton into third place in the Iowa caucuses, thus dealing a blow to her campaign from which it, and she, never entirely recovered. Finally, it was hard to avoid the suspicion, in the closing weeks of last October, that several of McCain's advisers must at the very least have been subconsciously working for an Obama victory. On the right, where febrile talk of Obama's "Marxism" is still to be heard, the rage and frustration reminds me of the way some on the left used to talk about Ronald Reagan in the age of "Teflon": a politi-cian seemingly immune from consequences and benefiting even from his own mistakes. (The locus classicus here would be the now-famous Philadelphia address on race and racism, which allowed Obama to turn the dross of his connection with the Reverend Jeremiah Wright into the gold of "the healing process.")

Our new president's charm is not merely superficial. It is com-pounded of two qualities that are distinctly rare in the political class: an apparently very deep internal equanimity, and an ability to employ irony at his own expense. Obama, one can tell, would not have been devastated if he had lost the contest for the White House. Nor was he ready to do or say absolutely anything to win it. In fact, I am convinced that he did not at first expect to win this time around (otherwise, as Jeremiah Wright himself once admitted, he would have taken his dis-tance from that South Side church as a prophylactic measure rather than a reactive or improvised one).

Should you desire to sample the combination of personal quali-ties I have just mentioned, read Obama's account, in *Dreams from My Father*, of his exchanges with his black teenage friend Ray while at prep school in Hawaii:

> Our rage at the white world needed no object, he seemed to be telling me, no independent confirmation; it could be switched on and off at our pleasure. . . . We weren't living in the Jim Crow South, I would remind him. We weren't consigned to some heatless housing project in Harlem or the Bronx. We were

in goddamned Hawaii. We said what we pleased; ate where we pleased: we sat at the front of the proverbial bus. None of our white friends . . . treated us any differently than they treated each other. They loved us, and we loved them back. Shit, seemed like half of 'em wanted to be black themselves. . . . Well, that's true, Ray would admit. Maybe we could afford to give the bad-assed nigger pose a rest. Save it for when we really needed it.

It's this same catlike lightness and gentle raillery that I believe communicated itself subliminally to many white and brown and Jewish voters, and even to those like myself who detest the idea of voting with the epidermis. It certainly leaves a man like David Freddoso repeatedly punching the air. His book, which I hope he won't mind if I describe as surprisingly good-tempered and measured (he did begin as a colleague of Ann Coulter's at *Human Events*), has the fairly easy task of showing that Obama comes from a far more "left" milieu than any Democratic nominee before him. I believe I could prove this by my own unaided efforts: when *Newsweek*'s Jon Meacham asked both presidential candidates for a sample of their reading matter, he got back a fairly strong list from each. Obama gave John Steinbeck's *In Dubious Battle* where someone else might have been content to put *The Grapes of Wrath*. Whereas the latter is about suffering and stoicism, the former is about how the field hands finally rebel, and how the "organizer" helps them to do so. I would have noticed this even had I not dined a few times in the Hyde Park district of Chicago, and briefly met William Ayers and known others of that set. And, though it is true that Obama has no memory of 1968 and the "Days of Rage," if only because he was seven, the turning of Grant Park into a sort of "people's park" on the night of his election brought a smile to more than one set of grizzled old cheeks, and contributed to the numinous and refulgent effect in which everything seemed briefly bathed. Forgotten was the association of the word "Chicago" with the terms "machine" and "South Side," two cognates that are in point of fact just as relevant as the cynical Rahm Emanuel to the start of Obama's trajectory.

Freddoso performs nobly by supplying a thesaurus of near-incredible citations of uncritical if not servile drool that, alas, I can confirm were indeed uttered by senior members of my profession. He is fair, if tight-lipped, in adding a number of testimonies from the right—thus anticipating the famous "Obamacon" defectors, from Peggy Noonan to Christopher Buckley, who were such a feature of the postconvention (i.e., post–Palin nomination) months of the campaign. But eventually he concedes, and bows to Obama's sheer luck, and even succumbs somewhat to his charm, and avers several times that no, of course Obama's not a Marxist or a terrorist sympathizer or anything of the sort. This more or less seems to license the conclusion that we have nothing to fear from Obama but Obama himself.

If you are looking for troubling flaws in the new hero, you will find them in the accounts of his editorship at the *Harvard Law Review*, where he won golden opinions for soliciting and publishing every view but his own. It may be true that, according to Freddoso, Obama dismissed the slogan "Yes we can" as "vapid and mindless" when it was first proposed to him, in 2004, but he liked it well enough in 2008, and then came the null emptiness of the phrase—"the audacity of hope"—that he annexed from a windy sermon by Jeremiah Wright. Or you may have already begun to have your fill of verbiage like this, taken from the bestseller of that name:

> No, what's troubling is the gap between the magnitude of our challenges and the smallness of our politics—the ease with which we are distracted by the petty and trivial, our chronic avoidance of tough decisions, our seeming inability to build a working consensus to tackle any big problem.

No consensus on making tough decisions! This is not even trying to have things both ways; it's more like having things no way. It puts me in mind of the utter fatuity of Obama's speech in Berlin, where he attributed the fall of the wall to the power of "a world that stands as one"—a phrase that stands no test. Or even worse, in his scant pages dealing with Iraq (a country we would have abandoned in 2006 if he had had his way): "When battle-hardened Marine officers suggest we pull out and skeptical foreign correspondents suggest that we stay, there are . . . " (close your eyes and guess what's coming) "no easy answers to be had." To some questions, there may not even be any *difficult* answers. The very morning after the US election, Russian president Dmitry Medvedev threatened to redeploy and retarget Russian short-range missiles against Poland; as recently as 2005, Obama and his Senate colleague Dick Lugar had contentedly watched as Russian long-range missiles were being stood down. Something more than luck will be required here.

It was, I think, Lloyd George who said of Lord Derby that, like a cushion, he bore the imprint of whoever had last sat upon him. Though Obama, too, has the dubious gift of being many things to many people, the difficulty with him is almost the opposite: he treads so lightly and deftly that all the impressions he has so far made are alarmingly slight. Perhaps this is the predictable downside of being a cat.

(*The Atlantic*, January/February 2009)

The Lovely Stones

THE GREAT CLASSICIST A. W. Lawrence (illegitimate younger brother of the even more famously illegitimate T. E. "of Arabia") once remarked of the Parthenon that it is "the one building in the world which may be assessed as absolutely right." I was considering this thought the other day as I stood on top of the temple with Maria Ioannidou, the dedicated director of the Acropolis Restoration Service, and watched the workshop that lay below and around me. Everywhere there were craftsmen and -women, toiling to get the Parthenon and its sister temples ready for viewing by the public this summer. There was the occasional whine of a drill and groan of a crane, but otherwise this was the quietest construction site I have ever seen—or, rather, heard. Putting the rightest, or most right, building to rights means that the workers must use marble from a quarry in the same mountain as the original one, that they must employ old-fashioned chisels to carve, along with traditional brushes and twigs, and that they must study and replicate the ancient Lego-like marble joints with which the master builders of antiquity made it all fit miraculously together.

Don't let me blast on too long about how absolutely heart-stopping the brilliance of these people was. But did you know, for example, that the Parthenon forms, if viewed from the sky, a perfect equilateral triangle with the Temple of Aphaea, on the island of Aegina, and the

Temple of Poseidon, at Cape Sounion? Did you appreciate that each column of the Parthenon makes a very slight inward incline, so that if projected upward into space they would eventually steeple themselves together at a symmetrical point in the empyrean? The "rightness" is located somewhere between the beauty of science and the science of beauty.

With me on my tour was Nick Papandreou, son and grandson of prime ministers and younger brother of the socialist opposition leader, who reminded me that the famously fluted columns are made not of single marble shafts but of individually carved and shaped "drums," many of them still lying around looking to be reassembled. On his last visit, he found a graffito on the open face of one such. A certain Xanthias, probably from Thrace, had put his name there, not thinking it would ever be seen again once the next drum was joined on. Then it surfaced after nearly 2,500 years, to be briefly glimpsed (by men and women who still speak and write a version of Xanthias's tongue) before being lost to view once more, this time for good. On the site, a nod of respect went down the years, from one proud Greek worker to another.

The original construction of the Parthenon involved what I call Periclean Keynesianism: the city needed to recover from a long and ill-fought war against Persia and needed also to give full employment (and a morale boost) to the talents of its citizens. Over tremendous conservative opposition, Pericles in or about the year 450 BC pushed through the Athenian Assembly a sort of stimulus package which proposed a labor-intensive reconstruction of what had been lost or damaged in the Second Persian War. As Plutarch phrases it in his *Pericles*:

> The house-and-home contingent, no whit less than the sailors and sentinels and soldiers, might have a pretext for getting a beneficial share of the public wealth. The materials to be used were stone, bronze, ivory, gold, ebony and cypress-wood; the arts which should elaborate and work up these materials were those of carpenter, molder, bronze-smith, stone-cutter, dyer,

veneerer in gold and ivory, painter, embroiderer, embosser, to say nothing of the forwarders and furnishers of the material. It came to pass that for every age almost, and every capacity, the city's great abundance was distributed and shared by such demands.

When we think of Athens in the fifth century BC, we think chiefly of the theater of Euripides and Sophocles and of philosophy and politics—specifically democratic politics, of the sort that saw Pericles repeatedly reelected in spite of complaints that he was overspending. And it's true that *Antigone* was first performed as the Parthenon was rising, and *Medea* not all that long after the temple was finished. From drama to philosophy: Socrates himself was also a stonemason and sculptor, and it seems quite possible that he, too, took part in raising the edifice. So Greece might have something to teach us about the arts of recovery as well. As the author of *The Stones of Athens*, R. E. Wycherley, puts it:

> In some sense, the Parthenon must have been the work of a committee. . . . It was the work of the whole Athenian people, not merely because hundreds of them had a hand in building it but because the assembly was ultimately responsible, confirmed appointments and sanctioned and scrutinized the expenditure of every drachma.

I have visited many of the other great monuments of antiquity, from Luxor and Karnak and the pyramids to Babylon and Great Zimbabwe, and their magnificence is always compromised by the realization that slaves did the heavy lifting and they were erected to show who was boss. The Parthenon is unique because, though ancient Greece did have slavery to some extent, its masterpiece also represents the willing collective work of free people. And it is open to the light and to the air: "accessible," if you like, rather than dominating. So that to its rightness you could tentatively add the concept of "rights," as

Periclean Greeks began dimly to formulate them for the first time.

Not that the beauty and symmetry of the Parthenon have not been abused and perverted and mutilated. Five centuries after the birth of Christianity the Parthenon was closed and desolated. It was then "converted" into a Christian church, before being transformed a thousand years later into a mosque—complete with minaret at the southwest corner—after the Turkish conquest of the Byzantine Empire. Turkish forces also used it for centuries as a garrison and an arsenal, with the tragic result that in 1687, when Christian Venice attacked the Ottoman Turks, a powder magazine was detonated and huge damage inflicted on the structure. Most horrible of all, perhaps, the Acropolis was made to fly a Nazi flag during the German occupation of Athens. I once had the privilege of shaking the hand of Manolis Glezos, the man who climbed up and tore the swastika down, thus giving the signal for a Greek revolt against Hitler.

The damage done by the ages to the building, and by past empires and occupations, cannot all be put right. But there is one desecration and dilapidation that can at least be partially undone. Early in the nineteenth century, Britain's ambassador to the Ottoman Empire, Lord Elgin, sent a wrecking crew to the Turkish-occupied territory of Greece, where it sawed off approximately half of the adornment of the Parthenon and carried it away. As with all things Greek, there were three elements to this, the most lavish and beautiful sculptural treasury in human history. Under the direction of the artistic genius Phidias, the temple had two massive pediments decorated with the figures of Pallas Athena, Poseidon, and the gods of the sun and the moon. It then had a series of ninety-two high-relief panels, or metopes, depicting a succession of mythical and historical battles. The most intricate element was the frieze, carved in bas-relief, which showed the gods, humans, and animals that made up the annual Pan-Athens procession: there were 192 equestrian warriors and auxiliaries featured, which happens to be the exact number of the city's heroes who fell at the Battle of Marathon. Experts differ on precisely what story is being told here, but the frieze was quite clearly carved as a continuous narrative. Except that half the cast of the tale is still in Bloomsbury, in London, having been sold well below cost by Elgin to the British government in 1816 for $2.2 million in today's currency to pay off his many debts. (His original scheme had been to use the sculptures to decorate Broomhall, his rain-sodden ancestral home in Scotland, in which case they might never have been seen again.)

Ever since Lord Byron wrote his excoriating attacks on Elgin's colonial looting, first in "Childe Harold's Pilgrimage" (1812) and then in "The Curse of Minerva" (1815), there has been a bitter argument about the legitimacy of the British Museum's deal. I've written a whole book about this controversy and won't oppress you with all the details, but would just make this one point: if the *Mona Lisa* had been sawed in two during the Napoleonic Wars and the separated halves had been acquired by different museums in, say, St. Petersburg and Lisbon, would there not be a general wish to see what they might look like if reunited? If you think my analogy is overdrawn, consider this: the body of the goddess Iris is at present in London, while her head is in Athens. The front part of the torso of Poseidon is in London, and the rear part is in Athens. And so on. This is grotesque.

To that essentially aesthetic objection the British establishment has made three replies. The first is, or was, that return of the marbles might set a "precedent" that would empty the world's museum collections. The second is that more people can see the marbles in London. The third is that the Greeks have nowhere to put or display them. The first is easily disposed of: The Greeks don't want anything else returned to them and indeed hope to have more, rather than less, Greek sculpture displayed in other countries. And there is in existence no court or authority to which appeals on precedent can be made. (Anyway, who exactly would be making such an appeal? The Aztecs? The Babylonians? The Hittites? Greece's case is a one-off—quite individual and unique.) As to the second: Melina Mercouri's husband, the late movie director and screenwriter Jules Dassin, told a British parliamentary committee in 2000 that by the standard of mass viewership the sculptures should all be removed from Athens and London and exhibited in Beijing. After these frivolous and boring objections have been dealt with, we are left with the third and serious one, which is what has brought me back to Athens. Where should the treasures be safeguarded and shown?

It is unfortunately true that the city allowed itself to become very dirty and polluted in the twentieth century, and as a result the remaining sculptures and statues on the Parthenon were nastily eroded by "acid rain." And it's also true that the museum built on the Acropolis in the nineteenth century, a trifling place of a mere 1,450 square meters, was pathetically unsuited to the task of housing or displaying the work of Phidias. But gradually and now impressively, the Greeks have been living up to their responsibilities. Beginning in 1992, the endangered marbles were removed from the temple, given careful cleaning with ultraviolet and infrared lasers, and placed in a climate-controlled interior. Alas, they can never all be repositioned on the Parthenon itself, because, though the atmospheric pollution is now better controlled, Lord Elgin's goons succeeded in smashing many of the entablatures that held the sculptures in place. That leaves us with the next-best thing, which turns out to be rather better than one had hoped.

About a thousand feet southeast of the temple, the astonishing new Acropolis Museum will open on June 20. With ten times the space of the old repository, it will be able to display all the marvels that go with the temples on top of the hill. Most important, it will be able to show, for the first time in centuries, how the Parthenon sculptures looked to the citizens of old.

Arriving excitedly for my preview of the galleries, I was at once able to see what had taken the Greeks so long. As with everywhere else in Athens, if you turn over a spade or unleash a drill you uncover at least one layer of a previous civilization. (Building a metro for the Olympics in 2004 was a protracted if fascinating nightmare for this very reason.) The new museum, built to the design of the French-Swiss architect Bernard Tschumi, has had to be mounted aboveground on one hundred huge reinforced-concrete pillars, which allow you to survey the remnants of villas, drains, bathhouses, and mosaics of the recently unearthed neighborhood below. Much of the ground floor is made of glass so that natural light filters down to these excavations and gives the effect of transparency throughout. But don't look down for too long. Raise your eyes and you will be given an arresting view of the Parthenon, from a building that has been carefully aligned to share its scale and perspective with the mother ship.

I was impatient to be the first author to see the remounted figures and panels and friezes. Professor Dimitrios Pandermalis, the head of the museum, took me to the top-floor gallery and showed me the concentric arrangement whereby the sculpture of the pediment is nearest the windows, the high-relief metopes are arranged above head height (they are supposed to be seen from below), and finally the frieze is running at eye level along the innermost wall. At any time, you can turn your head to look up and across at the architectural context for which the originals were so passionately carved. At last it will be possible to see the building and its main artifacts in one place and on one day.

The British may continue in their constipated fashion to cling to what they have so crudely amputated, but the other museums and galleries of Europe have seen the artistic point of reunification and restored to Athens what was looted in the years when Greece was defenseless. Professor Pandermalis proudly showed me an exquisite marble head, of a youth shouldering a tray, that fits beautifully into panel number five of the north frieze. It comes courtesy of the collection of the Vatican. Then there is the sculpted foot of the goddess Artemis, from the frieze that depicts the assembly of Olympian gods, by courtesy of the Salinas Museum, in Palermo. From Heidelberg comes another foot, this time of a young man playing a lyre, and it fits in nicely with the missing part on panel number eight. Perhaps these acts of cultural generosity, and tributes to artistic wholeness, could "set a precedent," too?

The Acropolis Museum has hit on the happy idea of exhibiting, for as long as following that precedent is too much to hope for, its own original sculptures with the London-held pieces represented by beautifully copied casts. This has two effects: it allows the visitor to follow the frieze round the four walls of a core "*cella*" and see the sculpted tale unfold (there, you suddenly notice, is the "lowing heifer" from Keats's "Ode on a Grecian Urn"). And it creates a natural thirst to see the actual reassembly completed. So, far from emptying or weakening a museum, this controversy has instead created another one, which is destined to be among Europe's finest galleries. And one day, surely, there will be an agreement to do the right thing by the world's most "right" structure.

(*Vanity Fair*, July 2009)

Edward M. Kennedy: Redemption Song

⁓⊗⊗⊗⁓

B Y THE TIME I came across the full-page ad in Sunday's *New York Times*, I had become so numb and habituated that the thing barely managed to register as grotesque. On an otherwise almost uncluttered expanse of paper appeared the words "The work goes on, the cause endures, the hope still lives, and the dream shall never die." There followed the name of the politician who once read those words aloud. As I say, this seemed perfectly in keeping with the determination of the American mass media not to give up until every child in the country, if not the world, could lisp the deathless words of Bob Shrum by heart. At the bottom of the page in smaller letters appeared the injunction "Let us continue his legacy of faith in the people and faith in the work that has yet to be done." That, too, could have come from almost any tribute uttered since August 26. Last of all came the Levi's logo and the blunt exhortation: "Go forth." (To do what? Multiply? Now that the Kennedys could all do.)

When mindlessly and endlessly reiterated, ordinary words begin to lose their anchorage in original meaning. "Dream" is now so vague as to be strictly without content, and, with strong assistance from Barack Obama, "hope" is rapidly going the same way. (Twice on Saturday I heard the closing words of the Roman Catholic funeral liturgy, which sonorously intone "the sure and certain hope of the resurrection." If this means anything, it means not that there is anything certain about the prospect of the resurrection but that people sure think that there is something certain about hoping for it.)

One of the many dreadful aspects of the Kennedy "legacy" is the now-unbreakable grip of celebrity politics, image-doctoring, stage management, and "torch passing" rhetoric in general. One of the film-archive obits showed an early moment when this began to happen. In 1962, despite having been all but fixed up by his family for the Massachusetts Senate seat, Edward Kennedy (as I feel I must call him since I didn't know the man) ran into a tough and articulate primary opponent named Edward J. McCormack, the state's attorney general. The old footage shows McCormack getting some mileage with his charge of family coattailing and carpetbagging—and then a sort of light coming on in Kennedy's eyes as he bluffs away and says that the election is nothing to do with his ability to peddle influence in Washington but instead concerns "the destiny" of the people of Massachusetts. As the cheap applause starts to rise and it hits McCormack that times have changed, you can almost see the hereditary senator-to-be thinking aloud: *This is too easy.*

The surviving family must have been thinking the same, as the whole Camelot replay rolled once again unchallenged across the national screen. But perhaps by now they take it as their due. Sure, the "tragedy" of Chappaquiddick had its necessary moment, but even in those days Barbara Walters was doing her damage control, and it was amazing to see a clip of Walter Cronkite referring deadpan to the "driving accident" that had kept Kennedy away from the Senate. It must take some ingenuity at the networks, even so, to simply airbrush the fascist sympathies and bootlegging background of Joseph Kennedy Sr., his sons' murder campaigns in Cuba, the recruitment of the mafia for same, the assassination of Ngo Dinh Diem in Vietnam, the increasingly frantic and pathetic narco-addictions of JFK, the exploitation of unstable broads like Marilyn Monroe, and so much else besides.

In some ways, this banana-republic coverage was a disservice even to the recently departed. After all, it was in part the case that the youngest brother had lived down the criminal and narcissistic and power-mad background of his family. His best biographer, Adam Clymer, wrote, on the morning after he died, that it was arguably wrong to see a discontinuity in Kennedy's career and that he had actually been a decent-enough legislator *before* abandoning any yearning for the White House after 1980. This may be true as far as it goes, but the obituaries would still have had to be somewhat different in tone, even given the servility of the journalistic profession, if Kennedy had died at the time of the Au Bar episode in Palm Beach, for instance, and had not decided to take some kind of a pull on himself and become a citizen again instead of a drone.

A former Senate staffer of his stopped by for a drink last week and told me that, without fanfare, the socialist president of Chile had come in person to the Kennedy home a few months ago to bestow one of her nation's highest human rights awards on him. His work on that subject alone was a part atonement for his siblings' deployment of what Lyndon Johnson himself called "a goddam Murder Incorporated" in the Southern Hemisphere. So, of course, was his labor on health care (where Richard Nixon had a better political track record than the Kennedy administration) and his last decision to keep looking life in the face for as long as he had breath. In those waning months, after being disgusted by malicious anti-Obama propaganda being spread in the Democratic primaries—later picked up and used by the right in the general election—he withdrew his support from a candidate whose victory would have meant the continuation of the dynastic politics represented by the family names Bush, Gore, and Clinton. What a favor he did us all by that repudiation! And how fitting that it should have been a Kennedy who did it. The political rhetoric of Obamaism, alas, is even more bloviating at times than Camelot was, but you can't have everything.

It is true, then, and not just in America, that people do instinctively respond to redemption, atonement, the making up for missed opportunities and squandered time. Call no man happy until he is dead, as the Greeks had it. Kennedy's very last year was quite possibly his best, and how many men or women will be able to say that?

(*Slate*, August 31, 2009)

Engaging with Iran Is Like
Having Sex with Someone
Who Hates You

———— ∞∞∞ ————

L IVING IN THE Islamic Republic," wrote Azar Nafisi in her book
Reading Lolita in Tehran in 2003, "is like having sex with a man
you loathe." This verdict has gathered extra force and pungency as
the succeeding years have elapsed and as more women have been
stoned, hanged, beaten, raped, and silenced. Lately has come the news
that Iranian men in prison are being raped, too, for trying to exercise
their right to vote. And now the US government has come to a point
where it must ask itself: What is it like to enter negotiations with a
man who loathes you and who every Friday holds public prayers that
call for your death?

Last Friday brought the news that the Obama administration had
accepted an offer from Tehran, delivered the preceding Wednesday, for
the holding of what the *New York Times* called "unconditional talks."
It was further reported that the administration had spent "less than
48 hours" deliberating whether to respond to the invitation, which
yields the interesting if minor detail that this must have been the most
significant decision taken by Obama's people on or about the eighth
anniversary of the attacks of September 11.

Well, I am all for talks without preconditions, and I have said several times in this space that I think we should offer the Iranians cooperation on a wide spectrum of topics, especially the very pressing one of helping to "proof" Iran against the coming earthquake that could devastate its capital city. There may even be areas of potential interest in our having common enemies in the Taliban and al-Qaeda. But things have changed a little since the president and his secretary of state were sparring over the word "unconditional" during the primaries. First, it has become ever clearer that Iran's uranium-enrichment and centrifuge program has put it within measurable distance of the ability to weaponize its nuclear capacity. Second, it has become obscenely obvious that the theocracy is prepared to govern by force alone and to employ the most appalling measures to remain in power without a mandate.

So it would be nice to know, even if no "conditions" or "preconditions" (this seems like a distinction without much difference) are to be exacted, whether the administration has assured itself on two points. The first of these is: Do we seriously expect the Islamic Republic to be negotiating in good faith about its nuclear program? And the second is: What do we know about the effect of these proposed talks on the morale and the leadership of the Iranian opposition?

One presumes that the Mahmoud Ahmadinejad regime had its own reasons for firing off a five-page document proposing negotiations and including Britain, France, Russia, Germany, and China—the much-stalled group of countries that have conducted business with Iran so far—in the offer. The letter was sent out in the same period that the Russian government opposed any further sanctions on Iran for noncooperation, in the same period that Ahmadinejad announced that Iran would never halt its nuclear fuel production, and in the run-up to Ahmadinejad's next appearance at the podium of the United Nations toward the end of this month.

Might it be possible—you will, I hope, forgive my cynicism—that this latest initiative from Tehran is yet another attempt to buy time or run out the clock?

Meanwhile, it is certainly the case that at least three of the six countries approached are being asked to negotiate under some kind of duress. In an unpardonable violation of diplomatic immunity (a phrase that may remind you of something), employees of the French and British embassies in Tehran have been placed under arrest and subjected to show trials since the convulsions that attended the coup mounted by the Revolutionary Guards in June. And the Iranian correspondent of *Newsweek* magazine—who is also a Canadian citizen—has been held incommunicado for almost the same length of time. Without overstressing any "preconditions," it doesn't seem too much to require of the Iranian regime that it not send out invitations to countries whose citizens or locally engaged diplomatic staff it is holding as hostages.

On the larger question of the breach by Iran of all its undertakings about nuclear weapons, and the amazing absence from its diplomatic note of any mention of its own program, one wasn't too reassured by the lazy phrasing of Susan Rice, the US ambassador to the United Nations. The Obama administration, she said, would not impose "artificial deadlines" on Ahmadinejad. Why is this not reassuring? Because it's impossible to tell what is meant by an "artificial deadline." Would one prefer a "genuine" deadline, whereby, for example, the United Nations required Iran to demonstrate compliance with the relevant Security Council resolutions on nuclear proliferation—we have a bushel of these—or face further UN-mandated sanctions? Certainly one would, but this isn't what Ambassador Rice appears to have meant.

From all appearances, then, this seems like another snow job from the mullahs. And did the State Department or the CIA take any soundings, in those forty-eight hours between receipt of the mullahs' letter and our response to it, among the leaders of Iranian civil society? Given the short interval, it seems that the thought did not even occur to them. Here is what I heard from Professor Abbas Milani, the director of Iranian studies at Stanford University:

When you read [the Iranian letter] and realize how empty of earnest negotiating positions it in fact is, you are left with no choice but to conclude that they are relying on their ally in Putin's Russia to veto any resolutions against them. For the Russians to be able to even pretend to be serious in their talk of no need for more pressure on the regime, Tehran has also to pretend to be serious in negotiation.

This analysis appears to conform to all the available facts as we know them. A bit too much like having sex with someone who loathes you.

(*Slate*, September 14, 2009)

Colin Powell:
Powell Valediction

⸺⣿⸺

A S I WAS completing this essay, I experienced one of those random moments that make my supposed profession worthwhile. I
had been invited for a Foggy Bottom chat with Ambassador Richard
Boucher, the State Department's chief spokesman. He took me deftly
over and around the various hurdles involved in any Colin Powell retrospect, and demonstrated the diplomatic adroitness that has endeared
him to so many correspondents, and seemed almost to smooth away
much of the jaggedness. And then we got to Darfur.

Boucher began a practiced response, speaking about "process" and
bargaining and about pipelines of food and medicine and all of that,
especially stressing the horrible fate of those herders and villagers
who had been "caught in the middle." I like to think that he saw the
question forming on my lips, but, before I could get any further, he
suddenly underwent a complete change of expression. "Actually," he
said, as if half-talking to himself, "they aren't 'caught in the middle.'
There is no middle. No middle to be caught in. The word 'middle'
doesn't apply." After a short pause I asked if that had been, or could
now be, for the record. He said "Yeah."

This was a useful tip-off to the content of Secretary Powell's tes-
timony on Capitol Hill about a week later, when he broke with the

cautious language that some had been employing and stated in more-or-less round terms that the conduct of the racist Arab-Muslim death squads in Darfur conformed to the definition of genocide. It is always encouraging when the department shakes off the dusty euphemisms that make up the small change of diplomatic habit. Taken together with the focus he has developed on the AIDS catastrophe now menacing Africa, it can be said of Darfur that Powell will be able to point to a monument, or at any rate a benchmark, for his time in office. It may also be said, of this high point, that few things became Secretary Powell's tenure more than the leaving of it.

Previously, a sense of dankness and exhaustion was palpable in the department. I might instance the uninspired announcement, shortly before I paid my call, that the secretary of state would not be traveling to Athens to represent the United States at the closing ceremony of the Olympic Games after all. The Department of State, which made the announcement only on the day of Powell's planned departure, gave various official and unofficial explanations for this extremely short-notice cancellation. No, the secretary was not especially concerned about security. (A demonstration of two thousand people organized by leftists and anarchists on the preceding Friday had been mild by Athenian standards, and much worse was predicted. The forces of international terrorism had stayed away altogether.) On the other hand, one State Department official said, the secretary "didn't want anything untoward and did not want the complications of any visit to distract from the end of a very successful Olympics." Poorly phrased as it was, this might have been an intelligible reason for declining to attend the ceremony in the first place. But as an excuse for withdrawing at the last possible moment, it sounded a bit hollow and graceless. Another State Department aide only made matters worse (and perhaps went somewhat "off message") when he revealed that Secretary Powell had been the one to ask the White House if he could represent the United States at the ceremony. It shows a fair degree of vanity to suppose that one's own presence, booked or unbooked, could by itself be a "distraction" from a global gala on the Olympic scale. And by this standard, if it is a standard, the United States should always avoid high-level attendance at major international gatherings.

Would I be straining the patience of the reader if I extended this example just a little further? The Greek authorities spent an estimated $1.2 billion on surveillance and security systems for the games, much of it at US urging. The newly enlarged NATO alliance contributed air, land, and sea forces to guarantee further protection. In addition to attending the ceremony, the secretary was to have met officials in Athens to review developments in Cyprus. And Colin Powell canceled just like that.

The combined weariness and solipsism of this behavior sent me back to read the profile of the secretary, by Wil Hylton in an issue of *GQ* two months earlier. Here we were told on the record by Powell's chief of staff, Larry Wilkerson, that the secretary was "tired. Mentally and physically. And if the president were to ask him to stay on—if the president is reelected and the president were to ask him to stay on, he might for a transitional period, but I don't think he'd want to do another four years." In addition to this, we gathered from Wilkerson, it had been a bit much putting up with all the neoconservatives the president had also seen fit to hire. A bit more than a bit much, to judge by this remark: "I don't care whether utopians are Vladimir Lenin on a sealed train to Moscow or Paul Wolfowitz." (This allusion to Washington Bolshevism is eclipsed in an undenied remark in Bob Woodward's *Plan of Attack*, in which the secretary himself refers to Dick Cheney supporters in the Pentagon as the "Gestapo office.")

From William Jennings Bryan to Cyrus Vance, history used to suggest a remedy for secretaries of state who became demoralized or disillusioned with the policies pursued by their presidents: resignation. More than just quitting, resignation also at least implies an acceptance of responsibility (as it did, for example, when Lord Carrington resigned as Prime Minister Margaret Thatcher's foreign secretary over the Falklands imbroglio). But with Powell, one has never been entirely sure whether he considers collective responsibility to be a part of his cabinet rank. Instead, he offers a grudging willingness to stay on, for

a little bit at least, if invited—no, make that pressed—to do so. This
attitude is normally associated either with insufferable guests, or with
people who appear to believe that they are performing the thankless
task of holding up the sky.

Neither a Bush nor—one assumes—a Kerry presidency will now
feature Colin Powell as secretary of state. So the time has come to
ask: Will he be as much missed as all that? What were the qualities
that defined his stewardship? One can be reasonably certain of what
the secretary, and his partisans, would want to have said of him. In
general, he preferred the arts of diplomacy, patience, and negotiation
to the murk of war and the yells of combat. Very well. How ably did
he vindicate this preference?

In the early months of the Bush administration, Powell certainly
did crucial work in defusing a potentially ugly and vertiginous conflict
that erupted suddenly after the April 1, 2001, collision of a US EP-3
spy plane with a perhaps overzealous Chinese fighter aircraft. Those in
Washington who had been undismayed by the idea of a confrontation
with Beijing on various matters of principle would probably now agree
that, whatever those matters of principle are and were, that would
not have been the ideal moment, or indeed pretext, at which to put
them to a trial of strength. And the bad moment passed, without the
United States having to humiliate itself by making too many apolo-
gies. One might wish for the return of the time when our world was
so easily managed.

But here is exactly what Powell's critics maintain: he does not
sufficiently understand that the world has since become more dangerous and less "manageable," and he is too willing to bargain with,
and perhaps even to apologize to, those who do not wish the United
States well. He may indeed favor the venerable traditions of negotiation and multilateralism. Yet what reward has this touching faith
brought him? The chief evidence against him would be his attempt
to prolong the political life of Yasir Arafat; his reluctance to believe
that Saddam Hussein was incorrigible short of war; his belief in the
good faith of the Saudis; and his willingness, right up until September

2004, to extend deadlines in Sudan. (Some on the Virginia side of the Potomac have duly noted that he had no difficulty recognizing a deadly enemy, and leaking accordingly, when that enemy was in the Department of Defense.)

There would be no need to mention the "Quartet"—the all-inclusive Powellite force that comprises (or comprised; it's hard to say) the United States, the United Nations, the European Union, and Russia—if its utter failure had only involved that cemetery of diplomacy, the Israeli-Palestinian conflict. More important to us is the question, Does the dogma of multilateralism outweigh all experience? Recent history suggests an answer. The Europeans failed their very first post–Cold War test, in directly neighboring Bosnia and Herzegovina, and had to implore American help. The Gulf Arabs, and their partial allies in Egypt and Syria, could not have recovered statehood for Kuwait on their own, and had to beseech the help of the United States, which—on that basis—was able to recruit an overpowering majority in the United Nations. Colin Powell as national security advisor and Colin Powell as chairman of the Joint Chiefs of Staff sternly opposed both rescue operations until the balance in Washington shifted decisively against him. On the issue of the former Yugoslavia, he had a celebrated confrontation with then UN Ambassador Madeleine Albright, who accused him of being unwilling to employ military superiority in any circumstances.

We have a fairly accurate picture of what this secretary thought, and did, after September 11, 2001. No serious person needs even to read between the lines of Woodward's two volumes, *Bush at War*, succeeded by the much superior *Plan of Attack*. To the annoyance of many within the administration, especially concerning the first book, Powell was to all intents and purposes being quoted firsthand.

But he was also being cited, in his own name and in real time, and in his own capacity, in public. It's true that directly after September 11, he expressed skepticism about Deputy Secretary of Defense Paul Wolfowitz's plan for "ending states who sponsor terrorism," and a more general skepticism about regime change, a skepticism quite consistent with his entire political past. But he also made the most cogent presentation of any cabinet member, right in front of the UN General Assembly and the entire world, making the case that time had run out for Saddam Hussein.

Here, then, might be the nub. Powell, and his most loyal subordinate Richard Armitage, assured us in minute detail that the secretary was not content to spout any form of words handed to him. He is known to have spent many painful hours winnowing and refining that presentation. George Tenet, then the director of US central intelligence, sat conspicuously behind him as if in confirmation that the two US government agencies most doubtful about regime change were, at any rate, of one mind about the regime in question. Yet, several months later, while being interviewed by NBC journalist Tim Russert, the secretary appeared to suggest that he had been led astray by opportunistic intelligence provided through the Iraqi National Congress of Ahmad Chalabi: a man who was a bête noire at State and CIA for many years. One need only imagine what Dean Rusk or Adlai Stevenson might have done, had they learned too late that someone had faked or "improved" the U-2 photography over Cuba that they waved in the face of the world and shook in the face of the Soviet delegation. Resignation would have been the least of it. And somebody would have been fired (which, strangely enough in this case, nobody has).

During this same period, the Department of State had every opportunity to prove the relative superiority of diplomacy and alliance building over "saber rattling," or whatever we agree to call it. European and other capitals could have been subject to a vast American effort of persuasion, and free media across the world could have been offered some "public diplomacy," too. Powell inaugurated his tenure at Foggy Bottom with a speech to the staff in which he had said that he would be a friend of the diplomatic corps. He even got the president to come to the department and speak encouraging words. Yet can anyone cite any effort, by any accredited American representative overseas, to make the administration's case? And can anyone recall, without acute embarrassment, the expensive and useless tactics of soft-core public relations and pseudo-MTV with which former Undersecretary of State for Public Diplomacy and Public Affairs Margaret Tutwiler and others briefly attempted to boost America's "image"? So dire was this defeat, in fact, that the lack of enthusiasm or allies was used as evidence in itself that the policy must somehow be wrong.

The official historian of the State Department has calculated that Powell will have traveled less than any secretary in more than three decades. His three immediate predecessors voyaged abroad an average of 45 percent more than him. "Shuttle diplomacy" may well have been overpromoted by Henry Kissinger, but a *politique de présence* has an importance of its own, and Powell should not forget that it was very largely his own personality—large, affable, calm, and, yes, originally Caribbean—that landed him the post to begin with. I myself doubt that a diplomatic "offensive" by Powell would have melted the heart of the Élysée, but he incurs criticism not for failing, but for not trying. And then he incurs further criticism for indicating dissent from a major policy, partly on the grounds that it did not command enough sympathy overseas.

So why didn't Powell resign? The kindest explanation would seem to be that it didn't cross his mind. He assumed himself unsackable, almost certainly correctly. And he could therefore continue to have things both ways, conducting his own private diplomacy through Woodward if things didn't suit him. This experience was not exactly a first: as chairman of the joint chiefs, he had expressed himself freely on matters more properly decided by civilian authority, such as the future of Bosnia or the role of homosexuals in the military. Indeed, it's thinkable that he exerted more influence on policy when he was not secretary.

To inquire about his stand on the principle of resignation is a bit like asking whether he'd ever have deigned to run for president. Here again, he felt entitled to be flirtatious and noncommittal, keeping the voters (or rather the book buyers) guessing until he'd finished his tour with the 1995 memoir, *My American Journey*. It was in those pages, incidentally, that he disclosed what has since become evident: "Having seen much of the world and having lived on planes for years, I am no longer much interested in travel."

It's not only the frequency, or lack of it, in Powell's trips. It's also the duration. By July of this year, he had spent less than twenty-four hours in Sudan. He may possibly have been right that the Sudanese authorities needed to be engaged rather than isolated, condemned, and subjected to hostile pressure, in respect to their conduct in Darfur and elsewhere. (He had better have been right: even as Powell cautioned against military intervention, Slobodan Milosevic employed similar breathing spaces to carry out ethnic cleansing in the former Yugoslavia.) But how much seriousness does this level of "engagement" show?

There is, one cannot help feeling, something in Colin Powell that likes to give away the store. While bidding, not too hard, for the Chilean vote at the United Nations, he stated during a televised town hall interview that the United States had nothing to be proud of in the 1973 overthrow of Chilean president Salvador Allende. When the terrible revelations from the Abu Ghraib prison were published, Powell, in the course of one interview, at first denied that he had ever seen anything like it in Vietnam, and then proceeded to evoke the memory of My Lai. This writer had better come clean and agree that it was high time to make an official statement about Chile, and indeed about My Lai. But perhaps not when vote-hunting in the Chilean case.

A more solemn and considered remark at an earlier or later date might have been more dignified. And perhaps not to pile on the agony as secretary of state in the Abu Ghraib case, where there had been neither a massacre nor a proven high-level cover-up. (And perhaps especially not if, as a young officer in Vietnam—as Powell was—one had been all too willing to dismiss early reports of atrocities.)

Colin Powell reportedly became incensed on January 20, 2003, when, after many exhausting negotiations at the United Nations, he discovered from Dominique de Villepin, then the French minister of foreign affairs, that Paris thought that "nothing! nothing!" justified the armed enforcement of Resolution 1441 compelling Iraq to yield to UN inspections. This, Powell felt, was something that he might well have been told before he wasted his time. But it is also something that he could have known before he wasted that time (and, dare one hint) the time of others, too. In a much-underreported speech to France's assembled ambassadors on August 26, 2004, the new French minister of foreign affairs Michel Barnier said that it was France that has become isolated, even "arrogant," and that it could not flourish without allies. He was noted for not even mentioning the United States in his cautious remarks.

Thus, one might mark the end of the Powell tenure by noting that there is always room for quiet diplomacy, but by adding that "quiet diplomacy" may not necessarily involve deniable smirks and disclaimers concerning a central policy; that such smirks and disclaimers are especially unpersuasive when the policy is in trouble; that to tell the hometown paper that your rivals and critics are Communists and Nazis isn't all that "diplomatic" in any case, and that faintness and ambiguity are not the same as patience, discretion, and reticence.

(*Foreign Policy*, October 26, 2009)

Shut Up about Armenians or We'll Hurt Them Again

—◦◦◦◦◦—

A PRIL IS THE cruelest month for the people of Armenia, who every year at this season have to suffer a continuing tragedy and a humiliation. The tragedy is that of commemorating the huge number of their ancestors who were exterminated by the Ottoman Muslim caliphate in a campaign of state-planned mass murder that began in April 1915. The humiliation is of hearing, year after year, that the Turkish authorities simply deny that these appalling events ever occurred or that the killings constituted "genocide."

In a technical and pedantic sense, the word "genocide" does not, in fact, apply, since it only entered our vocabulary in 1943. (It was coined by a scholar named Raphael Lemkin, who for rather self-evident reasons in that even more awful year wanted a legal term for the intersection between racism and bloodlust and saw Armenia as the precedent for what was then happening in Poland.) I still rather prefer the phrase used by America's then-ambassador to Turkey, Henry Morgenthau. Reporting to Washington about what his consular agents were telling him of the foul doings in the Ottoman provinces of Harput and Van in particular, he employed the striking words "race extermination." (See the imperishable book *The Slaughterhouse Province* for some of the cold diplomatic dispatches of that period.) Terrible enough in itself, Morgenthau's expression did not quite comprehend the later erasure of all traces of Armenian life, from the destruction of their churches and libraries and institutes to the crude altering of official Turkish maps and schoolbooks to deny that there had ever been an Armenia in the first place.

This year, the House foreign affairs committee in Washington and the parliament of Sweden joined the growing number of political bodies that have decided to call the slaughter by its right name. I quote now from a statement in response by Recep Tayyip Erdogan, the current prime minister of Turkey and the leader of its Islamist party:

> In my country there are 170,000 Armenians. Seventy thousand of them are citizens. We tolerate 100,000 more. So, what am I going to do tomorrow? If necessary I will tell the 100,000: OK, time to go back to your country. Why? They are not my citizens. I am not obliged to keep them in my country.

This extraordinary threat was not made at some stupid rally in a fly-blown town. It was uttered in England, on March 17, on the Turkish-language service of the BBC. Just to be clear, then, about the view of Turkey's chief statesman: if democratic assemblies dare to mention the ethnic cleansing of Armenians in the twentieth century, I will personally complete that cleansing in the twenty-first!

Where to begin? Turkish "guest workers" are to be found in great numbers all through the European Union, membership of which is a declared Turkish objective. How would the world respond if a European prime minister called for the mass deportation of all Turks? Yet Erdogan's xenophobic demagoguery attracted precisely no condemnation from Washington or Brussels. He probably overestimated the number of "tolerated" economic refugees from neighboring and former Soviet Armenia, but is it not interesting that he keeps a count in his head? And a count of the tiny number of surviving Turkish Armenians as well?

The outburst strengthens the already strong case for considering Erdogan to be somewhat personally unhinged. In Davos in January 2009, he stormed out of a panel discussion with the head of the Arab League and with Israeli president Shimon Peres, having gone purple and grabbed the arm of the moderator who tried to calm him. On that occasion, he yelled that Israelis in Gaza knew too well "how to kill"—which might be true but which seems to betray at best an envy on his part. Turkish nationalists have also told me that he was out of control because he disliked the fact that the moderator—David Ignatius of the *Washington Post*—is himself of Armenian descent. A short while later, at a NATO summit in Turkey, Erdogan went into another tantrum at the idea that former prime minister Anders Fogh Rasmussen of Denmark would be chosen as the next head of the alliance. In this case, it was cartoons published on Danish soil that frayed Erdogan's evidently fragile composure.

In Turkey itself, the continuing denial has abysmal cultural and political consequences. The country's best-known novelist, Orhan Pamuk, was dragged before a court in 2005 for acknowledging Turkey's role in the destruction of Armenia. Had he not been the winner of a Nobel Prize, it might have gone very hard for him, as it has for prominent and brave intellectuals like Murat Belge. Turkish-Armenian editor Hrant Dink, also prosecuted under a state law forbidding discussion of the past, was shot down in the street by an assassin who was later photographed in the company of beaming, compliant policemen.

The original crime, in other words, defeats all efforts to cover it up. And the denial necessitates continuing secondary crimes. In 1955, a government-sponsored pogrom in Istanbul burned out most of the city's remaining Armenians, along with thousands of Jews and Greeks and other infidels. The state-codified concept of mandatory Turkishness has been used to negate the rights and obliterate the language of the country's enormous Kurdish population and to create an armed colony of settlers and occupiers on the soil of Cyprus, a democratic member of the European Union.

So it is not just a disaster for Turkey that it has a prime minister who suffers from morbid disorders of the personality. Under these conditions, his great country can never hope to be an acceptable member of Europe or a reliable member of NATO. And history is cunning: the dead of Armenia will never cease to cry out. Nor, on their behalf, should we cease to do so. Let Turkey's unstable leader foam all he wants when other parliaments and congresses discuss Armenia and seek the truth about it. The grotesque fact remains that the one parliament that *should* be debating the question—the Turkish parliament—is forbidden by its own law to do so. While this remains the case, we shall do it for them, and without any apology, until they produce the one that is forthcoming from them.

(*Slate*, April 5, 2010)

Hezbollah's Progress

〜⧉〜

WRITING FROM SOUTHERN Lebanon in the mid-to-late 1970s, during the continuing war of attrition between Israel and the PLO and at a time when the country's long-relegated Shiite minority was just beginning to get itself organized, I noticed the presence of an almost unremarked token force of Iranian troops. These had been dispatched by the Shah of Iran, who (as we tend to forget) was ever-mindful of his title Shadow of God and of his anointed role as protector of the Shiites. Commenting more presciently than I knew, I said that these soldiers would probably be needed back home before too long to safeguard the peacock throne.

At that time, it would have been entirely impossible to picture any Iranian head of state visiting multicultural Lebanon as a plenipotentiary and being feted all the way to within yelling distance of the Israeli border. Yet last week President Mahmoud Ahmadinejad managed this feat almost without effort. A man who has managed to escape serious inconvenience for his illegal pursuit of nuclear weapons and who has pitilessly repressed and cheated his own people can appear on neutral soil as the patron of the Party of God because his regime shares that party's pitiless attitude toward the state of Israel and its biting contempt for all the Arab and Muslim "moderates" who would even consider a compromise with it.

In a way, an even more dramatic measure of the progress of Hezbollah and its patrons involves a comparison with only a few years ago. In February 2005, former Lebanese prime minister Rafik Hariri was blown to shreds in broad daylight, his murder capping a series of assassinations of politicians and journalists who had been critical of the Syrian presence in their country. So immense was the democratic popular revulsion against this criminality that Damascus was compelled to withdraw its occupying forces, and an international tribunal was convened to investigate the complicity of the Syrian Baathists, and by implication their holy Hezbollah proxy, and in turn that proxy's other supporter in Tehran. Aided, in my opinion, by the momentum created by the fall of Saddam Hussein, and encouraged even by French support for the relevant UN resolutions, the local prestige of the United States became very high.

Now mark the sequel. The leaders of all other parties and factions in Lebanon, from Christian to Druze, cringe with fear when the name of Hezbollah's leader, Hassan Nasrallah, is mentioned. The once-vaunted tribunal, long stalled, has been preempted by highly credible threats of violence if its belated findings turn out to be awkward for Syria or Hezbollah. The son of the murdered Hariri, like the son of the previously murdered Druze leader Kamal Jumblatt, has been forced to "make nice" in the most degrading fashion with the capo Bashar Assad, whose family almost certainly slew the heads of theirs. And the Party of God possesses two vetoes, one over the outcome of any Lebanese election it does not win and another on the timing of the next war with Israel to be launched from Lebanese territory.

What brought about this stark reversal? The first cause is Israel's crass intervention in Lebanon in 2006, responding to a clever Hezbollah provocation (a raid and a kidnap of Israeli soldiers) that was almost certainly designed to produce the response that it did. The second cause is the palpable loss of interest in Lebanon on the part of the United States. The March 14 coalition—named for the date of the triumphant intercommunal rally against Syria that followed Hariri's assassination—is splintering back into sectarianism and impotence. And what prudent Lebanese citizen, with Syria so nearby, Iran acting like a pre-nuclear regional superpower, and a humiliated Washington squandering all its effort on the predictable and pathetic failure of the Israel-Palestine "peace process," would not begin to adjust to the rugged new reality?

A depressingly excellent book on the contours of that new reality is provided by Thanassis Cambanis. *A Privilege to Die* lays out the near-brilliant way in which Hezbollah manages to be both the party of the downtrodden and the puppet of two of the area's most retrograde dictatorships. Visiting Beirut not long after Hezbollah had been exposed as an accomplice to Syria *and* as the party that had brought Israel's devastating reprisals upon the innocent, I was impressed, despite myself, by the discipline and enthusiasm of one of Nasrallah's rallies in the south of the city. Cambanis shows how the trick is pulled. With what you might call its "soft" power, the Party of God rebuilds the shattered slums, provides welfare and education, and recruits the children into its version of a Boy Scout movement, this time dedicated to martyrdom and revenge. With its "hard" power, it provides constant reminders of what can happen to anyone who looks askance at its achievements. Its savvy use of media provides a continual menu of thrilling racial and religious hatred against the Jews. And its frontline status on Israel's northern frontier allows it to insult all "moderate" regimes as poltroons and castrati unwilling to sacrifice to restore Arab and Muslim honor. Many Sunni Arabs hate and detest Hezbollah, but none fail to fear and thus to respect it, which Nasrallah correctly regards as the main thing.

In Greek legend there was a fighter named Antaeus who drew strength from the earth even when he was flung down. It took Hercules to work out his vulnerability as a wrestler. Hezbollah loves death, thrives on defeat and disaster, and is rapidly moving from being a state within a state to becoming the master of what was once the most cosmopolitan and democratic country in the Middle East. Meanwhile, a former superpower—no Hercules—is permitting itself to be made a hostage and laughingstock by a squalid factional fight within the Israeli right wing involving the time and scale of petty land theft by zealots and fanatics. Only a few years from now, this, too, will seem hard to believe, as well as shameful and unpardonable.

(*Slate*, October 18, 2010)

The Politicians We Deserve

ASKING MY HOSTS in Connecticut if there was anything worth
noting about the upcoming elections in their great state, I received the reply, "Well, we have a guy who wants to be senator who
lied about his record of service in Vietnam, and a woman who wants
to be senator who has run World Wrestling Entertainment and seems
like a tough lady." Though full enough of curiosity to occupy, say, one
course of lunch, that still didn't seem to furnish enough material to
keep the mind focused on politics for very long.

And this dearth—of genuine topics and of convincing or even plau-
sible candidates—appears to extend from coast to coast. In New York,
a rather shopworn son of one Democratic dynasty (and ex-member
by marriage of another) is "facing off," as people like to say, against a
provincial thug with a line in pseudo-tough talk. In California, where
the urgent question of something suspiciously like state failure is staring the electorate in the face, the Brown-Whitman contest hasn't yet
risen even to the level of the trivial.

Speaking of things that become blindingly obvious once you notice
them, it was only while being interviewed the other day that I came
to fully appreciate something that I already knew. I have lived in
Washington, DC, for almost three decades. My own generation is now
getting long in the tooth, having lived through some intensely politi-

cal decades, but when I reflect back, I can only think of two or three members of it who ever tried to run for Congress. Some of this had to do with a 1960s-based suspicion of what used to be dismissively called "electoral politics," but the general reluctance goes far deeper than that. And among the politically conscious who are decades younger and up-and-coming, the revulsion appears to be more profound still.

I could introduce you to dozens of enthusiastic and intelligent people, highly aware of "the issues" and very well informed on all questions from human rights to world trade to counterinsurgency, to none of whom it would occur to subject themselves to what passes for the political "arena." They are willing to give up potentially more lucrative careers in order to work on important questions and expand the limits of what is currently thinkable politically, but the great honor and distinction of serving their country in the legislature is only offered to them at a price that is now way too steep.

Consider: What normal person would consider risking their career and their family life in order to undergo the incessant barrage of intrusive questioning about every aspect of their lives since well before college? To face the constant pettifogging and chatter of Facebook and Twitter and have to boast of how many false friends they had made in a weird cyberland? And if only that was the least of it. Then comes the treadmill of fund-raising and the unending tyranny of the opinion polls, which many media systems now use as a substitute for news and as a means of creating stories rather than reporting them. And, even if it "works," most of your time in Washington would be spent raising the dough to hang on to your job. No wonder that the best lack all conviction.

This may seem to discount or ignore the apparent flood of new political volunteers who go to make up the Tea Party movement. But how fresh and original are these faces? They come from a long and frankly somewhat boring tradition of anti-incumbency and anti-Washington rhetoric, and they are rather an insult to anyone with anything of a political memory. Since when is it truly insurgent to rail against the state of affairs in the nation's capital? How long did it take Gingrich's "rebel" forces in the mid-1990s to become soft-bottomed incumbents in their turn? Many of the cynical veterans of that moment, from Dick Armey to John Boehner, are the effective managers and controllers of the allegedly spontaneous Tea Party wave we see today.

Populism imposes its own humiliations on anyone considering a run. How many times can you stand in front of an audience and state: "I will always put the people of *X* first"? (Quite a lot of times, to judge by recent campaigns.) This is to say no more than that you will be a megaphone for sectional interests and regional mood swings and resentment, a confession that, to you, all politics is yokel. Nothing makes this plainer than this season's awful rash of demagogic attacks on trade with China. In a replay of the stupidity about that "giant sucking sound" that marked the nadir of the Ross Perot populist bubble of two decades ago, educated American voters (and, indirectly, Chinese audiences) are exposed to cartoon clichés of dragons and portraits of Mao Zedong in an attempt to infuse xenophobia into the argument about free trade. Meanwhile, the Chinese are making the only tenders for contracts to build high-speed rail links in the United States, but in Connecticut a few nights ago, would-be Democratic senator Richard Blumenthal (whose main experience of Asia consists of his having lied about serving there) taunted his Republican opponent Linda McMahon for complicity in the manufacture of WWE action toys on the territory of the People's Republic! How low can it go? Much lower, just you wait and see.

(*Slate*, October 11, 2010)

Rosa Luxemburg:
Red Rosa

⸺◦◦◦⸺

THE GENERALLY ACCEPTED verdict on twentieth-century ideology—that its "totalitarian" character eclipses any of the ostensible differences between its "left" and "right" versions—is one that few wish to dispute. Indeed, the very term "totalitarian" was most probably coined by the dissident Marxist Victor Serge, to denote a uniquely modern form of absolutism that essentially sought to abolish the private life and the individual conscience. As with concepts, so with consequences: David Rousset's early classic, *L'Univers concentrationnaire*, foreshadowed the image of "the camp" as the place where the human surplus of brute Utopianism was disposed of, no matter what the claimed character of the regime.

This convergence or symmetry does not automatically translate into a strict moral equivalence. More people may have been consumed by the gulag than by the Nazi *lager* system. Yet Robert Conquest, the preeminent historian of Stalinism, when invited to pass a judgment, found the Hitlerite crimes to be more damnable. Pressed to enlarge

---

Review of *The Letters of Rosa Luxemburg* edited by Georg Adler, Peter Hudis, and Annelies Laschitza

on this, he replied: "I simply feel it to be so." I think the intuition of many morally intelligent people would be the same.

Another way in which a distinction might be drawn is this: we have no real record of any "dissident" writing by the minority of intellectuals who were drawn to fascism and National Socialism. Indeed, were it not for a certain sick fascination with the pornography of violence and racism, there would be scant point in studying the political writings of Louis-Ferdinand Céline, let alone of Alfred Rosenberg, at all. Martin Heidegger and Giovanni Gentile may have laid down an obfuscatory barrage of pseudo-historical justification for the cult of supreme national leadership, but it survives mainly as a curiosity. Most important: it is quite impossible to imagine any terms in which they could ever have formulated a critique of Hitler or Mussolini as having betrayed the original ideals of their respective movements. The ideologies blankly forbade and foreclosed any such contingency.

By contrast, even Lenin's wooden tome *The Development of Capitalism in Russia* constitutes some species of analysis and anatomy, of a kind that would be merely ridiculous to compare with the ravings of *Mein Kampf.* And from the many Marxists who took issue with Lenin, there proceeded a number of works of a high order of seriousness, and failing to scrutinize them would severely limit one's knowledge of modern history. To me, the most brilliant—and the most engaging—of these Marxist intellectuals was Rosa Luxemburg, the Polish-born Jew who was the most charismatic figure in the German Social Democratic Party (SPD).

Bertrand Russell's first book (evolved from a series of lectures he gave in 1896) was on the character of this historic party. Wedded to a rather formalist Marxism in theory, the party in practice provided millions of workers and their families with something like an alternative society within Germany: not merely trade unions but welfare associations, educational institutions, holiday camps, and women's associations. Strongly critical of Prussian militarism, it felt confident enough in 1912 to declare that in the event of war, it would call for strikes and protests, and endeavor to make alliances with fraternal parties in the other combatant nations. In the event, war hysteria proved so damnably potent that the majority of the party capitulated in August 1914 and voted to take part in the greatest fratricide the world had ever seen. (Lenin was so shocked by this that he at first refused to believe that the SPD had in fact deserted its position.) Luxemburg was one of the few of the party's leaders to maintain a stance against the kaiser, and was imprisoned as a consequence. The central tranche of this collection of her letters was written during that bleak incarceration, and that great political relapse. The confusion of the moment is caught in a letter from October 1914, in which she urgently seeks instruction on the best manner of forwarding information by way of Benito Mussolini, entirely unaware that this hitherto antiwar socialist editor had deserted the cause and begun his long swing to the fanatical right.

Slightly lamed since childhood, married only to gain the formalities of citizenship, and famous for the scornfulness of her polemics, Luxemburg was easy to portray as a thwarted and unfeminine personage. But her correspondence shows her to have been an active and ardent lover, as well as a woman constantly distracted from politics by her humanism and her love for nature and literature. In a single letter to her *inamorato* Hans Diefenbach (whose life was to be thrown away on the western front), written from a Breslau jail in the summer of 1917, there are tender and remorseful reflections on the deaths of parents; some crisp appraisals of the style of Romain Rolland; a recommendation that Diefenbach read Hauptmann's *The Fool in Christ, Emanuel Quint*; and some extended observations on the ingenious habits of wasps and birds, as observed through the windows of her cell. Another letter to him earlier in the same year is saturated with their common addiction to the works of Goethe and Schiller, and goes on to offer a spirited hypothesis of a possibly feminist Shakespeare, based on the figure of the unquenchable Rosalind in *As You Like It*. Her favorite word of opprobrium for the war-makers was "barbaric," and it becomes plain that by this she intended no ordinary propaganda slogan, but an intense conviction that European culture itself was being outraged and profaned. She was righter even than she knew.

Her internationalism was so strong that she despised anything to do with lesser or sectarian "identities." This led her to oppose any nationalist claims made by her fellow Poles and fellow Jews (in retrospect, perhaps, a somewhat questionable position for any German politician to have been taking). To her friend Mathilde Wurm, she wrote rebukingly:

What do you want with this theme of the "special suffering of the Jews"? I am just as much concerned with the poor victims on the rubber plantations of Putumayo, the Blacks in Africa with whose corpses the Europeans play catch. You know the words that were written about the great work of the General Staff, about Gen. Trotha's campaign in the Kalahari desert: "And the death rattles of the dying, the demented cries of those driven mad by thirst faded away in the sublime stillness of eternity." Oh that "sublime stillness of eternity," in which so many cries of anguish have faded away *unheard*, they resound within me so strongly that I have no special place in my heart for the ghetto. I feel at home in the entire world, wherever there are clouds and birds and human tears.

The quotation is from a conscience-stricken German soldier in the army of General Lothar von Trotha, who had in 1904 issued a general "extermination order" against the rebellious Herero tribe in what is now Namibia. One feels another crackle of premonition when reading again about this once-notorious atrocity: the imperial ethnologists in German South West Africa who conducted hideous medical experiments on the Herero included the mentors of Josef Mengele, and the first political governor of the province had been Hermann Goering's father. Von Trotha himself became a member of a race-myth cult group calling itself the Thule Society, which was one of the seedbeds of the early Nazi Party. For Luxemburg, the hecatomb of the European war was partly a projection of the brutality of empire back into its metropolis. Her prompting was always to the enlargement of the picture: the concept of the "global" did not in the least intimidate her. Indeed, she took it as her point of departure.

A prewar and pre-incarceration letter to another lover (Kostya Zetkin, son of Clara) is almost entirely devoted to a rhapsodic review of Bach's *Saint Matthew Passion*, ending with praise and thanks for some violets and a glimpse of the antics of her cat, Mimi, who features in many more missives. When jailed, Luxemburg decided with immense regret not to take the animal with her, deeming it wrong to imprison a feline. This may appear mawkish or sentimental, but consider this extract from my favorite of all her letters. Written to Sophie Liebknecht from the same Breslau jail in late December 1917, it describes some Romanian buffalo, pressed into service as beasts of burden by the German army. As they dragged their impossibly heavy load into the prison yard, they continued to be flogged with the blunt end of the whip handle by an exceptionally callous soldier:

Sonyichka, the hide of a buffalo is proverbial for its toughness and thickness, but this tough skin had been broken. During the unloading, all the animals stood there, quite still, exhausted, and the one that was bleeding kept staring into the empty space in front of him with an expression on his black face and in his soft, black eyes like an abused child. It was precisely the expression of a child that has been punished and doesn't know why or what for, doesn't know how to get away from this torment and raw violence. . . . All this time the prisoners had hurriedly busied themselves around the wagon, unloading the heavy sacks and dragging them off into the building; but the soldier stuck both hands in his trouser pockets, paced around the courtyard with long strides, and kept smiling and softly whistling some popular tune to himself. And the entire marvelous panorama of the war passed before my eyes.

That dry closing sentence, I submit, acquits the letter of mawkishness and makes its register of animal torture more like that of Dostoyevsky. It also assists in pointing up the deep contrast with Lenin, who famously distrusted his emotions and tried his best to silence the appeals of nature and art. Though he did once refuse to shoot a vixen because "really, she was so beautiful," he turned away from a performance of Beethoven's *Appassionata* lest its haunting loveliness distract him from the requirements of the struggle, and only emerged from an apparent reverie at the summit of a Swiss mountain to exclaim that the damned Mensheviks were hell-bent on spoiling everything.

Ever since the 1905 upheaval in Russia, Luxemburg had suspected Lenin's faction of what she scornfully termed a "barracks" mentality. A short while after the 1917 revolution, we find her writing a succession of letters, describing the situation in Russia as "abysmal" and the Bolsheviks as deserving of "a terrible tongue-lashing" for their repression of rival parties such as the Social Revolutionaries, and their unilateral decision to abolish the Constituent Assembly. She extends this condemnation to include the police mentality (concerning incessant foreign "conspiracies") that underlay Soviet foreign policy. She singles out a certain "Józef" as a particular exemplar of this attitude, and with yet another shock of premonition, one discovers that this was the "party name" of her fellow Pole Felix Dzerzhinsky, founder of the Cheka and later considered the father of the KGB. It was during this time that Luxemburg made her imperishable defense of free speech, boldly stating that the concept was meaningless unless it meant the freedom of "the one who thinks differently."

Still, her general optimism about the tide of revolution that obliterated the monarchs and empires that had started the war can give one a lump in the throat. Writing in December 1917, she exclaimed:

> In Russia the time of pogroms has passed once and for all. The strength of the workers and of socialism there is much too strong for that. . . . I can sooner imagine—pogroms against Jews here in Germany.

Perhaps aware that she was giving a hostage to fortune, she hastily added, "Anyhow an atmosphere conducive to that prevails here, one of viciousness, cowardice, reaction, and thick-headedness."

This last premonition was the most sobering of all. Released from prison by the strikes and mutinies that accompanied the abdication of the kaiser, Luxemburg was propelled to the center of revolutionary politics and journalism in Berlin. In January 1919 she was arrested, and her capacious skull splintered by a rifle butt in the hands of a member of the Freikorps, the debased militia that was to form the pattern and nucleus of the Brownshirts. "In her assassination," wrote Isaac Deutscher, "Hohenzollern Germany celebrated its last triumph and Nazi Germany its first." Over her corpse—later thrown into the Landwehr Canal—was to step a barbarism even more ruthless and intense than any she had dared to imagine. Had Germany gone the other way, is it completely fanciful to imagine an outcome that would have preempted not just Nazism but, by precept and example, Stalinism, too? However debatable that might be, one cannot read the writings of Rosa Luxemburg, even at this distance, without an acute yet mournful awareness of what Perry Anderson once termed "the history of possibility."

(*The Atlantic*, June 2011)

Joan Didion: Blue Nights

⎯⎯◦∞◦⎯⎯

L IKE THE EXPERIENCE of warfare, the endurance of grave or
terminal illness involves long periods of tedium and anxiety, punctuated by briefer interludes of stark terror and pain. This endurance
need not necessarily be one's own: indeed, the experience of watching over a sibling or mate in extremis can be even more acute. But
nothing, according to the experts, compares to the clutching, choking
nightmare that engulfs the one who is slowly bereft of a child.

It is horrible to see oneself die without children. Napoléon Bonaparte
said that.
What greater grief can there be for mortals than to see their children
dead. Euripides said that.
When we talk about mortality we are talking about our children.
I said that.

Joan Didion, here slightly syncopating in the Bob Dylan manner,
has striven with intense dignity and courage in *Blue Nights* to deepen
and extend the effect of *The Year of Magical Thinking*, her 2005 narrative of the near-simultaneous sudden death of her husband, John
Gregory Dunne, and the onset of the fatal illness of their daughter,
Quintana Roo Dunne Michael. In the course of setting it down, she

came to realize that she could no longer compose in the old style: the one that she had "supposed to be like writing music."

And what kind of music could this have been, except the blues? But blue is more than the shade of a symphony. It is where the "bolt" comes from, as Didion mordantly notes. It can register the transit of an entire evening, from the first, faint translucent gloaming to the near-inky cerulean black.

The long day wanes along a spectrum of blue. So did the short life of the keen, merry girl, who wasn't *too* spoiled by showbiz or room service, who shrewdly opposed her mother's choice of poem at her father's memorial service. And whose solemn recommendation about death was "Don't dwell on it."

That last choice is not available to her mother:

> Vanish.
> Pass into nothingness: the Keats line that frightened her.
> Fade as the blue nights fade, go as the brightness goes.
> Go back into the blue.
> I myself placed her ashes in the wall.
> I myself saw the cathedral doors locked at six.
> I know what it is I am now experiencing.
> I know what the frailty is, I know what the fear is.
> The fear is not for what is lost.
> What is lost is already in the wall.
> What is lost is already behind the locked doors.
> The fear is for what is still to be lost.
> You may see nothing still to be lost.
> Yet there is no day in her life on which I do not see her.

In this supremely tender work of memory, Didion is paradoxically insistent that as long as one person is condemned to remember, there can still be pain and loss and anguish.

The True Spirit of Christmas

EVER SINCE TOM Lehrer recorded his imperishable anti-Christmas ditty all those years ago, the small but growing minority who view the end of December with existential dread has had a seasonal "carol" all of its own:

Christmas time is here by golly: disapproval would be folly.
Deck the halls with hunks of holly, fill the cup and don't say
* when.*
Kill the turkeys, ducks and chickens, mix the punch, drag out the
* Dickens.*
Even though the prospect sickens—brother, here we go again.

I used to know all the words to this song and can still recall most of them, but unless I am mistaken, the religious character of the festivities is barely if at all mentioned. I suppose there is the line, "Angels we have heard on high, tell us to go out—and buy."

Yet this is hardly subversive at all. Religious sermons against the "commercialization" of Christmas have also been a staple of the season ever since I can remember. A root-and-branch resistance to the holiday spirit would have to be a lot tougher than that. It's fairly easy to be a charter member of the Tom Lehrer Club, which probably embraces a fair number of the intellectual classes and has sympathizers even in the most surprising families.

But the thing about the annual culture war that would probably most surprise those who want to "keep the Christ in Christmas" is this: the original Puritan Protestants regarded the whole enterprise as blasphemous. Under the rule of Oliver Cromwell in England, Christmas festivities were banned outright. The same was true in some of the early Pilgrim settlements in North America.

Last year I read a recent interview with the priest of one of the oldest Roman Catholic churches in New York, located downtown and near Wall Street. Taking a stand in favor of Imam Rauf's "Ground Zero" project, he pointed to some parish records showing hostile picketing of his church in the eighteenth century. The pious protestors had been voicing their suspicion that a profane and popish ceremonial of "Christ Mass" was being conducted within.

Now, *that* was a time when Americans took their religion seriously. But we know enough about Puritans to suspect that what they really disliked was the idea of a holiday where people would imbibe strong drink and generally make merry. (Scottish Presbyterians did not relax their hostility to Yuletide celebrations until well into the twentieth century.) And the word "Yule" must be significant here as well, since pagans of all sorts have been roistering at the winter solstice ever since records were kept, and Christians have been faced with the choice of either trying to beat them or join them.

In their already discrepant accounts of the miraculous birth, the four gospels give us no clue as to what time of year—or even what year—it is supposed to have taken place. And thus the iconography of Christmas is ridiculously mixed in with reindeer, holly, snow scenes, and other phenomena peculiar to northern European myth. (Three words for those who want to put the Christ back in Christmas: Jingle Bell Rock.) There used to be an urban legend about a Japanese department store that tried too hard to symbolize the Christmas spirit, and to show itself accessible to Western visitors, by mounting a display of a Santa Claus figure nailed to a cross. Unfounded as it turned out, this wouldn't have been off by much.

You would have to be religiously observant and austere yourself, then, to really seek a ban on Christmas. But it can be almost as objectionable to be made to take part in something as to be forbidden to do so. The reason for the success of the Lehrer song is that it so perfectly captures the sense of irritated, bored resignation that descends on so many of us at this time of year. By "this time of year," I mean something that starts no later than Thanksgiving (and often sooner) and pervades the entire atmosphere until December 25.

If you take no stock in the main Christian festival of Easter, or if you are a non-Jew who has no interest in atoning in the fall, you have an all-American fighting chance of being able to ignore these events, or of being only briefly subjected to parking restrictions in Manhattan. But if Christmas has the least tendency to get you down, then lots of luck. You have to avoid the airports, the train stations, the malls, the stores, the media, and the multiplexes. You will be double-teamed by Bing Crosby and the herald angels wherever you go. And this for a whole unyielding month of the calendar.

I realize that I do not know what happens in the prison system. But I do know what happens by way of compulsory jollity in the hospitals and clinics and waiting rooms, and it's a grueling test of any citizen's capacity to be used for so long as a captive audience.

I once tried to write an article, perhaps rather straining for effect, describing the experience as too much like living for four weeks in the atmosphere of a one-party state. "Come on," I hear you say. But by how much would I be exaggerating? The same songs and music played everywhere, all the time. The same uniform slogans and exhortations, endlessly displayed and repeated. The same sentimental stress on the sheer joy of having a Dear Leader to adore. As I pressed on I began almost to persuade myself. The serried ranks of beaming schoolchildren, chanting the same uplifting mush. The cowed parents, in terror of being unmasked by their offspring for insufficient participation in the glorious events. . . . "Come on," yourself. How wrong am I?

Compulsory bad taste isn't a good cultural sign either. In their eagerness to show loyalty, entire families compose long letters of confessional drool, celebrating the achievements of the previous year and swearing to surpass them in the next. These letters are delivered and sometimes, to the shame of their authors, also read aloud. As if to celebrate some unprecedented triumph in the agricultural sphere, of the sort that leads to an undreamed-of surplus, the survivors (and, one sometimes suspects, the sick and wounded) of the nation's turkey-camps are rounded up and executed for a second great annual immolation.

Then there's another consideration, again deftly touched-upon by Lehrer:

Relations sparing no expense'll
Send some useless old utensil.
Or a matching pen-and-pencil: just the thing I need, how
    nice . . .

One of my many reasons for not being a Christian is my objection to compulsory love. How much less appealing is the notion of obligatory generosity. To feel pressed to give a present is also to feel oneself passively exerting the equivalent unwelcome pressure upon other people.

I don't think I have been unusually unfortunate with my family and friends, but I present as evidence my tie rack. Nobody who knows me has ever seen me wear a tie except under protest, and the few that I do possess of my own volition are accidental trophies, "given" to me by the maitre d's of places where neckwear is compulsory. Yet somehow I possess a drawerful of new, unopened examples of these useless items of male apparel.

Nobody derived any pleasure from either the giving or the receiving, and it's appalling to see what some stores feel they can charge for a tie. Do I blush to think of some of my reciprocal gestures? Sure I do. Don't pretend not to know what I am talking about. It's like the gradual degradation of another annual ritual, whereby all schoolchildren are required to give valentines to everybody in the class. Nobody's feelings are hurt, they tell me, but the entire point of sending a valentine in the first place has been deliberately destroyed. If I feel like giving you a gift I'll try and make sure that (a) it's worth remembering and (b) that it comes as a nice surprise. (I like to think that some of my valentines in the past packed a bit of a punch as well.)

But the Christmas cycle imposes a deadening routine and predictability. This is why the accidental genius of Charles Dickens is to have made, of Ebenezer Scrooge, the only character in the story who has any personality to him—and the one whose stoic attempt at a futile resistance is invoked under the breath more than most people care to admit. And when the author of *A Christmas Carol* was writing, the great clanking machinery of a Ramadan-length Christmas had not got into gear, and English people reserved December 26 ("Boxing Day") for the exchange of tokens.

There is a contradiction in my position, because many of the crimes against taste and proportion this month are effectively secular and material in tone, and have unmoored themselves from whatever is supposed to have happened in Bethlehem in the reign of Caesar Augustus. (Visit Bethlehem today and linger in awe in "Manger Square" if you want to see kitsch defined.)

Indeed, a soggy version of multiculturalism has mandated that "the holidays" also take in a dubious episode from the Jewish apocrypha as well as Kwanzaa, an Afrocentric fabrication that comes to us courtesy of Ron Karenga, who we must also thank as the inventor of "ebonics." This adds, of course, to the sheer length and dutiful inclusiveness of the business. When Christmas was still Christmas, a paid-up Jewish liberal like Anthony Lewis could get seasonal outrage out of Nixon's and Kissinger's bombardment of Vietnam, referring with high-minded irony to the "Christmas bombing," almost as if hardened Vietnamese Marxists would have preferred to be strafed on Labor Day.

But making the celebrations confessionally pluralistic, and leaching them of their Christian monopoly, does not make them any less religious. Thus to the most Scrooge-like of all questions: Is there a constitutional issue here?

Much as one might want to avoid an annual freshet of legalism, it is very hard to argue that there is not. I have no idea how many churches and synagogues there are in the United States (there seem to be quite a number, many of them tax-exempt), but if the "holy days" were only celebrated on these premises, or on boards and signs visible from them, the effect would already be very impressive. The same is true if we limit the effect to the number of believers whose homes display candles, lights, symbols, Scandinavian wildlife and vegetation, and whatever else the spirit moves them to exhibit.

But what is all this clutter doing on the White House lawn or in the public rooms of the executive mansion, or on public property and in public schools? Quite apart from the clear stipulations of the First Amendment, this seems to me to violate the Tocquevillian principle that American religion is strictly based on the voluntary principle and neither requires nor deserves any taxpayer-funded endorsement.

It also offends—by being so much in my face, without my having requested it and in spite of polite entreaties to desist—another celebrated precept about the right to be let alone. A manger on your lawn makes me yawn. A reindeer that strays from your lawn to mine is a nuisance at any time of year. Angels and menorahs on the White House lawn are an infraction of the Establishment Clause, which is as much designed to prevent religion from being corrupted by the state as it is to protect the public square from clerical encroachment.

The "wall of separation" has to be patrolled in small things as well as big ones. When President Jefferson wrote his famous letter to the Baptists of Danbury, Connecticut, assuring them of the protection of this very wall, it was because they had written to him, afraid of persecution by the Congregationalists of Danbury, Connecticut. This now seems as remote to us as a Calvinist anti-Christmas protest outside a Catholic church in Manhattan. But it is only remote because such scruple and consistency were employed to defend the principle in matters great and small.

At this time of year, Mr. Jefferson would close his correspondence in words dry enough to be characteristic of him, yet somehow convivial enough to be thinkable in the mouth of Mr. Pickwick: "With the compliments of the season." I wouldn't want to be tempted any further than that.

(*The Wall Street Journal*, December 24, 2011)

Charles Dickens's Inner Child

〰️

THOSE WHO STUDY Charles Dickens, or who keep up the great cult of his admiration, had been leading a fairly quiet life until a few years ago. The occasional letter bobs to the surface, or a bit of reminiscence is discovered, or perhaps some fragment of a souvenir from his first or second American tour. The pages of that agreeable little journal the *Dickensian* remained easy to turn, with little possibility of any great shock. At least since *The Invisible Woman*, Claire Tomalin's definitive, 1991 exposure of the other woman in Dickens's life—the once enigmatic Nelly Ternan—there hasn't been any scandal or revelation.

And then, in late 2002, the *Dickensian* carried a little bombshell of a tale: it seemed that in 1862, during Fyodor Dostoyevsky's visit to London, he had met Dickens. And not only met him but elicited from him the exact admission that we would all have wanted the great man to make. Here is how it goes in English, as summarized by Dostoyevsky in an 1878 letter to a certain Stepan Dimitriyevich Yanovsky. According to this, the two men met at the offices of Dickens's own personal magazine, *All the Year Round*. And here's how the confessional session went:

He told me that all the good simple people in his novels, Little Nell, even the holy simpletons like Barnaby Rudge, are what he wanted to have been, and his villains were what he was (or rather, what he found in himself), his cruelty, his attacks of causeless enmity towards those who were helpless and looked to him for comfort, his shrinking from those whom he ought to love, being used up in what he wrote. There were two people in him, he told me: one who feels as he ought to feel and one who feels the opposite. From the one who feels the opposite I make my evil characters; from the one who feels as a man ought to feel I try to live my life. Only two people? I asked.

So convenient and neat was this package that many first-time recipients endorsed it without even bothering to cut the ribbon, let alone ask why something as tasty as a Dostoyevsky original had lain unscrutinized for so long. Original? Come to think of it, where is the Russian version? Between 1862 and 1878—in other words, the dates of the meeting and the report of it—what was S. D. Yanovsky doing to busy himself? We know little about him, other than that he treated the great writer's hemorrhoids. The Russian version of their correspondence doesn't seem at all traceable now.

So it was sweet while it lasted, the rumor of a meeting between two great literary titans: an encounter that one of them didn't even find interesting enough to put in a letter. It could have happened, but I doubt it.* That's the wonderful thing about the celebration of Charles Dickens: he truly is ranked among our immortals, and it truly doesn't matter if the legend should sprout and then drop a Dostoyevsky or two.

We can certainly count the coincidences between his biography and his fiction among the things that make Dickens eternally fascinating. Opening his own memoir, the most inept fictional narrator

---

*Publisher's note: Subsequent to the publication of this essay, the Dickens–Dostoyevsky meeting was proved to be a hoax. See *Times Literary Supplement*, "When Dickens Met Dostoevsky," April 10, 2013.

of my generation showed that he was out of his depth by dismissing "all that David Copperfield kind of crap." Mr. Holden Caulfield may one day be forgotten, but the man who stumbled across the little boy trapped in the sweatshop basement, and realized their kinship, will never be. In the second chapter of *David Copperfield*, and not in any tongue-in-cheek exchange with the expert on the lower depths of St. Petersburg, is where we find the clue:

> This may be fancy, though I think the memory of most of us can go farther back into such times than many of us suppose; just as I believe the power of observation in numbers of very young children to be quite wonderful for its closeness and accuracy. Indeed, I think that most grown men who are remarkable in this respect, may with greater propriety be said not to have lost the faculty, than to have acquired it; the rather, as I generally observe such men to retain a certain freshness, and gentleness, and capacity of being pleased, which are also an inheritance they have preserved from their childhood.

Charming, is it not—seductive even—the manner in which that somewhat overpunctuated Victorian sentence suddenly gives way and yields a deposit of "freshness, and gentleness, and capacity of being pleased." It is all there to emphasize the one central and polar and critical point that Dickens wishes to enjoin on us all: whatever you do—hang on to your childhood! He was true to this in his fashion, both in ways that delight me and in ways that do not. He loved the idea of a birthday celebration, being lavish about it, reminding people that they were once unborn and are now launched. This is big-hearted, and we might all do a bit more of it. It would help me to forgive, perhaps just a little, the man who helped generate the Hallmark birthday industry and who, with some of his less imposing and more moistly sentimental prose scenes in *A Christmas Carol*, took the Greatest Birthday Ever Told and helped make it into the near Ramadan of protracted obligatory celebration now darkening our Decembers.

But imagine the power that Dickens had. By a few brilliant strokes of the pen, he revived and restored a popular festival and made it into a sort of social solidarity: a common defense against the Gradgrinds and the Bounderbys and the men who had been responsible for the misery of the Hungry Forties. For the first time, the downtrodden English people were able to see a celebrity, a man of wealth and fame, who was *on their side*. We have verbatim reports—sometimes in letters from the author himself—of the speeches he made to enthusiastic crowds in halls across the nation, just as we have the author's cue cards for the electrifying evenings in 1869 when he staged the murder of Nancy by Bill Sikes, so it's clear that Dickens had the sort of demagogic power that could have been dangerous in other hands. It's also quite clear that he can't have modeled a villain like Sikes, or a heroine like Nell, on his own character. No, he was drawing on much wider and deeper sources of potency. The main one was the sheer stubborn existence of so many people whom the system had disregarded. Begin thinking about it and you start to whisper a list to yourself: the pathetic Jo, the crossing sweeper; Smike; Mr. Micawber; Amy Dorrit; Mr. Dick—all of them with pain to feel and a life to lead, and many of them kept going (like poor Dick Swiveller) only by a certain unique sense of humor and the absurd. Dickens was able to mine this huge resource of London life, becoming its conductor and chronicler like nobody since Shakespeare himself, and always remembering, as he noted in the last stages of *The Old Curiosity Shop*, to "keep the child in view."

And here's my birthday or anniversary present to you. You can forget that sense of guilt you have. The one about being not quite sure which character is from which book. None of us really knows, and there is no shame in it. Probably Dickens himself wasn't certain much of the time. As Jane Smiley notices in *Charles Dickens*:

> The first ten parts of *Oliver Twist* were written at the same time Dickens was writing the last ten parts of *Pickwick*. Each section of *Oliver Twist* ran to about eight thousand words, and each section of *Pickwick* ran to about that or a bit more, so Dickens

was writing ninety pages a month of these novels, while also working on other essays, articles, speeches, and plays. Evidence is that he would write the dark, ironic chapters of *Oliver Twist* first, then the light, comic chapters of *Pickwick*.

So it's all right to confuse Podsnap and Pecksniff, or to ask whether the incident of the mutton chops in the fireplace is at Mrs. Todgers's establishment or Mrs. Jellyby's, and whether the missing baby belongs to either or both of them, or to Mrs. Gamp—a character over whom Dickens quite lost control. The same goes for the settings: the Circumlocution Office and the High Court of Chancery—indeed the whole vast apparatus of the Jarndyce-and-Jarndyce lawsuit—are all part of the same narrative. Cut into it at any point and you have taken a simultaneous tranche out of Sydney Carton and the "infant phenomenon." That Dickens should have had the nerve to call himself, simply, "the Inimitable" may seem conceited. All right then, so it was.

We can't hope to "read" all of Dickens by the light of this single candle of access to boyhood. He showed his biographer John Forster a section from the autobiography he never completed that said quite a lot about his apprenticeship to the grime and shame of the blacking factory so that Forster could write about "the attraction of repulsion" as the spring of *David Copperfield*, and indeed of everything he wrote. This leaves a nice little area of darkness in which we can speculate about the motives of the lad as he maneuvers for his liberty. On the other hand, we don't have so much guidance on which to rely when it comes to the pallid, worried, wraithlike little girl who slips disturbingly through so much of Dickens's fiction, taking here the shape of Little Dorrit, and of Florence Dombey with her brother, and then the infant Agnes and—above all—Little Nell. It seems impossible that no such rapidly evaporating diminutive female haunted Dickens's own life at some stage. Possibly he simply and shrewdly "knew" that Victorian guilt about the endangerment of such creatures was a continuous "draw" ("Is Nell dead?" they say the New York crowds cried out as the dreaded installment of *The Old Curiosity Shop* was freighted to the waiting wharf), but we have to draw our own conclusions from scanty evidence.

For instance, and from a deep boiling layer of anxiety and rage that goes well beyond anything Dostoyevsky might or might not have been told about, we have the Dickens who wrote to his best female friend, Angela Burdett-Coutts, in 1857, telling her of his yearnings to "exterminate" the Indian rebels against British rule. We have the Dickens who joined his friends Thomas Carlyle and John Ruskin against Charles Darwin, T. H. Huxley, J. S. Mill, and the other Victorian humanitarians, to support Governor Eyre of Jamaica in his war of torture and execution and reprisal against the rebels of that country. We have—this is in some ways the most depressing of all—Dickens's surreptitious hatred for Americans, even as he was making his way from one scene of their immense hospitality to the next in the 1840s. Admittedly, he had a qualified beef with those Yankee publishers who wouldn't part with royalties, but this hardly licenses what he wrote in private to his friend the actor William Macready about America's being "a low, coarse and mean nation" that was "driven by a herd of rascals . . . Pah! I never knew what it was to feel disgust and contempt, 'till I travelled in America." The Dickens mean streak is quite something when you strike it.

This renders it all the more impressive when he tries to make restitution. For instance, he was obviously very impressed when a prominent Jewish lady, Mrs. Eliza Davis, wrote him an anguished letter after the 1838 publication of *Oliver Twist*. She was obviously terribly upset about the character of Fagin and was not even quite willing to concede that some Jews had been involved in the stolen-goods racket. At any rate, Dickens went into the matter and convinced himself that he'd been part of an injustice. He thereupon did three things: he softened the description of Fagin in later versions of the book. When he himself took part in public "readings" from the story, he downplayed the "Jewish" characteristics of the villain. And he then created a whole new character to order. In *Our Mutual Friend*, we encounter a Jewish moneylender named Mr. Riah, who is friendly and helpful to Lizzie Hexam and Jenny Wren. I admit that I find this personage almost too altruistic to be true, but it says something for Dickens, surely, that he would take someone who had the same occupation as the infamous Shylock, but none of Shylock's vices, and insert him at the heart of business, at a time when vulgar prejudice was easy to stir up. The story isn't as well known as it ought to be.

The next instance of the victory of the large spirit comes from his second visit to the United States, in 1867. Dickens did his very best to clean up after himself, once again accepting lavish hospitality, but this time not taking revenge for it in a nasty, boring novel named *Martin Chuzzlewit* or a cruel and hastily written travelogue named *American Notes for General Circulation*, in which the not-too-clever pun suggests that American currency is bankrupt. Having successfully miscalculated the exchange rate, Dickens publicly offered to include a speech of praise for the USA in reprints of his two books about the country— and actually kept the promise even after the wild applause had died away and he had gone back home to England. Possibly he would not be an American hero if he had not performed this now forgotten act. But then, the "attraction-repulsion" principle, of which he spoke so readily, seems to have meant that he could sometimes let himself be "claimed" by those—from his neglected children to the mobs that he so feared—who loved him in spite of himself.

(*Vanity Fair*, February 2012)

G. K. Chesterton:
The Reactionary

⸺ ◈ ⸺

PROFESSOR KER'S SPIRITED and double-barreled attempt at a rehabilitation of his cherished subject is enjoyable in its own right, and takes in such matters as G. K Chesterton's dialectical genius for paradox, the authority of the Father Brown stories in the detective genre, and the salience of Charles Dickens in the English canonical one. But for him to show that his hero was the protagonist of a superior form of English democratic virtue, Ker would have to meet me where we are at agreement: on the high quality of Chesterton's poems. It's at exactly this sublime point, though, that he comes undone.

In his obituary, T. S. Eliot alluded to GKC's capacity for "first-rate journalistic balladry," and this high praise I think almost insufficient, because it understates his magic faculty of being unforgettable. Selecting from "one of his handful of good serious poems," Ker makes important use of "Lepanto," the verses of which Chesterton employed to mark off a certain English Protestant memory from a Roman Catholic one. Inspired by GKC's friend Father John O'Connor, the poem shows

---

Review of *The Everyman Chesterton* edited by Ian Ker; and *G. K. Chesterton: A Biography* by Ian Ker

how the great 1571 battle of the papacy against the Ottoman Porte was, and is, a minor Rorschach blot for a discrepant national memory.

Aiming off an early line ("The cold queen of England is looking in the glass") as a kind of establishing shot, Chesterton presses on to conscript all the images of sullen northern Protestant indifference in the face of the sultan's mobilization:

> *St. Michael's on his Mountain in the sea-roads of the north*
> (Don John of Austria is girt and going forth.)
> *Where the grey seas glitter and the sharp tides shift*
> *And the sea-folk labour and the red sails lift.*
> *He shakes his lance of iron and he claps his wings of stone;*
> *The noise is gone through Normandy; the noise is gone alone;*
> *The North is full of tangled things and texts and aching eyes,*
> *And dead is all the innocence of anger and surprise,*
> *And Christian killeth Christian in a narrow dusty room,*
> *And Christian dreadeth Christ that hath a newer face of doom,*
> *And Christian hateth Mary that God kissed in Galilee,—*
> *But Don John of Austria is riding to the sea.*

In one rather gallant stave, then, the finer aspects of Christendom detach themselves from the frigid dogmas of the Reformation, and re-proclaim the magnificence of the Crusades. In a separate but intimately related poem, "The Secret People" (the historic refrain of which is "Smile at us, pay us, pass us; but do not quite forget / For we are the people of England, that never have spoken yet"), Chesterton summarizes the woes and dispossessions of his fellow-countrymen in this way:

> *Our patch of glory ended; we never heard guns again.*
> *But the squire seemed stuck in the saddle; he was foolish, as if in*
> *   pain.*
> *He leaned on a staggering lawyer, he clutched a cringing Jew,*
> *He was stricken; it may be, after all, he was stricken at Waterloo.*

Or perhaps the shades of the shaven men, whose spoil is in his
   house,
Come back in shining shapes at last to spoil his last carouse:
We only know the last sad squires ride slowly towards the sea,
And a new people takes the land and still it is not we.

Thus, and in a few small phrases, Chesterton hopelessly under-mines his own project of defending England against the secular pallor of Protestantist greed. Instead, by making it seem as if they were to be condemned for their neutrality and abstention at Lepanto, he confines his chosen people inside the enclave that had been fashioned for them by some rather strict Catholic intellectuals: intellectuals who were later to get themselves on the wrong side of Europe's most important quarrel by being shady on the question of fascism. (Professor Ker somewhat confidingly, if not devastatingly from his own viewpoint, adds that this poem "could hardly have been more Catholic in its view of English history.") One might also note that Chesterton wrote his jaw-dropping line about the "cringing Jew" at a time when England was becoming preoccupied by the so-called Marconi case, involving the "scandal" of Jewish commerce in politics, and thus helped to ce-ment the idea that there was a connection between the two. At any rate, I don't think even the best of the poetic quotations can redeem Chestertonianism from the reactionary implications of the prosaic ones: they put one too much in mind of another critique of his work by T. S. Eliot. Reviewing him on Robert Louis Stevenson in 1927, Eliot found him suffering "under a misunderstanding that we are not likely to labor under," "attacking misconceptions which we had not heard of and in which we are not interested," and putting forth "a style exasperating to the last point of endurance."

Chesterton's overbuilt reputation for paradox was founded on his Paradox of Conservatism, which was to the effect that if you want to be a conservative, you had better not be *too much* of one. He gave us this, which he deemed to be a distillation of Cardinal John Henry Newman's "theory of development":

All conservatism is based upon the idea that if you leave things alone you leave them as they are.

But you do not. If you leave a thing alone you leave it to a torrent of change. If you leave a white post alone it will soon be a black post. If you particularly want it to be white you must be always painting it again; that is, you must be always having a revolution. Briefly, if you want the old white post you must have a new white post.

(One wishes, as on other occasions, that he had not reserved his recommendation of brevity until the last. The old buzzard could be a master of prolixity.)

So there was GKC's enduring problem. Instead of occupying massive portions of the landscape ("there came a sound like that of Mr G. K. Chesterton falling onto a sheet of tin") for his meditative verses and polemics, he was compelled to be active so that his fellow reactionaries could be involved in something worth calling a movement. For an instance of the operations of paradox in practice, incidentally, we may examine the founding of the only movement that ever bore the name he gave it: that of "Distributism." This scheme for a more equitable sharing of existing property took form in late 1926, the year of class convulsion that saw the defeat of the General Strike and the mobilization and demobilization of millions of British workers. The initial founders of the Distributist League could fit into one hall in the Strand, and could not at once decide upon a unifying name. An early suggestion was "The Cow and Acres," which sounded to GKC rather too much like a pub. Another was "The League of the Little People," which with its air of plaintive populism also retained the aura of a fairy glen. It was later generally agreed that the only genuine disagreement concerned the question of whether a true Distributist should also be a Roman Catholic.

GKC himself took heart from the launch of this frail bark, despising the niceties of theory and nomenclature because in his own mind an essential point had already been established. Disputes about machinery and capital were to be put on one side. The English people had already been shorn of their property rights before the advent of industrial capital. This is a clear reference to the lines, in "The Secret People," about the "men of the new religion, with their Bibles in their boots," who had "eaten the abbey's fruits." The Protestant revolution, in other words, had been an act of theft and not an action of redistribution. To Chesterton's bucolic conservatism, and his view that a certain kind of revolution was necessary to keep the counterrevolution in action, was to be added a working alliance with Roman Catholic conservatism. In the late 1920s and early 1930s, this was actually an unpromising initiative, as Chesterton failed to note when he traveled to Rome and saw Mussolini and formed the verdict that while fascism could be criticized as hypocritical to the point of flagrance, the same could surely be said of liberal democracy. This shows the moth-eaten fringe of absurdity that always hung around his political reflections, as it did his vastly draped and histrionic form.

Let us try some of his other paradoxes and see how they hold up. The first one states that those who affirm that they conduct themselves by "the spirit of Christianity" rather than its outward dogmas do in fact keep "some of the words and terminology, words like Peace and Righteousness and Love; but they make these words stand for an atmosphere utterly alien to Christendom; they keep the letter and lose the spirit." It would be just about as useful to say that GKC could reinfuse the higher concepts of faith by restoring them to upper and lower case: we are all fully familiar with the religious practitioner who can't or doesn't live up to the merits of his creed. There's nothing innately paradoxical in that. Any solution, however, is a bit like the Golden Rule: the creed is only as morally strong as the person who happens to be uttering it. If Chesterton ever managed the feat of preserving the letter *and* the spirit, or knew anyone who had, or anyone who could temporarily separate letter and spirit, he would have done well to inform us. (Professor Ker, sadly, describes the above effort as "one of [Chesterton's] most brilliant paradoxes.")

Had he been tempted down to cases, GKC might have extracted

more profit from his mischievous idea that the book of Job portrayed god as "paradoxically" atheist, but this, when compared with other and mightier speculations on that text, was a trifle thin. His American tour yielded a small handful of what one might call minor ironies or contradictions (he began ostentatiously to call himself "a democrat" and "an equal"), while on the larger point, he missed a critical chance. It was unfortunate, Chesterton asserted, that although America had "a great political idea . . . it had a small religious idea." This came out as follows:

> This "individualism in religion" explained why Americans were not proper republicans in the sense of every man having "a direct relation to the realm or commonweal, more direct than he has to any masters or patrons in private life": in America the individual made "good in trade, because it was originally the individual making good in goodness; that is, in salvation of the soul."

One has immediately the sense of a big chance being forfeited, with the elements of paradox being discarded along the way. The opposition is not between a small and a large concept in any case, Mr. Chesterton, sir: the United States is its own guarantee of some kind of noble scale in the business. How annoying it is that a certain kind of English voice seems so determined to condescend to Americans. No, it is the *simple ingenuity* (if I might be allowed a paradoxical locution) of the Jefferson/Madison religious signpost, with its clearly made pointer to Danbury, Connecticut, that is so graspable by the minds of the simplest as well as the most superior persons. Given time, the symbol of a simple wall of separation has fashioned and established itself inside our own crania, so that almost every American has an approximate idea that they are entitled to a great degree of "freedom of," as well as a marked amount of "freedom from," with a good deal of debatable latitude in between. This is not a small or inert legacy.

Some of GKC's other half-developed insights have the unintended result, like the post-Falstaffian bulk problem, of straining and breaking the branch on which he leaned for effect. (An irresistible digression: in 1908, GKC rented a house in Rye, East Sussex, adjacent to that of Henry James. James was aghast that such a mind was "imprisoned in such a body," and the regular viewing of "the unspeakable Chesterton" with his awful pachydermatous silhouette horrified James, who otherwise admired GKC. To picture The Master in such a predicament . . .) He could not understand why anti-Catholics accused their foes of forming secret societies while forming them—like the KKK—in their own right. But this in turn meant that he never "got" the appeal of camp and sinister formations like Opus Dei.

Chesterton hoped to show that the English had seen through the Protestant Reformation, and would survive it because they liked those who laughed. Yet the life of the great Samuel Johnson, we learn, was constrained because of "the absence of the pleasures of religion" in it. There's something weirdly self-regarding about that formulation, especially coming as it does from a man who believed that the great English strength—deployed all along a rampart of joviality and confidence that extends from Chaucer's Tabard Inn to Charles Dickens's own prospect of Kent and the Medway—is founded on mirth. The sort of mirth that puffs away fanaticism and narrowness need have no connection to "the pleasures of religion." Behind this crude camouflage, we can see being wheeled into position a large block of stone or paper, incised or authored by Cardinal John Henry Newman but helped along by Chesterton's own main force, on which all the needs and promptings and moral suasions of the English people will need to be sternly written down. And yes, Messrs. Johnson and Dickens may well be casting around themselves for the exits. It may be true that the Protestant Reformation delivered the poor and the squires into the bondage of the "new, unhappy lords" who raised their grievous rent, but this does not mean any general English nostalgia for the old regime of throne and altar and the incineration of martyrs. And

Chesterton did end up by wrestling his own block of moral admonition into shape, and publishing it as a sort of summa. Here's Ker's version of GKC's account:

> The previous year Chesterton had contributed a brief chapter to *Twelve Modern Apostles and their Creeds*, entitled "Why I am a Catholic," which began with the assertion that there were ten thousand reasons, "all amounting to one reason: that Catholicism is true." The Catholic Church simply was "catholic"—"not only larger than me, but larger than anything in the world . . . indeed larger than the world." It was the only "corporate mind in the world" that was "on the watch to prevent minds from going wrong." The church, "looking out in all directions at once," was "not merely armed against the heresies of the past or even of the present, but equally against those of the future, that may be the exact opposite of those of the present." She carried "a sort of map of the mind which looks like the map of a maze, but which is in fact a guide to the maze." Uniquely, she constituted "one continuous intelligent institution that has been thinking about thinking for two thousand years." The resulting map marked clearly "all the blind alleys and bad roads."

Chesterton rested this on the relatively small paradox that few young people by then regarded the old wars and divisions of Christianity as important: one could be a Roman Catholic or Protestant almost as according to taste. (A brief pause for a moment to reflect on what it took to attain to that compromise after centuries of war and torment. . . .) The idea of a body that actually did all the official thinking was probably not unrelated to the Mussolini concept of the corporate state. This would be repulsive to the English and American tradition. If there was a collectivity that "did" all the thinking, in England it was expressed in the definite skepticism concerning such matters as the Inquisition, the Spanish Armada, and the question of papal infallibility. In America it was still the durable sign system pointing to Danbury, Connecticut. In neither case was there any requirement for that minatory block of text or stone, forever guarding the outer doors of orthodoxy and unsleepingly seeking to entrap or expel the heretic and the dissident. The more that attempts were made to codify truth, the more elusive truth became. Chesterton became part of a forgettable rear-guard operation against the age of uncertainty, which has now definitively become our age. It seems that there are no rules, golden or otherwise, even natural or otherwise, by which we can define our place in the universe or the cosmos. Those who claim to know the most are convicted of claiming to know the unknowable. There is a paradox, if you like.

As to the durability or importance of GKC as a fictionist: the late Sir Kingsley Amis once told me that he reread *The Man Who Was Thursday* every year, and on one of his annual visitations wrote a tribute. That novel, with its evocation of eeriness and solitude, and its fascination with anonymity, has been credited by some with a share of influence on Franz Kafka. *The Napoleon of Notting Hill* is not in the same class, and may even be drawn to a meaner scale in order to attenuate the frame of "rights." Father Brown I give up and return to you. The character is deliberately vacant and the scheme of plot little more than a clanking trolley. A figure named Father Bond makes a brief reappearance—the only one I think he merits—on what must be intended as the shelf of a good Catholic schoolboy in Amis père's well-wrought anti-Vatican and anti-castration fantasy *The Alteration*. The debt is overwhelmingly to Conan Doyle, with no indebtedness to any of the great formulas of detective fiction. As a consequence, the little priest's summings-up are usually arid and often iffy. When told of a minor crisis in his financial affairs, we are informed by Ker, the proprietor of *G.K.'s Weekly* would reply: "'Oh, well. We must write another Father Brown story,' and this would be done at lightning speed a day or two later from a few notes on the back of an envelope." It showed, I fear. Evelyn Waugh may have been able to squeeze part of a *Brideshead* evening out of a phrase of Brown's—about "a twitch upon the thread"—but my conjury is not equal to his.

Then at last we come to the sordid but inescapable question: Why did GKC feel the imperative to drape that drooping English squire in that cringing Jew? I could have done it in one blow, and simply said that Chesterton wrote and believed that Englishmen, if they wished to be "chosen" as public servants like Sir Rufus Isaacs, should agree to wear a different national dress and thus to signify their apartness. This was the direct ancestor of the yellow star, even if applied more selectively, and it made the same point: Jews were a foreign nation and should have a state of their own. GKC was more of a Christian Zionist than an anti-Semite, let alone an exterminationist or eliminationist one. Thus, one cannot quite place him in the yellow-star camp as we have come to think of it.

But he and his fellow Distributists and other stray reactionaries did get themselves on the wrong side of the debate about Nazism. And they did so, furthermore, because of self-imposed blinders in their own view of matters ethnic and ideological and confessional. For instance, in search of a good taunt, Chesterton decided that the Protestant Reformation was originally Jewish! And that the concept of a "chosen race" came to us as a Jewish one; and, not content with this, that it also descended through Protestantism. Thus, through an obsession with the covenant with Israel had come "the great Prussian illusion of pride, for which thousands of Jews have recently been rabbled or ruined or driven from their homes." So that the laugh, here, comes at the expense of the Jews.

An even more extensive, not to say wild, rewriting of history involved GKC's view that Hitlerism was a last attempt to Protestantize the old Bismarckian empire. Professor Ker has the integrity to step in at this stage, if only to adumbrate the fact that the führer who grabbed Austria as a limb of a future "Greater Germany" was himself an Austrian Catholic. But Chesterton would not be persuaded:

The racial pride of Hitlerism is of the Reformation by twenty tests; because it divides Christendom and makes all such divisions deeper; because it is fatalistic, like Calvinism, and makes superiority depend not upon choice but only on being of the chosen; because it is Caesaro-Papist, putting the State above the Church, as in the claim of Henry VIII; because it is immoral, being an innovator of morals touching things like Eugenics and Sterility; because it is subjective, in suiting the primal fact to the personal fancy, as in asking for a German God, or saying that the Catholic revelation does not suit the German temper; as if I were to say that the Solar System does not suit the Chestertonian taste. I do not apologise, therefore, for saying that this catastrophe in history has been due to heresy.

In that closing, Chesterton missed one or two opportunities for wit and ducked a couple of openings for a tu quoque (especially on the matter of Henry VIII and church-state compromises). But he most of all sacrificed his duty to moral courage and historical truth, blaming Nazism on the wrong culprits. And this was because he put his theocratic allegiance higher than those claims, and at a time when civilization was in danger from the men of the Hitler-Vatican concordat. Another way of phrasing it might be to say that, when the hour really struck, Chesterton could not detect a paradox when it truly reared up to confront him and his prejudices. Harsher but correct would be the verdict that his Catholicism made him morally frivolous about Hitlerism; a judgment that Professor Ker strives to avoid but is, I think, in part compelled to admit. Confrontation with GKC has been enjoyable, even if the main elements of the debate have come to seem extraordinarily archaic.

The verdict one must pass on GKC, then, is that when he was charming, he was also deeply unserious and frivolous (as with the pub revolution to set off the Distributist revolution); when he was apparently serious, he was really quite sinister (as in calling Nazism a form of Protestant heresy and Jews a species of conspicuous foreigner in England); and when he was posing as a theologian, he was doing little more than ventriloquizing John Henry Newman at his most "dogmatic." For the time and hour in which he lived, "Chestertonian-ism" came to represent a minor but still important failure to meet a distinct moral challenge.

(*The Atlantic*, March 2012)

The Importance of Being Orwell

⸻ꔷ⸻

A T VARIOUS POINTS in his essays—notably in "Why I Write" but also in his popular occasional column As I Please—George Orwell gave us an account of what made him tick, as it were, and of what supplied the motive for his work. At different times he instanced what he called his "power of facing unpleasant facts"; his love for the natural world, "growing things," and the annual replenishment of the seasons, and his desire to forward the cause of democratic socialism and oppose the menace of fascism. Other strong impulses include his near-visceral feeling for the English language and his urge to defend it from the constant encroachments of propaganda and euphemism, and his reverence for objective truth, which he feared was being driven out of the world by the deliberate distortion and even obliteration of recent history.

As someone who had been brought up in a fairly rarefied and distinctly reactionary English milieu, in which the underclass of his own society and the millions of inhabitants of its colonial empire were regarded with a mixture of fear and loathing, Orwell also made an early decision to find out for himself what the living conditions of these remote latitudes were really "like." This second commitment,

Introduction to *George Orwell Diaries*

to acquaint himself with the brute facts as they actually were, was to prove a powerful reinforcement of his latent convictions.

Read with care, George Orwell's diaries from the years 1931 to 1949 can greatly enrich our understanding of how Orwell transmuted the raw material of everyday experience into some of his best-known novels and polemics. They also furnish us with a more intimate picture of a man who, committed to the struggles of the mechanized and "modern" world, was also drawn by the rhythms of the wild, the rural, and the remote. (He barely survived into the first month of the second half of the twentieth century, dying of the sort of poverty-induced disease that might have killed a character out of Dickens. Yet despite his Edwardian and near-Victorian provenance he remains more contemporary and relevant to us than many authors of a much later date.)

These diaries are not by any means a "straight" guide, or a trove of clues and cross-references. It would be rather difficult to deduce, for example, that it was during his sojourn in Morocco in 1938–1939 that Orwell conceived and composed the novel *Coming Up for Air*. This short and haunting work involves an evocation of a lost bucolic England set in the barely imaginable years before the drama of the First World War. For it to have been written amid the torrid souk of Marrakech and the arid emptiness of the Atlas Mountains must have involved some convolutions of the creative process into which he gives us little or no insight. But he was also in Morocco—in addition to being in search of a cure for his gnawing tuberculosis—to make notes and take soundings about the conditions of North African society.

Indeed, the thirties were the decade during which Orwell took up the task of amateur anthropologist, both in his own country and overseas. Sometimes attempting to disguise his origins as an educated member of the upper classes and former colonial policeman (he is amusing about his attempts to flatten his accent according to the company he was keeping), he set off to amass notes and absorb experiences. His family background, the income of which depended on the detestable opium trade between British-ruled India and British-influenced China, had at first conditioned him to fear and despise the "locals" and the "natives." One of the many things that made Orwell so interesting was his self-education *away* from such prejudices, which also included a marked dislike of the Jews. But anyone reading the early pages of these accounts and expeditions will be struck by how vividly Orwell still expressed his unmediated disgust at some of the human specimens with whom he came into contact. When joining a group of itinerant hop-pickers he is explicitly repelled by the personal characteristics of a Jew to whom he cannot bear even to give a name, characteristics which he somehow manages to identify as Jewish. He is unsparing about the sheer stupidity and dirtiness of so many of the proletarian families with whom he lodges, and is sometimes condescending about the extreme limitations of their education and imagination. The failure of *The Road to Wigan Pier* was partly attributable to a successful Communist campaign to defame it (and him) for saying that "the working classes smell." Orwell never actually *did* say this, except in the oblique context of denouncing those who did, but his own slightly wrinkled nostrils must have helped a little in the spread of the slander.

It may not be too much to claim that by undertaking these investigations, Orwell helped found what we now know as "cultural studies" and "postcolonial studies." His study of unemployment and poor housing in the north of England stands comparison, with its careful statistics, with Friedrich Engels's *Condition of the Working Class in England*, published a generation or two earlier. But with its additional information and commentary about the reading and recreational habits of the workers, the attitudes of the men to their wives, and the mixtures of expectation and aspiration that lent nuance and distinction to the undifferentiated concept of "the proletariat," we can see the accumulation of debt that later "social" authors and analysts, such as Michael Young and Richard Hoggart, owed to Orwell when they began their own labors in the postwar period. We can also feel, in the increasingly stubborn growth of his egalitarian and socialist principles during these years, the germination of one of the most famous lines of *Nineteen Eighty-Four*: "If there is hope, it lies in the proles." From a detail in the life of the British coal miner—does he have the right to a cleansing bath at the pithead, and if so, does he pay for it out of his own wages and in his own time?—Orwell illustrates the potential power of the working class to generate its own resources out of an everyday struggle, but also to generalize that quotidian battle for the resolution of greater and nobler matters such as the ownership of production and the right to labor's full share.

Similarly, in North Africa, Orwell continued down the track on which he had begun when he declared his own independence from the British colonial system in Indochina. (It is often forgotten that one of his first published researches, written in French and published by a small radical house in Paris, was about the way in which Britain's exploitation perpetuated the underdevelopment of Burma.) The sexual and racial implications of the exertion of colonial power he reserved for his first novel—*Burmese Days*—but he never lost sight of the importance of the economic substratum and, in his comparatively brief sojourn in Morocco, was also highly interested in the ethnic composition of the population and in such seemingly arcane matters as the circulation wars between the different language groups and political factions, as reflected in the sales of local newspapers. Again, though, one notices a certain fastidious preoccupation with the stench of poverty and squalor, including some pungent reflections on the discrepant scents of Jewish and Arab ghettos.

The most searing and formative experience of Orwell's engagement with the thirties was his enlistment on the Republican side in the Spanish Civil War, during which he took a bullet in the throat from the fascist side and—very nearly—another one in the back from the Communists. If there is a diary covering this intense period it almost certainly reposes in the archives of the Russian secret police in Moscow, having been seized from Orwell and his wife during a Communist police raid on his Barcelona hotel in 1937. However, references to Spain, and to the agony of its defeat at the hands of a military rebellion backed by Hitler and Mussolini, are scattered throughout every section of these English and Moroccan journals.

In England, Orwell concentrates on attitudes about the war among workers and intellectuals and draws on his friendship with other radical British volunteers from the educated classes to propose a "Peoples' Army," along the lines of the Spanish militias, to defend Britain in the event of a German invasion. With the help of some seasoned veterans like Tom Wintringham, Humphrey Slater, and Tom Hopkinson, the idea of a "Home Guard" for precisely this purpose was actually officially implemented, contributing considerably to the quiet egalitarian revolution which swept Britain during the war and helped evict the Conservatives from power as soon as it ended.

From this period also dates some of Orwell's best and most mordant egalitarianism. Readers who have followed the "99 per cent" campaign of response to the mixture of crime and capitalism on Wall Street in 2011 may be amused at the exactitude of Orwell's observation in this culling from the press.

From a letter from Lady Oxford to the *Daily Telegraph*, on the subject of war economies:

> "Since most London houses are deserted there is little entertaining . . . in any case, most people have to part with their cooks and live in hotels."
>
> Apparently nothing will ever teach these people that the other 99% of the population exist.*

Franco's invasion of Spain was initially launched from Madrid's colony in Morocco and reinforced by the deployment of several Moorish colonial regiments. Orwell's interest in the territory, then, was also heavily strategic. He thought that the Allies should declare in favor of Moroccan independence and then set up a provisional antifascist

---

*It perhaps counts as an irony of British society that the little Oxfordshire churchyard in which Orwell was laid to rest, in the village of Sutton Courtenay, became also the "last resting place" of Margot Asquith's husband, the former prime minister and Earl of Oxford and Asquith. Equality between the one and the ninety-nine was attainable at least in death.

Spanish government in exile, thus taking Franco in the rear both militarily and politically. However, knowing the generally pro-imperial mentality of the British establishment, and its obdurate shortsightedness in preferring Franco to a victory of the Spanish left, he was sure that London would lack the imagination for such an emancipating move (and he was right). Nonetheless, it deserves to be remembered that, throughout the course of a protracted war which concentrated attention on the grand Atlantic and Pacific "theaters" and on the huge battles in Western Europe and Russia, Orwell always sought to focus attention on the liberation of Abyssinia (now Ethiopia), on the independence of India and Burma, on the sufferings of the Maltese under Axis bombardment, on the aspirations of Arab nationalism, and in general on the end of imperialism. This was an outcome which he foresaw, and worked for, long before most intellectuals—even many leftist ones—could be convinced that the days of a white-ruled globe were over.

It was from his time making wartime broadcasts to India for the BBC that Orwell began to concentrate on the idea of history and falsification. He could see events being mutated into propaganda before his very eyes, even in the information headquarters of an ostensible democracy. Thus in the summer of 1942, when the British authorities resorted to massive force in order to put down demonstrations and riots in India, he noticed that the hitherto respectable name of Nehru—once the British favorite for the Indian leadership—had somehow become blacklisted: "Today the reference to Nehru was cut out of the announcement—N. being in prison and therefore having become Bad." This is a slight but definite prefiguration of the scenes in the Ministry of Truth in *Nineteen Eighty-Four*, where certain political figures are suddenly deemed to be "unpersons" and where rapid changes of wartime allegiance necessitate the hectic rewriting of recent history.

The culture of censorship and denial also necessitated a coarsening of attitudes to language and truth; earlier in the same year he had written:

We are all drowning in filth. When I talk to anyone or read the writings of anyone who has any axe to grind, I feel that intellectual honesty and balanced judgment have simply disappeared from the face of the earth. Everyone's thought is forensic, everyone is simply putting a "case" with deliberate suppression of his opponent's point of view, and, what is more, with complete insensitiveness to any sufferings except those of himself and his friends.*

One has to use a certain amount of decoding to identify literary transitions like this, as they move from Orwell's private to his published writing, whereas other sources of inspiration and provocation are more blunt and obvious. In 1939 he takes a "miscellaneous" diary note from the agricultural journal *Smallholder*: "Rat population of G.Britain estimated at 4–5 million." Who knows in what part of his cortex he stored away *that* random finding, against the day when it would help form one of the most arresting images of terror in all of his fiction. Indeed, the whole leprous moral and social texture of "Airstrip One," his dystopian name for a future totalitarian Britain, is taken from the dank, smelly, depressing, and undernourished society ("drowning in filth" in a less metaphorical sense) that he had been observing at close hand in peace and war. It was this that called upon his growing capacity "to see the world in a grain of sand / and heaven in a wild flower."**

This need to *know* things at the level of basic experience, and the reluctance to be fobbed off by the official story or the popular rumor,

---

*This is a very acute register of what Orwell himself called "a power of facing unpleasant facts." Netted in a world of lies, he wanted not to be spared the bad news or coddled by victory propaganda at his place of work. And he despised the alternative flow of information and insight, which was gossip and rumor. Like Winston Smith, he was first and foremost activated by a raging thirst to know: a thirst that could only be slaked by a personal quest for the least varnished version of the truth.

**It is from this poem of William Blake's that Orwell also claimed one of his favorite lines, and one of the clues to his personality: "A truth that's told with bad intent / Beats all the lies you can invent."

was a part of the "infinite capacity for taking pains" that Thomas Carlyle once described as the constituent of genius. Hearing a rumor in 1940 that "Jews greatly predominate among the people sheltering in the Tubes [London underground stations]," Orwell minutes, "Must try and verify this." Two weeks later, he is down in the depths of the transport system to examine "the crowds sheltering in Chancery Lane, Oxford Circus and Baker Street stations. *Not* all Jews, but, I think, a higher proportion of Jews than one would normally see in a crowd of this size." He goes on, with almost cold objectivity, to note that Jews have a way of making themselves conspicuous. Again, this is not so much an expression of prejudice as a form of confrontation with it: a stage in Orwell's own evolution. Only a few days after he expresses the misanthropic and even xenophobic view that European refugees, including Jews, secretly despise England and surreptitiously sympathize with Hitler, he excoriates the insular-minded British authorities for squandering the talents of the Jewish Central European émigré Arthur Koestler. When he contradicts himself, as he very often does, he tries his best to be aware of the fact and to profit from it.*

A good small example of the ways in which Orwell could discover virtues even in matters of which he disapproved is provided by an observation he makes during this same period of bombardment, while surveying the near destruction by the Nazis of London's most beloved cathedral:

> Appalled today by the havoc all round St. Paul's, which I had not seen before. St. Paul's, barely chipped, standing out like a

---

*It deserves to be said that Orwell went on to write several analyses and condemnations of anti-Semitism and to attack contemporary writers like G. K. Chesterton who exploited it in their work. Among his colleagues and friends at the socialist weekly *Tribune* he numbered two Jewish colleagues, Jon Kimche and T. R. "Tosco" Fyvel. Not to recycle any corny allusion to "some of my best friends," but Fyvel regarded Orwell as free from prejudice and even as having been slightly prescient in his misgivings about Zionism, then a popular cause on the left. (Orwell thought that even if it were a just cause it would necessitate a garrison state to defend itself against the rival nationalism that it had defeated.)

rock. It struck me for the first time that it is a pity the cross on top of the dome is such an ornate one. It should be a plain cross, sticking up like the hilt of a sword.

This forms an admirable example of what I have elsewhere described as Orwell's version of the Protestant ethic and the Puritan revolution. In his essays, he generally ridiculed the Christian religion and displayed an especial animus toward its Roman Catholic version, but he admired the beauty of the Anglican liturgy and knew much of the King James Bible and the Cranmer Book of Common Prayer by heart. In this image of a possible St. Paul's, drawn almost from the rhetoric of John Milton and Oliver Cromwell, he evinces an understanding that certain traditional values may become useful for radical purposes: the ceremonial symbol pressed into service as a weapon of popular struggle. (His ambitions for the Home Guard clearly drew on his admiration for Cromwell's "New Model Army.")

The Protestant revolution was partly centered on the long battle to have the Bible made available in the English vernacular and removed from the control of the linguistic priesthood or "Inner Party." So it is perhaps surprising, given his lifelong near-obsession with the subject, that Orwell does not appear to expend much energy here in his famous preoccupation with the mutations of the English language for purposes of propaganda. There is one vivid example, but it has more to do with another element of "Newspeak": the need for compression in order to produce journalistic neologism. In the early days of the bombing of London, he observes that "the word 'blitz' now used everywhere to mean any kind of attack on anything. . . . 'Blitz' is not yet used as a verb, a development I am expecting." Three weeks later he laconically records that "the *Daily Express* has used 'blitz' as a verb." At a slightly later stage, while analyzing the way in which he finds himself scouring the press for deeper sources of interpretation, he decides that "nowadays, whatever is said or done, one looks instantly for hidden motives and assumes that words mean anything except what they appear to mean." So the outline of a discourse in which, for example, "freedom is slavery," was slowly taking shape in his mind. This is not a thesaurus of eurekas, in other words, so much as a gradual and often arduous set of connections being slowly pieced together.

It seems to be an open question whether that very weight—the strain and tedium and approximation of everyday existence—was a hindrance to Orwell or an assistance. He himself seems to have thought that the exigencies of poverty, ill health, and overwork were degrading him from being the serious writer he might have been and had reduced him to the status of a drudge and pamphleteer. Reading through these meticulous and occasionally laborious jottings, however, one cannot help but be struck by the degree to which he became, in Henry James's words, one of those upon whom nothing was lost. By declining to lie, even as far as possible to himself, and by his determination to seek elusive but verifiable truth, he showed how much can be accomplished by an individual who unites the qualities of intellectual honesty and moral courage. And, permanently tempted though he was by cynicism and despair, Orwell also believed in the latent possession of these faculties by those we sometimes have the nerve to call "ordinary people." Here, then, is some of the unpromising bedrock—hardscrabble soil in Scotland, gritty coal mines in Yorkshire, desert landscapes in Africa, soulless slums and bureaucratic offices—combined with the richer soil and loam of ever-renewing nature, and that tiny, irreducible core of the human personality that somehow manages to put up a resistance to deceit and coercion. Out of the endless attrition between them can come such hope as we may reasonably claim to possess.

(Reprinted, in slightly different form, in *Vanity Fair*, August 2012)

What Is Patriotism?

———⌾———

PATRIOTIC AND TRIBAL feelings belong to the squalling childhood of the human race, and become no more charming in their senescence. They are particularly unattractive when evinced by a superpower. But ironies of history may yet save us. English language and literature, oft-celebrated as one of the glories of "Western" and even "Christian" civilization, turn out to have even higher faculties than used to be claimed for them. In my country of birth the great new fictional practitioners have in their front rank names like Rushdie, Ishiguro, Kureishi, Mo. This attainment on their part makes me oddly proud to be whatever I am, and convinces me that internationalism is the highest form of patriotism.

(*The Nation*, July 15/22, 1991)

Index

Note: Page numbers in **boldface** *indicate the subjects of reviews or prose pieces.*

absolutism, 273
Abu Ghraib prison, 258
Acheson, Dean, 92, 96
Acropolis, 238, 240
Acropolis Museum, 240–42
Acropolis Restoration Service, 235
Adamic, Louis, 26
Adams, John, 44
Adler, Georg, et al., eds., *The Letters of
        Rosa Luxemburg*, **273–79**
Afghanistan, war in, 119–20
Africa, Guevara in, 13–14, 15
"After Strange Gods" (Eliot), 80
*After the Victorians: The Decline of
        Britain in the World* (Wilson),
        91–96
Age of Jackson, The (Schlesinger), 202
Ahmadinejad, Mahmoud, 248, 249,
        265
AIDS, 252
Akçam, Taner, 35
Akhmatova, Anna, 150
Alamo, 80
Albright, Madeleine, 255
Alexander the Great, 3
" 'Alimentary, Dr. Leiter': Anal Anxiety
        in *Diamonds Are Forever*" (Allen),
        97–98

Al Jazeera, 106–7, 112
Allen, Dennis W., " 'Alimentary, Dr.
        Leiter': Anal Anxiety in *Diamonds
        Are Forever*," 97–98
Allen, George, 75
Allende, Salvador, 17, 160, 258
Allingham, Margery, 167
All the Year Round, 291–92
al-Qaeda, 66, 105, 111, 120, 248
Altenberg, Peter, 150
Alter, Victor, 22
Alteration, The (Amis), 307
American Civil Liberties Union
        (ACLU), 106, 110, 112, 226
American Enterprise Institute, 194
American Nazi Party, 110
American Notes for General Circulation
        (Dickens), 297
American Revolution, 55
Americans for Democratic Action
        (ADA), 116, 118, 120
Amis, Kingsley
        The Alteration, 307
        The James Bond Dossier, 98
Amristar massacre (1919), 93, 206
Anderson, John, 200
Anderson, Jon Lee, *Che Guevara: A
        Revolutionary Life*, **1–18**

Anderson, Perry, 279
  English Questions, 27
Andress, Ursula, 99
Angola, Cuban expedition to, 6
Animal Farm (Orwell), 23, 24, 28
Antaeus (Greek legend), 267–68
Anti-Defamation League (ADL),
  124–25
Antigone (Sophocles), 237
Anti-Suffrage League, 154
Antiterrorism and Effective Death
  Penalty Act (1996), 112, 226
Aplin, Hugh, transl., *A Hero of Our
  Time* (Lermontov), 57, 62
Arafat, Yasser, 136, 254
Arbenz, Jacobo, 8, 9–10, 11, 14
Area of Darkness, An (Naipaul), 221
Armas, Castillo, 9
Armenia, **261–64**
Armey, Dick, 271
Armitage, Richard, 256
Aron, Raymond, 148
Ashcroft, John, 108, 111
Ashe, Arthur, 73
Assad, Bashar, 266
Assad, Hafez al-, 128
Astor, Nancy, 93
As You Like It (Shakespeare), 275–76
Atatürk, Kemal, 34–35, 36–37
Atlantic, The
  "A. N. Wilson: Downhill All the
    Way" (January/February 2006),
    91–96
  "Arthur Schlesinger: The Courier"
    (December 2007), 197–202
  "Barack Obama: Cool Cat" (Janu-
    ary/February 2009), 229–34
  "Blood for No Oil!" (May 2006),
    115–21
  "Clive James: The Omnivore"
    (April 2007), 147–51
  "Edmund Wilson: Literary Com-
    panion" (September 2007),
    163–68
  "Gertrude Bell: The Woman Who
    Made Iraq" (June 2007), 153–58
  "G. K. Chesterton: The Reaction-
    ary" (March 2012), 299–310
  "Ian Fleming: Bottoms Up" (April
    2006), 97–103
  "Imperial Follies" (December 2006),
    141–46
  "Mikhail Lermontov: A Doomed
    Young Man" (June 2005), 57–62

  "On Becoming American" (May
    2005), 53–55
  "Orhan Pamuk: Mind the Gap"
    (October 2004), 29–37
  "Paul Scott: Victoria's Secret" (Janu-
    ary/February 2008), 203–9
  "Rosa Luxemburg: Red Rosa" (June
    2001), 273–79
  "Salman Rushdie: Hobbes in the
    Himalayas" (September 2005),
    63–69
  "V. S. Naipaul: Cruel and Unusual"
    (November 2008), 217–24
Audacity of Hope, The (Obama), 230–31
Auden, W. H., 149
Aung San Suu Kyi, 150
Authorization for Use of Military
  Force (AUMF), 108
Axelrod, David, 230
Ayers, William, 232

Baden-Powell, Robert, 16
Bailey, Peter, 221
Baker, James A. III, 128–29, 216
Baldwin, James, 229
Balfour Declaration, 156
Balkenende, Jan Peter, 194
Bamford, James
  Body of Secrets, 111
  The Puzzle Palace, 111
Banderas, Antonio, 3
Barnier, Michel, 259
Barr, Bob, 112
Batista, Fulgencio, 3, 8, 10, 11
Bayle, Pierre, 193
BBC, 1, 262
Beauvoir, Simone de, 174
Beinart, Peter, *The Good Fight: Why
  Liberals—and Only Liberals—Can
  Win the War on Terror and Make
  America Great Again*, **115–21**
Belge, Murat, 263
Bell, Aimee, 183
Bell, Gertrude, **153–58**
  "A Review of the Civil Administra-
    tion of Mesopotamia," 157
Bend in the River, A (Naipaul), 219
Benedict XVI, Pope, 139–40
Bennett, Alan, *The History Boys*, 141
Bergen, Peter, 111
Beria, Lavrenty, 143
Berlin, Isaiah, 27, 148, 199
Berman, Paul, 118
Bernal, J. D., 28

Betancourt, Ingrid, 150
Bethune, Norman, 160
Bevan, Aneurin, 146
Beyond Belief (Naipaul), 222
Bhagavad Gita, 68
Bhowani Junction (Masters), 205
Bhutto, Zulfikar Ali, 135
bin Laden, Osama, 132
Bitter Fruit (Schlesinger and Kinzer), 8
Black and Tans, 93
Black Caucus, 230
Black Jacobins, The (James), 223
Black Panthers, 111
Blackwell, Kenneth, 50
Blair, Tony, 96, 106, 112
Blake, William, 317n
Blue Nights (Didion), **281–82**
Blumenthal, Richard, 271
Blunt, Wilfred, 158
Bobbitt, Philip, 72
Body of Secrets (Bamford), 111
Boehner, John, 271
Bolívar, Simón, 7
Bolivia, Guevara's death in, 7, 15–17
Borges, Jorges Luis, 166
Bosnia, 119, 193, **215–16**, 255
Boston Massacre, 206
Boucher, Richard, 251
Boxer, Barbara, 120
Bradlee, Ben, 138
Bradley, Doug, 74
Brasillach, Robert, 150
Brideshead Revisited (Waugh), 168, 308
Britain's Secret Propaganda War (Lashmar and Oliver), 19–20
British Empire, end of, **141–46**, 203–4
British Empire Exhibition (1924), 92
British Museum, 239
Broaddrick, Juanita, 213
Brookhiser, Richard, 137
Bruce, Evangeline, 199
Bryan, William Jennings, 253
Brzezinski, Zbigniew, 200
Buchan, John, 155
Buchanan, James, 76
Buchanan, Patrick J., 53, 55, 105, 116
Buchwald, Art, 87
Buckley, Christopher, 233
Buckley, William F., Jr., 73, 137
Burdett-Coutts, Angela, 296
Burke, Edmund, 42
Burke and Hare, 160
Burmese Days (Orwell), 205, 314
Burns, John, 110–11

Bush administration (W.), 107–9, 111, 121, 127–29, 213, 254
Bush at War (Woodward), 255
Bush, George H. W., 17, 72, 119–20, 128, 216, 226
Bush, George W.
    bombing proposal by, 106, 112
    and elections, 48, 50, 225
    medal awarded by, 109
    and Middle East wars, 106, 120, 227
    and September 11 attacks, 109, 226
    speeches of, 30, 226
    and warrantless surveillance, 107, 108, 109, 111
Bush, Laura, 226
Byron, George Gordon, Lord, 58, 59, 60, 62
    "Childe Harold's Pilgrimage," 239
    "The Curse of Minerva," 239
Byzantine Empire, 238

Cambanis, Thanassis, *A Privilege to Die,* 267
Campbell, Joseph, and Henry Morton Robinson, *A Skeleton Key to Finnegans Wake,* 165
Camus, Albert, 151
    The Rebel, 149
Capra, Frank, 46
Carlyle, Thomas, 296, 318
Carr, Allen, 178, 186, 188
Carr, E. H., 21
Carrington, Lord, 253
Carter, Jimmy, 118, 199–200, 202
Carter, John P., 77
Casanova complex, 62
Case Against Barack Obama, The (Freddoso), **229–34**
"cash nexus," 1
Casino Royale (Fleming), 99, 102
Castro, Fidel, 4, 100, 149
    and Guevara, 10, 11
    lynch trials ordered by, 11
    and revolution, 1, 9, 10, 12
Castro, Raúl, 11
Cave of the Patriarchs, Hebron, 161
Céline, Louis-Ferdinand, 21, 274
Chalabi, Ahmad, 256
Chamberlain, Joseph, 95
Chamberlain, Neville, 95
Chandler, Raymond, 167
Chanel, Coco, 148
Channon, Henry "Chips," 200
Chappaquiddick, 137, 244

Charterhouse of Parma, The (Stendhal), 20

Chaucer, Geoffrey, 305

Che Guevara: A Revolutionary Life (Anderson), **1–18**

Chekhov, Anton, 36

Cheney, Dick, 48, 50, 128, 253

Chesterton, G. K., **299–310**, 318n
on Distributism, 302–3, 308, 309
Father Brown stories, 299, 307–8
"Lepanto," 299–300, 301
The Man Who Was Thursday, 307
and Marconi case, 301
The Napoleon of Notting Hill, 307
and Nazism, 308–10
on paradoxes, 301, 303–4, 306–7, 309
Paradox of Conservatism, 301
poems by, 299
"The Secret People," 300–301, 303
"Why I Am a Catholic," 306

"Childe Harold's Pilgrimage" (Byron), 239

Childers, Erskine, *The Riddle of the Sands*, 155

Chinese fighter aircraft collision (2001), 254

Chirac, Jacques, 96

Christie, Agatha, *Who Killed Roger Ackroyd?*, 167

Christmas, **87–89**, 202, **283–89**

Christmas Carol, A (Dickens), 287, 293

"Christmas Carol, A" (Lehrer), 283–84, 285, 286

Chung, Connie, 138

Church, Frank, 111

Churchill, Winston, 92, 93, 142, 144, 153

CIA, 3, 113
and Castro, 100
and Congress for Cultural Freedom, 201
and Guatemala, 8, 11
and Guevara, 4, 7, 16–17
and Hungary, 144
and Middle East, 109, 111

Cienfuegos, Camilo, 10

Cities of Salt quintet (Munif), 29

civil rights, 198–99

Clinton administration, 72, 202, 216

Clinton, Bill, 41, 54, 125, 227
Antiterrorism and Effective Death Penalty Act, 112, 226

and election campaign, 216
and Hillary, 211, 212
and Schlesinger, 202
and sex, 202, 212–13
and TV, 137

Clinton, Chelsea, 216

Clinton, Hillary, 121, **211–14**, **215–16**, 230–31

Clymer, Adam, 245

Codebreakers, The (Kahn), 111

Cold War, 117, 119, 121

Colefax, Sybil, 95

Coleridge, Samuel Taylor, "Khubla Khan," 36

colonialism, 145

Coming Up for Air (Orwell), 312

Communism, fall of, 141

Communist Party
in Britain, 21, 22–23, 24, 27
in Cuba, 10, 11, 13
in Spain, 21, 22

Condit, Gary, 138

Condition of the Working Class in England, The (Engels), 313

Congress for Cultural Freedom, 201

Connally, C. Ellen, 48

Connery, Sean, 99

Connor, "Bull," 199

Conquest, Robert, 273–74

Constitution, U.S., 105, 106, 108

Coppola, Peter, 189

Cortázar, Julio, 6

Coughlin, Father, 54

Coulter, Ann, 232

Council on American-Islamic Relations, 110

Coward, Noël, 99, 102

Craig, Daniel, 99

Crick, Bernard, 20

Croly, Herbert, *The Promise of American Life*, 168

Cromwell, Oliver, 89, 284, 319

Cronkite, Walter, 244

Crosby, Bing, 285

Crossman, Richard, 26

Crump, Ed "Boss," 43

Cuba
Castro revolution in, 1, 9, 10, 12
Communist Party in, 10, 11, 13
Guevara in, 11–13
legal currencies in, 1–4
Ministry of Tourism, 2

Cuban missile crisis, 12

Cuban National Bank, 1
Cultural Amnesia: Necesssary Memories From History and the Arts (James), **147–51**
Cunninghame Graham, R. B., 158
"Curse of Minerva, The" (Byron), 239
Curzon, Lord, 98
Cyprus, 263
Czechoslovakia, Soviet occupation of, 23–24

Daily Telegraph, 19, 20
Daily Worker, 22
Dangerfield, George, *The Strange Death of Liberal England*, 93
Dante Alighieri, 165
Darfur, 251–52, 258
Dark Green, Bright Red (Vidal), 8
Darwin, Charles, 296
Dassin, Jules, 239
David Copperfield (Dickens), 293, 295
Da Vinci Code, The (Brown), 166
Davis, Eliza, 296
Day of the Scorpion, The (Scott), 204
Dean, James, 6
death penalty, 42
Debray, Régis, 7
Decembrist revolution (1825), 58, 62
de Gaulle, Charles, 142
Democratic Convention (1968), 202
Dershowitz, Alan, 125
Descartes, René, 193
detoxification, 173–74
Deutscher, Isaac, 26, 27, 94, 279
Development of Capitalism in Russia, The (Lenin), 274
DeVoto, Bernard, 167
Dewey, Thomas, 116
Diamond, Larry, 110
Diamonds Are Forever (Fleming), 97, 98
Dickens, Charles, **291–97**, 299, 305
   American Notes for General Circulation, 297
   A Christmas Carol, 287, 293
   David Copperfield, 293, 295
   Martin Chuzzlewit, 297
   The Old Curiosity Shop, 294, 295
   Oliver Twist, 294–95, 296
   Our Mutual Friend, 296–97
   The Pickwick Papers, 294–95
Dickensian, 291
Didion, Joan, 201

Blue Nights, **281–82**
The Year of Magical Thinking, 281
Diebold voting machines, 50–52
Diefenbach, Hans, 275
Dink, Hrant, 263
"disappeared persons," 4
Distributism, 302–3, 308, 309
Disuniting of America, The (Schlesinger), 202
Division of the Spoils, A (Scott), 205
Doctorow, E. L., 45
Donaldson, Sam, 137
Dostoyevsky, Fyodor, 278, 291–92, 295
Doughty-Wylie, Dick, 153
Doyle, Sir Arthur Conan, 166, 307
"Dream of H. C. Earwicker, The" (Wilson), 164
Dreams from My Father (Obama), 231–32
Driberg, Tom, 26
Drieu de Rochelle, Pierre, 21
Dr. No (Fleming), 99
Dubinsky, David, 116
Dulles, Allen, 9
Dulles, John Foster, 9, 145, 146
Dumont, René, 13
Dunne, John Gregory, 201, 281
Dyer, Reginald, 93, 206
Dylan, Bob, 281
Dzerzhinsky, Felix, 278

Earnhardt, Dale, 74
East India Company, 203
Eastman, Max, *The Literary Mind*, 164
Eco, Umberto, 103, 147
Eden, Sir Anthony, 100, 142, 144–45, 146
Edward VIII, king of England, 92
Edwards, John, 48, 230–31
Egypt, 142, 143–45, 146
Einstein, Albert, 30, 95
Eisenhower administration, 144, 145, 198
Eisenhower, Dwight D., 72, 100, 144–45, 146, 197
Elgin, Lord, 238–39, 240
Eliot, T. S., 178, 299
   "After Strange Gods," 80
Elizabeth II, queen of England, 92
Elton, Ben, 94
Emancipation Proclamation (Lincoln), 71, 109
Emanuel, Rahm, 232

Emmert, Kirk, 45
empire, 19; *see also* Great Britain
Encounter magazine, 201
Ends of British Imperialism: The Scramble for Empire, Suez, and Decolonialization (Louis), **141–46**
Engels, Friedrich, *The Condition of the Working Class in England*, 313
English Patient, The (film), 154
English Questions (Anderson), 27
Enigma of Arrival, The (Naipaul), 217
Enlightenment, 120, 193
Erdogan, Recep Tayyip, 262–64
Erlich, Henryk, 22
Establishment Clause, 288–89
Eugene Onegin (Pushkin), 61
Euripides, 237, 281
European Union, 262
Everyman Chesterton, The (Ker), **299–310**
Evita (Lloyd Webber), 3
exercise, 174, 190–91
Exner, Judith Campbell, 199
Eyre, Edward John, 296

Failed Illusions: Moscow, Washington, Budapest, and the 1956 Hungarian Revolt (Gati), **141–46**
Faisal, King (Saudi Arabia), 155, 157
Falklands War, 253
Fallaci, Oriana, **131–40**
  Inshallah, 138
  Interview with History, 134
  The Rage and the Pride, 139
Falwell, Jerry, 72
Fan-Mail (James), 151
Farabundo Martí Liberation Front, 2, 3
Farrakhan, Louis, *Final Call*, 84
fascism, 19
FBI, 109–10
Fekkai, Frédéric, 189
feminism, 150–51, 195
Fillmore, Millard, 76
Final Call (Farrakhan), 84
financial system, collapse of, 227
Financial Times, 187
Finnegans Wake (Joyce), 164–65
Firbank, Ronald, 167
Fireflies (S. Naipaul), 224
Firing Line (TV), 137–38
First Amendment, 54, 87, 89, 106, 107, 110, 112, 288
Fitzgerald, F. Scott, 171

Flanders and Swann, 43
Flaubert, Gustave, 151, 167
Fleming, Ian, **97–103**
  Casino Royale, 99, 102
  Diamonds Are Forever, 97, 98
  Dr. No, 99
  For Your Eyes Only, 101, 103
  "From a View to Kill," 103
  From Russia with Love, 100
  State of Excitement (unpubl.), 97
  You Only Live Twice, 98, 101
Flowers, Gennifer, 213
Fonda, Henry, 134
Foner, Eric, 82
Fool in Christ, Emanuel Quint, The, (Hauptmann), 275
Foote, Paul, 57
Ford, Gerald R., 200, 201
Foreign Intelligence Surveillance Act (FISA), 107–8, 111
Foreign Policy, "Colin Powell: Powell Valediction," 251–59
Forman, Miloš, 147
Forrestal, Mike, 199
Forster, E. M., 23, 93
  A Passage to India, 204, 205, 206, 207
Forster, John, 295
For Your Eyes Only (Fleming), 101, 103
Four Seasons Biltmore resort, Santa Barbara, 172–75
Fourth Amendment, 106, 112
Fowles, John, 81
Foxman, Abraham, 125
Fox News, 89
Franco, Francisco, 315–16
Franken, Al, 43
Franklin, Benjamin, 84–85, 88, 111, 113
Freddoso, David, *The Case Against Barack Obama*, **229–34**
Freedom Defense Committee, 23
Freeman, John, 136
French, Patrick, *The World Is What It Is: The Authorized Biography of V. S. Naipaul*, **217–24**
Freud, Sigmund, 41, 94
Friedman, Kinky, 80
"From a View to Kill" (Fleming), 103
From Russia with Love (Fleming), 100
Frost, David, 136
Frost, Martin, 173, 175
Fyvel, T. R., 318n

Galbraith, John Kenneth, 66
Gallipoli, 36, 153

Galloway, George, 102
Gandhi, Indira, 135
Gandhi, Mohandas K. (Mahatma),
    80–81, 207
Garbo, Greta, 151
García Márquez, Gabriel, 5–6
    "Operation Carlota," 6
Gates, Robert, 127, 128
Gati, Charles, *Failed Illusions: Moscow,*
    Washington, Budapest, and the
    1956 Hungarian Revolt, **141–46**
Gehlen, Reinhard, 117
Gellhorn, Martha, 2
Gellner, Ernest, 24
Genovese, Eugene and Elizabeth, 82
Gentile, Giovanni, 274
George V, king of England, 92
George Orwell Diaries, **311–20**
Gertrude Bell: Queen of the Desert,
    Shaper of Nations (Howell),
    153–58
Gettysburg Address (Lincoln), 84
Giancana, Sam, 2
Gingrich, Newt, 270–71
G. K. Chesterton: A Biography (Ker),
    299–310
Glezos, Manolis, 238
"God Bless the USA" (song), 76
Goering, Hermann, 276
Goethe, Johann Wolfgang von, 275
Goldstein, Baruch, 161
Goldstein, Cary, 186
Goldwater, Barry, 72
Gombrich, E. H., 27
Gonzales, Alberto, 113
Goodbye to a River (Graves), 81
Good Fight, The: Why Liberals—
    and Only Liberals—Can Win
    the War on Terror and Make
    America Great Again (Beinart),
    115–21
Good Soldier Schweik, The (Hašek), 39
Gorbachev, Mikhail, 119
Gordimer, Nadine, 223
Gore, Al, 50, 120, 213, 225, 226, 227
GQ, 253
Granma, 10, 166
Grapes of Wrath, The (Steinbeck), 232
Graves, John, *Goodbye to a River,* 81
Great Britain
    Arab Bureau of, 154
    Communist Party in, 21, 22–23,
        24, 27
    Empire of, 92, **141–46**, 156, **203–9**

General Strike (1926), 302
    and India, *see* India
    MI5 and MI6, 100
Great Leap Forward (China), 13
Greenbrier resort, White Sulphur
    Springs, 76–77
Greene, Graham, 81
    Stamboul Train, 160
Greenwood, Lee, 76
Guantanamo Bay, 226
Guatemala
    coup in, 9–10
    Guevara in, 8–10
Guerrillas (Naipaul), 221
Guerrilla Warfare (Guevara), 7
Guevara, Ernesto Che, **1–18**
    cult of, 3–5, 17–18
    death of, 3–4, 6, 7, 15–17
    early years of, 6–7
    Guerrilla Warfare, 7
    health of, 6–7, 15
    as internationalist, 7–11, 13–15
    in later years, 14–16, 17
    leper colonies visited by, 5
    medical training of, 5, 7, 8, 9, 160
    The Motorcycle Diaries: A Journey
        around South America, 5, 7–16
    rationalizations by, 11–12
    sense of humor in, 14
    wife and children of, 7
    writings of, 6
"Guide to Finnegans Wake, A" (Wil-
    son), 165
Guillén, Nicolás, 6

Habibi, Emile, *Saeed the Pessoptimist,*
    29, 117
Haile Selassie, 135
Hale, Patricia, 218, 222
Halliburton, 120
Hamdi, Yaser Esam, 108, 109
Hamilton, Alexander, 73
Hamilton, Ian, 177–78
Hamilton, Lee, 128
Hanley, Jennifer, 211
Hardy, Oliver, 93
Hariri, Rafik, 266, 267
Harriman, Averall, 198, 202
Harvard Law Review, 233
Hašek, Jaroslav, *The Good Soldier Sch-*
    weik, 39
Hastings, Warren, 203
Hauptmann, Gerhart, *The Fool in*
    Christ, Emanuel Quint, 275

Havel, Václev, 24
"Haw-Haw, Lord" (Joyce), 93
Hayden, Michael, 110
Hayes, Rutherford B., 45
Hazlitt, William, 149
health care, **159–62**, 245
Hegel, Georg Wilhelm Friedrich, 142,
    148
Heidegger, Martin, 274
Heine, Heinrich, 149, 151
Heller, Joseph, 65
Hemingway, Ernest, 2
Henry VIII, king of England, 309
Hercules, 267–68
Herero tribe, 276
Hero of Our Time, A (Lermontov),
    57–62
Herzl, Theodor, 124
Herzog, Werner, 5
Hezbollah, 128, **265–68**
Hikmet, Nâzim, 34
Hill, Christopher, 91
Hillary, Sir Edmund, 211–12
Hippocratic principles, 159–61
Hirohito, Emperor (Japan), 206
Hirsi Ali, Ayaan, 150, **193–98**
    Infidel, 195
History Boys, The (Bennett), 141
Hitler, Adolf, 117, 149, 150, 238,
    308–9, 318
    and Catholicism, 309
    Mein Kampf, 274
    Soviet alliance with, 21, 115, 116
    and Spanish Civil War, 314
Hoffman, Abbie, 200
Hoggart, Richard, 313
Hoggart, Simon, 181
Homer, *Odyssey*, 164
Hooters, 76
Hoover, J. Edgar, 110
Hopkinson, Tom, 315
House for Mr. Biswas, A (Naipaul), 220
Howe, Julia Ward, 116
Howell, Georgina, *Gertrude Bell: Queen
    of the Desert, Shaper of Nations*,
    153–58
"How to Write about Lenin—and
    How Not To" (MacIntyre),
    148–49
Huch, Ricarda, 150
Hudis, Peter, 273
Hughes, Karen, 107
Hull, Blair, 230
Humphrey, Hubert H., 116

Hungarian Revolt (1956), 141, 142–46,
    202
Hussein, Saddam, 49, 254
    and Bush (H. W.) administration,
        120, 128–29, 213, 226
    connections of, 37, 102, 123
    and Iran, 129
    and Kuwait, 119
    opposition to, 105, 120, 129, 213,
        227
    removal of, 227, 266
    and September 11 attacks, 120, 226
    TV interview of, 131, 132
Hutton, Barbara, 91, 96
Huxley, Thomas, 296
Hylton, Wil, 253

*Ian Fleming & James Bond: The Cultural
    Politics of 007* (symposium), 97
Ibn Saud, 155, 156
"If the South Woulda Won (We'd a
    Had It Made)" (song), 74
Ignatius, David, 263
I Married a Communist (Roth), 116
In a Free State (Naipaul), 223
India
    Amritsar massacre, 93, 206
    colonial leadership in, 156, 203–4
    end of the Raj in, 93, 143–44, 203–9
    and partition, 206
    riots in, 316
In Dubious Battle (Steinbeck), 232
Infidel (Hirsi Ali), 195
Information Research Department
    (IRD), British Foreign Office,
    19, 20, 24, 27
Inquisition, 306
Inshallah (Fallaci), 138
internationalism, 321
Interview with History (Fallaci), 134
Invisible Woman, The (Tomalin), 291
Ioannidou, Maria, 235
Iran, 129, 227, **247–50**, 265, 267
Iran-Contra, 17
Iraq, **153–58**
    birth of, 154, 155, 156
    inspections in, 258–59
    as Mesopotamia, 154, 155, 157
    war in, 120, **127–29**, 212, 213, 227
Iraq Study Group (ISG), 127, 129
Ireland, Ulster mutiny (1914), 93
Islam, Yusuf (formerly Cat Stevens),
    110
Israel, 255, 265–68

Jackson, Henry "Scoop," 118
Jackson, Leslie, 75
Jagger, Mick, 200
James, Clive
  *Cultural Amnesia: Necesssary Memo-
    ries from History and the Arts,*
    147–51
  Fan-Mail, 151
James, C. L. R., *The Black Jacobins,* 223
James, Henry, 93, 305, 320
James Bond Dossier, The (Amis), 98
Japanese imperialism, 206, 207
Jefferson, Thomas, 44, 54, 55, 73, 78,
    288–89
Jesus of Nazareth, 81, 109
Jewish Fundamentalism in Israel (Shahak
    and Mezvinsky), 161
Johnson, Lyndon B., 72, 199, 245
Johnson, Magic, 75
Johnson, Samuel, 305
Journals: 1952–2000 (Schlesinger),
    197–202
Joyce, James, 81
  Finnegans Wake, 164–65
  Ulysses, 164
Joyce, William "Lord Haw-Haw," 93
J Sisters, 181–83
Judgment of Paris, The (Vidal), 180
Judt, Tony, 124–26
Jumblatt, Kamal, 266
Jünger, Ernst, 149
Justice Department, U.S., 106, 108

Kabila, Laurent-Désiré, 3
Kafka, Franz, 167, 307
Kahane, Meir, 125
Kahn, David, *The Codebreakers,* 111
Karenga, Ron, 287
Kashmir, 63–67, 69
Keats, John, "Ode on a Grecian Urn,"
    242
Kemal, Mustafa (Atatürk), 34–35,
    36–37
Kennedy, Edward M. (Ted), 137, 200,
    202, 243–46
Kennedy, John F., 117–18
  and ADA, 118
  assassination of, 71
  and Cuba, 7, 12, 100, 117, 198, 244
  health of, 244
  and Schlesinger, 197–99, 200
Kennedy, Joseph, Sr., 244
Kennedy, Robert F., 199
Kennedy family, 198, 244

Kentucky Derby, 79
Kenyon College, Ohio, 45, 46
Keogh, David, 106, 107
Ker, Ian, ed., *The Everyman Chesterton*
    and *G. K. Chesterton: A Biography,*
    299–310
Kerouac, Jack, 6
Kerry, John, 17, 40, 42, 48, 49, 50, 52,
    225, 254
Keyes, Alan, 230
Khomeini, Ayatollah, 135
Khrushchev, Nikita, 12, 142, 144, 198
Kimche, Jon, 318n
King, Florence, *Wasp, Where Is Thy
    Sting?,* 73
King, Larry, 137
King, Martin Luther, Jr., 110, 199
Kinzer, Stephen, 8
Kipling, Rudyard, 58, 92, 93
Kirwan, Celia, 24–25
Kissinger, Henry A., 127, 128, 133–34,
    201, 257, 287
Klein, Melanie, 27
Klein, Morton, 123–24
Koestler, Arthur, 24, 94, 318
Kołakowski, Leszek, *Main Currents of
    Marxism,* 149
Koran, 36
Korda, Alberto, 3
Kovály, Heda, 150
Kraus, Karl, 150
"Kubla Khan" (Coleridge), 36
Kulwicki, Alan, 76
Kundera, Milan, 166
Kuwait, 119, 129, 255
Kuwait Oil Company, 97–98

Lamb, Brian, 137
Laschitza, Annelies, 273
Lashmar, Paul, and James Oliver,
    Britain's Secret Propaganda War,
    19–20
Latitudes del Silencio (Pesce), 7
Laurel, Stan, 93
Lawrence, A. W., 235
Lawrence, D. H., 81
Lawrence, T. E., 153, 154, 157, 158
Learmont, George, 59
Lebanon, 265–67
Le Bourgeois Gentilhomme (Molière), 72
Lee, Robert E., 78
Left Behind series, 166
Lehrer, Tom, "A Christmas Carol,"
    283–84, 285, 286

Lemkin, Raphael, 261
Lenin, V. I., 275, 278
  *The Development of Capitalism in
    Russia*, 274
  tomb of, 4
Leninism, 9, 11
"Lepanto" (Chesterton), 299–300, 301
Lermontov, Mikhail
  A Hero of Our Time, **57–62**
  "No, I'm Not Byron," 58
  "On the Death of the Poet," 61
Lessing, Doris, 62
Letters of Rosa Luxemburg, The (Adler et
    al., eds.), **273–79**
Lewinsky, Monica, 213
Lewis, Anthony, 287
Library of America, 164
Lichtenberg, Georg Christoph, 149
Lieberman, Joseph, 120, 226
Liebknecht, Sophie, 277
Lincoln, Abraham
  Emancipation Proclamation, 71,
    109
  Gettysburg Address, 84
  habeas corpus suspended by, 108
  second inaugural address, 84
Lindbergh, Charles, 54, 116
Lindh, John Walker, 109
Lin Piao, 12
*Literary Essays and Reviews of the
    1920s* and *Literary Essays and
    Reviews of the 1930s* (Wilson),
    163–68
Literary Mind, The (Eastman), 164
Lituchy, Gregg, 180, 182, 186
Lloyd George, David, 234
Lloyd Webber, Sir Andrew, *Evita*, 3
Locke, Richard, 218
Lodge, Henry Cabot, 146
Los Angeles riots (1992), 68
Louis, Wm. Roger, *Ends of British
    Imperialism: The Scramble for
    Empire, Suez, and Decoloniza-
    tion*, **141–46**
Loved One, The (Waugh), 168
Lowell, Robert, 45, 81, 177
Lowenberg, Marc, 180
Lugar, Dick, 234
Lumumba, Patrice, 14
L'Univers concentrationnaire (Adler et al.,
    eds.), **273–79**
Luxemburg, Rosa, 11, 150, **273–79**
Lycett, Andrew, 97
Lyssarides, Vassos, 160

Macaulay, Thomas Babington, Lord, 204
MacDiarmid, Hugh, 27
MacIntyre, Alasdair, 7
  "How to Write about Lenin—and
    How Not To," 148–49
Macready, William, 296
MAD (mutual assured destruction),
    118–19
Mahfouz, Naguib, 29
Mailer, Norman, 81
Main Currents of Marxism
    (Kołakowski), 149
Makarios III, Archbishop, 134
Malenkov, Georgy, 143
Malinowski, Bronisław, 27
Malle, Louis, 147
Mandela, Nelson, 17, 81
Mandelstam, Nadezhda, 150
Man Who Was Thursday, The (Chester-
    ton), 307
Maoists, 12
Mao Zedong, 160, 271
March on Washington, 199
Marconi case, 301
Marks, Herman, 10–11
Marshall Plan, 116
Martí, Farabundo, 6n
Martí Liberation Front, 2, 3
Martin, Kingsley, 26
Martin Chuzzlewit (Dickens), 297
Marx, Karl, 7
Marxism, 8, 13, 149, 274
Mason-Dixon Line, 73
Masters, John, *Bhowani Junction*, 205
Matos, Huber, 12
Matthews, Herbert, 11
Maugham, Somerset, 81
Mayan *indigenes*, 8
McCain, John, 231
McCarthy, Joseph, 26, 28
McCormack, Edward J., 244
McCurdy, Dave, 118
McCuskey, Madeline, 173
McGovern, George, 199–200
McMahon, Linda, 271
McMurtry, Larry, 81
Meacham, Jon, 232
Mearsheimer, John, 125
Medea (Euripides), 237
medical profession, **159–62**
Medvedev, Dmitry, 234
Meet the Press (TV), 14
Mein Kampf (Hitler), 274
Mencken, H. L., 79, 150

Mengele, Josef, 160, 161, 276
Menuhin, Yehudi, 94
Mercouri, Melina, 239
Meredith, James, 198
Mesopotamia, as Iraq, 154, 155, 157
Mexico, Guevara in, 10
Mezvinsky, Norton, 161
Michael, Quintana Roo Dunne, 281–82
Midnight's Children (Rushdie), 64
MI5 and MI6, 100
Miguel Street (Naipaul), 223
Milani, Abbas, 249–50
Mill, John Stuart, 296
Miłocz, Czesław, 148
Milosevic, Slobodan, 258
Milton, John, 165, 319
Mimi (cat), 277
Mishra, Pankaj, 67
Mladic, Ratko, 193
Mobutu Sese Seko, 3, 15
Modern Quarterly, The, 28
Molière, *Le Bourgeois Gentilhomme*, 72
Molotov, Vyacheslav, 22n
Monroe, Marilyn, 199, 244
Montesquieu, 141, 145
Moore, Henry, 23
Moore, Michael, 51, 118
Morgan, Peter, 136
Morgenthau, Henry, 261–62
Morozov, Pavlik, 21–22
Mosley, Sir Oswald, 22, 94
Mother Jones, 118
Motorcycle Diaries: A Journey around South America (Guevara), 5, 7–16
Mount Everest, 211
Moynihan, Daniel Patrick, 66, 71–72
Mudd, Roger, 137
mudslinging, **39–44**
Muggeridge, John, 95–96
multilateralism, 255
Munich (Spielberg), 99
Munif, Abdelrahman, Cities of Salt quintet, 29
Murrow, Edward R., 136
Mussolini, Benito, 274, 275, 303, 306, 314
My American Journey (Powell), 257–58
My Name Is Red (Pamuk), 30

Nabokov, Vladimir, 57, 59, 60, 62
Nader, Ralph, 48, 50
Nafisi, Azar, *Reading Lolita in Tehran*, 247
Nagy, Imre, 145

Naipaul, Seepersad, 220, 223
Naipaul, Shiva, 223–24
Fireflies, 224
North of South, 224
Naipaul, V. S., **217–24**
An Area of Darkness, 221
A Bend in the River, 219
Beyond Belief, 222
The Enigma of Arrival, 217
Guerrillas, 221
A House for Mr. Biswas, 220
In a Free State, 223
Miguel Street, 223
A Way in the World, 223
Namier, Lewis, 27
Napoléon Bonaparte, 3, 230, 281
Napoleon of Notting Hill, The (Chesterton), 307
NASCAR, 73–76, 79
Nasrallah, Hassan, 266, 267
Nasser, Gamal Abdel, 37
Nation, The, "What Is Patriotism?" (July 15/22, 1991), 321
National Association of Criminal Defense Lawyers, 110
National Rifle Association (NRA), 112
National Security Agency (NSA), 106, 107, 109, 110, 111
National Security Council (NSC), 145
NATO, 30, 253, 264
Nazism, 308–10, 318
Nehru, Jawaharlal, 207, 316
Neruda, Pablo, 6n
Neurach, Eva, 94–95
New Deal, 116, 198
New Frontier, 71, 117
New Left, 117, 141
Newman, Cardinal John Henry, 301–2, 305, 310
Newman, Paul, 45
New Republic, 27, 163
New Review, 177
Newsweek, 232, 249
New Yorker, 165
New York Review of Books, The, 124, 222
"Che Guevara: Goodbye to All That" (July 17, 1997), 1–18
"Orwell's List" (September 26, 2002), 19–28
Pamuk as contributor to, 30
reports from Kashmir in, 67
New York Times, 3, 11, 40, 88, 243, 247
Ngo Dinh Diem, 244

Nicholas I, Czar, 61
Niebuhr, Reinhold, 116–17
Nineteen Eighty-Four (Orwell), 19, 20, 22, 313–14, 316
Niven, David, 99
Nixon, Richard M., 41, 136, 198, 245
 and elections, 72, 200–201
 Ford's pardon of, 201
 and Hungary, 145
 and impeachment, 111
 and Schlesinger, 200–201
 and Vietnam, 201, 287
"No, I'm Not Byron" (Lermontov), 58
Noonan, Peggy, 233
No One Left to Lie To (Hitchens), 213
Norgay, Tenzing, 211
Norquist, Grover, 112
North Korea, 227
North of South (S. Naipaul), 224
Nouvelle Revue Française, 21
Nugent, S. Georgia, 46

Obama administration, 247, 249
Obama, Barack Hussein, 225, **229–34**, 243
 The Audacity of Hope, 230–31
 Dreams from My Father, 231–32
O'Brien, Conor Cruise, 201
O'Connor, Father John, 299
O'Connor, Leo, 106, 107
O'Dell, Walden, 50, 51
"Ode on a Grecian Urn" (Keats), 242
O'Dwyer, Michael, 93
Odyssey (Homer), 164
Office of Strategic Services (OSS), 100
O'Hara, Damian, 178–79
Ohio, election (2004) in, **45–52**
Oklahoma City bombing, 112, 226
Old Curiosity Shop, The (Dickens), 294, 295
Old Mortality (Scott), 59
Oliver, James, 19–20
Oliver Twist (Dickens), 294–95, 296
Olivetti, 3
Olympic Games, 252–53
"On the Death of the Poet" (Lermontov), 61
"Operation Carlota" (García Márquez), 6
Oppenheimer, Robert, 68
Opus Dei, 305
Orwell, George, 3, **19–28**, 148
 Animal Farm, 23, 24, 28
 As I Please column by, 311

Burmese Days, 205, 314
Coming Up for Air, 312
George Orwell Diaries, introduction, **311–20**
 Nineteen Eighty-Four, 19, 20, 22, 313–14, 316
 The Road to Wigan Pier, 94, 313
 and Spanish Civil War, 314, 315–16
 "Why I Write," 311
Oswald, Lee Harvey, 71
Ottoman Empire, 238, 261
Our Mutual Friend (Dickens), 296–97

Padilha, Janea, 181, 182
Pahlavi, Mohammad Reza, Shah of Iran, 131–33, 265
Paine, Thomas, 42, 78
País, Frank, 10
Pakistan, 63–67, 69, 205, 206, 208
Palestine, 156, 255, 266
Palin, Sarah, 233
Pamuk, Orhan, 263
 My Name Is Red, 30
 Snow, **29–37**
Pandermalis, Dimitrios, 241
Papandreou, Nick, 236
Parthenon, **235–42**
Partisan Review, 20, 148
Passage to India, A (Forster), 204, 205, 206, 207
Patriot Act, 112
patriotism, **53–55**, **321**
Paxman, Jeremy, 136
Pepper, Claude, 28
Peres, Shimon, 263
Pericles (Plutarch), 236–37
Peron, Juan, 5, 6
Perot, H. Ross, 41, 271
Pesce, Hugo, *Latitudes del Silencio*, 7
Peter Rabbit (Potter), 150
Pevsner, Nikolaus, 94
Phidias, 238, 240
Pickwick Papers, The, (Dickens), 294–95
Pierce, Franklin, 76
Pillars of Hercules (Soho pub), 177
Pinckney, Darryl, 188
Plan of Attack (Woodward), 253, 255
Pledge of Allegiance, 42, 75, 80
PLO, 265
Plot Against America, The, (Roth), 116
Plutarch, *Pericles*, 236–37
polymath, 147–48
Popper, Karl, 27, 94

Potter, Beatrix:
  Peter Rabbit, 150
  The Tale of Mr. Tod, 150
  The Tale of Pigling Bland, 150
Pound, Ezra, 21
Powell, Anthony, 61, 62, 149, 217
Powell, Colin, 112, **251–59**
  My American Journey, 257–58
POW/MIA, 74
President We Deserve, The (Walker), 54
Priestley, J. B., 26
Privilege to Die, A (Cambanis), 267
Promise of American Life, The (Croly), 168
Protestant Reformation, 305, 308–9
Proust, Marcel, 148
Pushkin, Alexander, 58–59, 60–61, 62
  Eugene Onegin, 61
Putin, Vladimir, 250
Puzzle Palace, The (Bamford), 111

Qaddafi, Muammar, 133
Quakers, 111
Quixote, Don (fict.), 7

Radio Free Europe, 145
Raft, George, 2
Rage and the Pride, The (Fallaci), 139
Raj Quartet, The (Scott), 63, **203–9**
Rákosi, Mátyás, 143
Ram Leela (Indian epic), 65
Randolph, A. Philip, 199
Ransom, Harry, 81
Ransom, John Crowe, 45
Rashid, Ahmed, 222
Rasmussen, Anders Fogh, 263
Rather, Dan, 131, 132
Rauf, Imam, 284
Raven, Simon, 102
Reading Lolita in Tehran (Nafisi), 247
Reagan, Ronald, 118–19, 121, 199, 231
Rebel, The (Camus), 149
Red Brigades, 148
Rees, Richard, 20, 24, 25
reflexology, 172
Reformation, 305, 308–9
regime change, 255–56
rehabilitation, **169–75**, **177–83**,
  185–91
  Brazilian keratin hair treatment,
    188–89
  Brazilian waxing technique, 181–83
  dentistry, 180–81, 186
  exercise, 174, 190–91
  manicure, 187

  memory loss, 187–88
  professional report and opinion,
    169–71
  scorecard, 191
  smoking cessation, 178–80, 186–88,
    191
  spa, 172–75
  unforeseen consequences of, 187
Rehnquist, William, 45
Reid, Harry, 120
Reid, Jerry, 76
Republican Jewish Coalition, 123–24
Republic of Letters, 165, 167
Reuther, Walter, 116
Revolution
  American, 55
  and Counter-Revolution, 7
  Decembrist, 58, 62
  expectations of, 8
  non-Soviet model sought in, 12
  readiness to die in, 10
Rice, Susan, 249
Rich, Marc, 125
Riddle of the Sands, The (Childers), 155
Rilke, Rainer Maria, 151
Road to Wigan Pier, The (Orwell), 94, 313
Robertson, Geoffrey, 107
Robeson, Paul, 27
Robinson, Henry Morton, 165
Roche, Dennis, 188, 189
Rockwell, Norman, 85
Rodriguez, Felix, 16–17
Rogers, Will, 201
Rognoni, Virginio, 148
Rolland, Romain, 275
Romero, Anthony, 106, 110
Roosevelt, Eleanor, 116
Roosevelt, Franklin, 150
Roosevelt, Theodore, 7, 43
Rose, Charlie, 137
Rosenberg, Alfred, 274
Roth, Philip
  I Married a Communist, 116
  The Plot Against America, 116
Rousset, David, *L'Univers concentration-*
  naire, 273
Rubin, Barnett, 110
Rumsfeld, Donald, 127, 128
Rushdie, Salman, 110, 321
  Midnight's Children, 64
  Shalimar the Clown, **63–69**
  Shame, 64
Rusk, Dean, 256
Ruskin, John, 296

Russell, Bertrand, 274
Russert, Tim, 137, 256
Rustin, Bayard, 116
Ryan, Jack, 230

Sadat, Anwar el-, 37, 201
Saeed the Pessoptimist (Habibi), 29, 117
Safire, William, 125
St. Paul's Cathedral, London, 95,
    318–19
Saklatvala, Shapurji, 92
Salinas Museum, Palermo, 241
Salinger, J. D., 177
Sandinistas, 3, 118
San Martín, José de, 6n
San Salvador, 2
Santiago, Cuba, massacre in, 1
Sartre, Jean-Paul, 148, 174
Saunders, Frances Stonor, *Who Paid the
    Piper?*, 26
Sayers, Dorothy L., 166
Scarborough Country (MSNBC), 87–88
Schiller, Friedrich von, 275
Schlesinger, Arthur, Jr., 116, 117
    The Age of Jackson, 202
    The Disuniting of America, 202
    Journals: 1952–2000, **197–202**
    A Thousand Days, 198
Schlesinger, Stephen, and Stephen
    Kinzer, *Bitter Fruit*, 8
Scholl, Sophie, 150
Schröder, Gerhard, 96
Scott, Paul, 65
    The Day of the Scorpion, 204
    A Division of the Spoils, 205
    The Raj Quartet, 63, **203–9**
Scott, Sir Walter, *Old Mortality*, 59
Scowcroft, Brent, 105
Sebestyen, Victor, *Twelve Days: The
    Story of the 1956 Hungarian Revo-
    lution*, **141–46**
Second Amendment, 112
"Secret People, The" (Chesterton),
    300–301, 303
Sellers, Peter, 99
September 11 attacks, 30, 247
    and Afghanistan-Iraq wars, 119–20,
        255
    and Fallaci, 139
    and intelligence agencies, 109
    and legislation, 108
    as life-changing event, 55, 105, 119,
        226
    and *W.* (film), 225–26

Serge, Victor, 273
Shahak, Israel, and Norton Mezvinsky,
    Jewish Fundamentalism in Israel, 161
Shakespeare, William, *As You Like It*,
    275–76
Shalimar the Clown (Rushdie), **63–69**
Shame (Rushdie), 64
Shrum, Bob, 243
Silva, Hector, 2–3
Simpson, Wallis, 92
Singer, Isaac Bashevis, 81
Sir Vidia's Shadow (Theroux), 221
Sitwell, Osbert, 23
60 minutes (TV), 136
Skeleton Key to Finnegans Wake, A
    (Campbell and Robinson), 165
Slate
    "Ayaan Hirsi Ali: The Price of Free-
        dom" (October 8, 2007), 193–96
    "Bah, Humbug" (December 20,
        2005), 87–89
    "The Case against Hillary Clinton"
        (January 14, 2008), 211–14
    "Edward M. Kennedy: Redemption
        Song" (August 31, 2009), 243–46
    "Engaging with Iran Is Like Having
        Sex With Someone Who Hates
        You" (September 14, 2009),
        247–50
    "Hezbollah's Progress" (October 18,
        2010), 265–68
    "How Uninviting" (October 23,
        2006), 123–26
    "Look Who's Cutting and Running
        Now" (November 20, 2006),
        127–29
    "No Regrets" (January 19, 2009),
        225–27
    "Physician, Heal Thyself" (July 9,
        2007), 159–62
    "The Politicians We Deserve" (Oc-
        tober 11, 2010), 269–71
    "Shut Up about Armenians or We'll
        Hurt Them Again" (April 5,
        2010), 261–64
    "The Tall Tale of Tuzla" (March 31,
        2008), 215–16
Slater, Humphrey, 315
Slaughterhouse Province, The (Davis),
    261
Smallholder, 317
Smith, Winston, 317n
smoking cessation, 178–80, 186–88,
    191

Smolka, Peter, 23
Smollett, Peter, 25
Snow (Pamuk), **29–37**
Socialist Leader, 23
Socrates, 237
Solti, Sir George, 94
Somoza, Anastasio, 8, 9
Sontag, Susan, 119, 147
Sophocles, 237
South, the, **71–82**
  "Bible Belt," 79
  redefining itself, 82
  rednecks in, 73
  Texas, 80–82
Soviet Union
  and Cold War, 120
  "Doctors' Plot" in, 159
  Guevara's criticism of, 12–13
  Hitler's alliance with, 21, 115, 116
  and Hungarian Revolt, 141, 142–46
Spain, Communist Party in, 21, 22
Spanish Armada, 306
Spanish Civil War, 115, 314, 315–16
Spanish Republic, 10
Spender, Stephen, 26
Sperber, Manès, 148
Spielberg, Steven, *Munich,* 99
Spinoza, Baruch, 193
Spurling, Hilary, 205
Stalin, Joseph
  death of, 142, 149
  and "Doctors' Plot," 159
  and Guevara, 9
  and Hitler, 115, 116
  and Orwell, 27, 28
Stalinism, 19, 22, 95, 161–62
Stamboul Train (Greene), 160
"Star-Spangled Banner, The" (anthem),
  74
State Department, U.S., 251–57
State of Excitement (Fleming, unpubl.),
  97
Steinbeck, John
  The Grapes of Wrath, 232
  In Dubious Battle, 232
Stendhal, *The Charterhouse of Parma,* 201
Stevens, Cat (aka Yusuf Islam), 110
Stevenson, Adlai E., 43, 72, 199, 256
Stone, I. F., 14, 27, 117
Stone, Oliver, 225–26
Stones of Athens, The (Wycherley), 237
Stoppard, Tom, 81
Strange Death of Liberal England, The
  (Dangerfield), 93

Straw, Jack, 107
Submission (film), 194
Suez Canal, 100, 142, 143–45, 146,
  202
Suphi, Mustafa, 34
Sykes, Sir Mark, 157
Sykes-Picot Agreement, 156
Syria, 266, 267

Tale of Mr. Tod, The (Potter), 150
Tale of Pigling Bland, The (Potter), 150
Taliban, 105, 222, 248
Tammany Hall, 51–52
Tea Party, 270–71
Temple of Aphaea, 235
Temple of Poseidon, 236
Tenet, George, 109, 110, 256
Tennant, Stephen, 217
Texas, 80–82
Thanksgiving, **83–85**, 87
Thatcher, Margaret, 96, 119, 253
Theroux, Paul, *Sir Vidia's Shadow,* 221
Thompson, Edward, 158
Thousand Days, A (Schlesinger), 198
Thule Society, 276–77
Timerman, Jacobo, 166
Titanic, 96
Tomalin, Claire, *The Invisible Woman,*
  291
totalitarian, use of term, 273
To the Finland Station (Wilson), 165
Transition magazine, 164
Trotha, Lothar von, 276
Trotsky, Leon, 10, 15
Trujillo, Rafael, 8
Truman administration, 27, 117
"truth commissions," 4
Tschumi, Bernard, 240
Turgenev, Ivan, 62
Turkey
  and Armenia, **261–64**
  as bridge between East and West,
    30, 31
  and Byzantine Empire, 238
  Gallipoli, 36, 153
  and Mesopotamia, 155
  national identity of, 35, 37
  Ottoman Empire, 238, 261
Turlington, Christy, 180, 181, 182
Tutwiler, Margaret, 257
Twelve Days: The Story of the 1956
  Hungarian Revolution (Sebestyen),
    141–46
Tyler, John, 76

Ulysses (Joyce), 164
United Fruit Company, 9
United Nations (UN)
  and Guevara, 13
  and Hungary, 141, 146
  and Hussein, 123, 227, 256, 266
  and Iran, 248, 249
  and Iraq, 258–59
  "oil for food" program of, 123
  and Powell, 249, 258–59
United States
  Bill of Rights, 105, 113
  Constitution, 105, 106, 108
  South, **71–82**
  as superpower, 141

Van Buren, Martin, 76
Vance, Cyrus, 253
van Gogh, Theo, 194
Vanity Fair, 112, 218
  "Charles Dickens's Inner Child"
    (February 2012), 291–97
  "The Importance of Being Orwell"
    (August 2012), 311–20
  "Joan Didion: Blue Nights" (June
    2011), 281–82
  "The Lovely Stones" (July 2009),
    235–42
  "My Red-State Odyssey" (Septem-
    ber 2005), 71–82
  "Ohio's Odd Numbers" (March
    2005), 45–52
  "On the Limits of Self-improve-
    ment, Part I: Of Vice and Men"
    (October 2007), 169–75
  "On the Limits of Self-
    improvement, Part II: Vice
    and Versa" (December 2007),
    177–83
  "On the Limits of Self-improve-
    ment, Part III: Mission Ac-
    complished" (September 2008),
    185–91
  "Oriana Fallaci and the Art of the
    Interview" (December 2006),
    131–40
  "Power Suits" (April 2006), 105–13
Vatican
  collection of, 241
  and Hitler, 309
  papal infallibility, 307
Vidal, Gore, 116, 150, 201
  Dark Green, Bright Red, 8
  The Judgment of Paris, 180

Vietnam War, 15, 40, 42, 111, 117, 199,
  201, 258, 287
Villein, Dominique de, 258
Virgil, 165
von Braun, Wernher, 117

W. (film), 225–26
Wałęsa, Lech, 133
Walker, Martin, *The President We
  Deserve*, 54
Wallace, Chris, 137
Wallace, George, 73
Wallace, Henry, 27, 28, 116, 117, 118,
  120
Wallace, Mike, 136
Wall Street Journal:
  "The True Spirit of Christmas"
    (December 24, 2011), 283–89
  "The Turkey Has Landed" (Novem-
    ber 23, 2005), 83–85
Walmart, 89
Walt, Stephen, 125
Walters, Barbara, 137, 244
Warner, Mark, 75
war on drugs, 42
War on Terror, 112
warrantless surveillance, 106–8, 109–11
Warsaw Pact, 12, 144
Washington, George, 44, 78, 88
Washington and Lee University, 78
Wasp, Where Is Thy Sting? (King), 73
Waugh, Evelyn, 81, 95, 136, 149, 167,
  307–8
  Brideshead Revisited, 168, 308
  The Loved One, 168
waxing technique, 181–83
Way in the World, A (Naipaul), 223
Wells, H. G., 160
White, Pippa, 46
White, Theodore, 198
White Rose resistance circle, 150
"Who Cares Who Killed Roger Ack-
  royd?" (Wilson), 167
Who Paid the Piper? (Saunders), 26
"Why I Am a Catholic" (Chesterton),
  306
"Why I Write" (Orwell), 311
Wilkerson, Larry, 253
Willey, Kathleen, 213
Williams, Hank, Jr., 74
Williams, Marjorie, 138
Wilson, A. N., *After the Victorians: The
  Decline of Britain in the World*,
  91–96

Wilson, A. T., 156
Wilson, Edmund
  "The Dream of H. C. Earwicker,"
    164
  "A Guide to Finnegans Wake," 165
  *Literary Essays and Reviews of the
    1920s* and *Literary Essays and
    Reviews of the 1930s*, **163–68**
  To the Finland Station, 165
  "Who Cares Who Killed Roger
    Ackroyd?," 167
  The Wound and the Bow, 164
Wilson, Sir Henry, 93
Wilson, Woodrow, 34, 156
Wilson Quarterly, The, "Bring on the
  Mud" (Autumn 2004), 39–44
Winters, Jonathan, 45
Wintringham, Tom, 315
Wolfowitz, Paul, 255
Wolfson, Howard, 216
Woodward, Bob, 257
  Bush at War, 255
  Plan of Attack, 253, 255
Woolf, Leonard, 94
Woollcott, Alexander, 163–64
*World Is What It Is, The: The Autho-
  rized Biography of V. S. Naipaul*
  (French), **217–24**
World Trade Center, 1993 attack on,
  68
World War I, 154

World War II, 95, 318–19
  Pearl Harbor in, 150
Wound and the Bow, The (Wilson), 164
Wren, Christopher, 95
Wright, Ann, transl., *The Motorcycle
  Diaries: A Journey around South
  America* (Guevara), 1n
Wright, Rev. Jeremiah, 231, 233
Wurm, Mathilde, 276
Wycherley, R. E., *The Stones of Athens*,
  237

Xanthias of Thrace, 236

Yanovsky, Stepan Dimitriyevich,
  291–92
Year of Magical Thinking, The (Didion),
  281
Yeats, William Butler, 149
yoga stretching, 173
Young, Michael, 313
You Only Live Twice (Fleming), 98, 101
Yugoslavia, former, 258

Zaire, 3
Zeitlin, Maurice, 11, 13
Zetkin, Kostya, 277
Ziegler, Philip, 93
Zilliacus, Konni, 26
Zionist movement, 156, 157, 308, 318n
Zionist Organization of America, 123

About the Author

Christopher Hitchens was born April 13, 1949, in England and graduated from Balliol College at Oxford University. The father of three children, he was the author of more than twenty books and pamphlets, including collections of essays, criticism, and reportage. His book *god Is Not Great: How Religion Poisons Everything* was a finalist for 2007 National Book Award and an international bestseller. His bestselling memoir, *Hitch-22*, was a finalist for the 2010 National Book Critics Circle Award for autobiography. His 2011 bestselling omnibus of selected essays, *Arguably*, was named by the *New York Times* as one of the ten best books of the year. A visiting professor of liberal studies at the New School in New York City, he was also the I. F. Stone professor at the Graduate School of Journalism at the University of California, Berkeley. He was a columnist, literary critic, and contributing editor at *Vanity Fair, The Atlantic, Slate, The Times Literary Supplement, The Nation, New Statesman, World Affairs*, and *Free Inquiry*, among other publications. He died in Houston on December 15, 2011. The following year, Yoko Ono awarded him the Lennon-Ono Grant for Peace.